BREAK & UNTANGLE

*DISCOVER THE FREEDOM TO BE YOU
DESPITE THE INHERITED MINDSETS
HOLDING YOU BACK*

CHAD PEEVY

GET THE FREE BREAK & UNTANGLE COMPANION COURSE

To help guide you through Break & Untangle, I have created an online companion course that includes bonus videos, worksheets, and other resources that are mentioned throughout the book. Some of the material presented in the book will be better experienced through the supplemental materials. To enhance your reading experience, I highly recommend that you go sign up now. It's free and easy.

Go to **ChadPeevy.com/book** for access.

*Dedicated to all the people who helped me
break & untangle the cycle I inherited,
and to all those who have the courage to
break & untangle theirs.*

CONTENTS

SOCIAL

how to connect and relate to other people

PREFACE

This project took me more than four years to complete. It took me so long because it was difficult for me to write what I'm sharing with you in these pages. Throughout the process, I struggled greatly with sharing intimate details about my family and myself. I spent many sleepless nights second-guessing myself, wondering if my recollections were accurate, wondering if what I remembered had actually happened. I wonder if there are other things my subconscious is still protecting me from. I worried about the impact this book will have on my family. I worried what my husband would think of me when he read this book—since many of these things I had never shared with him until this book was written. My heart was heavy throughout the process, and the fear of facing and exposing the truth was often paralyzing.

Nonetheless, I wrote the book anyway. I wrote it because I wanted to share with you what I've learned about surviving, thriving, and experiencing what I call *personal freedom*. I wrote it because I wanted to share with you the path that I discovered for a better life. I wrote it to create a movement of people who were willing to break the cycle of abuse and trauma that has plagued families like mine for generations. In order for me to continue my own journey of healing, I have to do all I can in this life to help others along the way.

I hope you recognize and heed the calling of this book so you can:

- ▶ step into who you truly are;
- ▶ recognize your own greatness;
- ▶ recognize your power to make a difference in others' lives;
- ▶ realize that your own healing lies in the service of helping others; and
- ▶ break the cycle of abuse that you've endured.

Finally, I hope that you give yourself permission to live fully as the person you have worked so hard to become.

All my best,
Chad

P.S. All of our experiences are different, unique, and require individual evaluation and reflection. Although my intention is to help you explore and evaluate your life's journey, my book, online courses, and coaching programs should not be seen as a substitute for the help of a licensed professional or medication when prescribed by your doctor.

INTRODUCTION

My past is my fuel, not my excuse.

~ Chad Peevy

From the outside looking in, it seems like some people are born with the wind at their back—the beneficiaries of cultural, genetic, and environmental inheritances that make their lives a little easier. For these people, life just seems to go their way. They're comfortable in their own skin, find it easy to be around other people, make friends, make money, and even fall in love. Their life fits the mold of "normal." Sure, they experience struggles like anyone else, but they face those setbacks with more tools: a surplus of emotional intelligence, confidence, social skills, and life skills. Even though we can't know for sure, it seems that they've inherited a set of healthy mindsets that have served them well in life.

The rest of us inherited something different. This inheritance didn't come with great role models or mentors. Life, for us, feels hard, and things don't come as easily as we think they should.

The universe seems to almost insist that we learn every lesson the hard way. A lot of our life feels lonely and isolating, like our past is dragging us down, robbing us of a bright future. On the hardest days, we find ourselves asking if this is all there is to life and if it's worth the effort. This inheritance gets passed down, imprisoning each generation with its shackles of toxicity.

This book is about rejecting those inherited toxic and sabotaging mindsets—those ways of thinking that block you from your true self, that block you from seeing yourself and the world as they really are. It's about making the decision to break the cycle of thinking that has kept you blocked, to free you to do things differently. It's a guide for people like you and me, who have the courage to untangle the things that hold us back. For those who have nothing left to lose. It's a framework to help you self-coach on life's most difficult days. It's about breaking free and experiencing personal freedom: a life full of purpose, meaning, and joy. In the pages that follow, I'll share with you my journey of overcoming the lingering impact of being the beneficiary of generational physical and emotional abuse coupled with the pain and isolation of being an outsider. I'll share how I have learned to manage the depression, anxiety, and loneliness. Furthermore, I'll offer you a guide for what I call "break and untangle:" a process that helped me better understand myself and my place in the world. The circumstances we were born into are not our fault; we can't be blamed or blame ourselves for the things we have learned by circumstance or inheritance. However, once we become aware that a way of thinking or doing something isn't good for us or for the people in our lives, we have a responsibility to break that cycle. I was able to do that by untangling how that way of thinking (or belief) came to be and replaced it with a more supportive idea. To break and untangle is a process involving twelve mindset methods that helped me discover my own personal freedom. Personal freedom is a knowing sense

I carry around with me. This sense of freedom assures me I have the tools necessary to face the world and my circumstances unencumbered by the constraints of my past that instilled those toxic mindsets. Personal freedom is the result of the work I'm sharing in this book. My newfound freedom gives me the space to be authentically me. My hope is that by embarking on this journey, you, too, will find the flexibility to discover and uncover your authentic self.

My need to reject this inheritance of toxic mindsets became obvious to me during the 2008 recession. During this time period, I lost my business, my income dried up, I was forced to lay off all my employees, and my car was repossessed. On top of that, my parents divorced after thirty years of marriage. I had begged my mother to divorce my dad when I was a child. I was in my late twenties when she finally did, and their divorce affected me in an unexpectedly profound way. What their relationship meant for how I saw myself was unclear to me at the time, and it didn't become clear to me until I did the work outlined in the pages to come. I was angry, and my relationship with both parents got worse, even hostile.

I was severely depressed. I had battled depression for most of my life, but this was the most depressed I had ever been. I lay in bed for almost six months, only spending an hour or two out of bed every day. My boyfriend at the time, Pasha, tried to get me up and out of the house. I was able to sit up in bed, and he would put my clothes on the nightstand next to me. But the only energy I could muster up was to put one leg of my pants on. Then, I would resign, slide the pants off, and crawl back into bed. I was at rock bottom.

We were broke, which meant I had access to no therapy and no pharmaceuticals. I could probably have found some help, but I had fallen far from grace, a faint reflection of who I had been just a year prior. I was so ashamed of myself. Plus, depression and anxiety carried such a stigma that I didn't want to open up to anyone about it, even if talking about it would mean feeling better.

My life was supposed to be totally different. I had graduated from one of the nation's best universities, started a decent business, and run a couple of nonprofits that brought me pride and satisfaction. But almost overnight I lost my family unit, my identity, my money, my motivation, and my sanity. Everything was happening to me all at once. My circumstances were revealing to me that my lifetime inheritance of toxic mindsets was like living in a house without a foundation. I didn't have a solid enough base to withstand the winds of the world. But it wasn't until this perfect tornado of circumstances hit that I realized how unstable my foundation was.

Pasha had just finished his doctorate degree in violin at The University of Texas at Austin. He was playing weddings, teaching a few classes at the public schools, and subbing with the Austin Symphony just so we could make ends meet. We lived in a really run-down duplex in south Austin; there were hardly any windows, and the bathroom was so small you could barely turn around in it. But the rent was really cheap; it was all we could afford.

During this time, I was terrified that Pasha was going to break up with me. I knew that if he did, I would be in a world of trouble. On the days I would make it out of the house, I considered the city in a new way, scouting bridges that would be suitable for me to live under should Pasha dump me. I even found a decent spot, on the northbound side of the I-35 interstate highway, where the top portion meets the bottom. I felt so lonely, so ashamed of myself, and so depressed that my thought process was one that whispered, *Live under a bridge instead of reach out for help.* But Pasha didn't leave me. Ultimately, it was his love that pulled me through the depression, because I didn't have the tools to do it on my own. Even when I was at my lowest point, he saw something in me, and he never gave up. If there is such a thing as a soul mate, Pasha is mine. When same-sex marriage became legal in 2015, we got married.

As time went on, things got a little better. The economy

improved, and more opportunities started to appear for us both. Pasha was getting consistent work, and an old friend approached me about opening an in-house marketing firm for real estate agents at the world's largest real estate office.

Once I got well enough, I quickly realized that I never wanted to go through an experience like that again. I knew I couldn't allow circumstances to dictate the severity of my depression. I needed to understand myself better and get to the root of what was going on so I could build a better foundation. I had to learn a better way to approach how I was experiencing life. So, I began to read and research what had been observed and studied about people who had similar experiences to mine. I started this journey of personal development to save myself.

I'm the first son of an angry and abusive father and a young, ill-equipped mother. I was raised in Alma, a rural town of about 2,700 people in western Arkansas. Alma is too small to have a hospital, so I was born in Fort Smith, about twenty minutes away. My parents took me home to a single-wide trailer atop a mountain on land that belonged to my dad's parents.

We were surrounded on the top of that mountain by immediate and extended family—nothing between us all but some barbed-wire fences, dogs, chickens, horses, and a few goats. As a kid, I cut a path through the field to get to my grandparent's house, collecting every chigger on the way. I would sit with my granddaddy and watch *The People's Court* and *Jeopardy!* Then we would doze off for an afternoon nap, with him laid out on the sofa and me curled up in the big comfy chair that got smaller as I got older. You might have also found us piddling around in the garden, collecting eggs from our chickens, or just sitting in front of the window A/C unit. When Granny got home from working the assembly line at the furniture factory, she would cook dinner, and I would help. We would eat together, then I would head back home to my parents' trailer across the field.

Part of what makes the breaking and untangling process difficult is the confusion that ensues. Rarely are our experiences all bad or all good. There are some good memories from those days in the trailer.

It was in that trailer that I got my first Red Ryder BB Gun. I was too short to hold it, so my dad sawed off several inches of the stock so I could shoot.

My first seven birthday parties were in that trailer. One year, I had a cake in the shape of Garfield, and my cousins were there to celebrate. I was so happy to be surrounded by other kids.

The trailer was also where I would get up and turn the clunky knob on the TV to change the channel. It was hard for my little hands to turn it, but I loved to try.

There are also some painful memories.

I remember being in the car with my drunk father and his friends. I don't remember where they took me, but I do remember their foul smell, how loud they were, and my fear.

I also remember an ice chest in the trailer; it was red on the outside and white on the inside. I don't know what happened with it, but the memory haunts me and gives me chills. The thought of it still makes me sick to my stomach.

The trailer is where my father's torture of me began. It's where I first inherited my toxic mindsets. And it's also the source of great confusion as I try to reconcile my happy memories with my miserable ones.

My own process of untangling took me back to the days I spent in that trailer as a boy. That's where the process had to begin for me to better understand myself and how I was showing up in the world. It's where I had to begin if I was going to finally break the cycle that had driven me to become bedridden with depression and anxiety.

First, I had understand how I went from a little kid in rural

Arkansas, to drum major of The University of Arkansas Razorback Marching Band, to a graduate student at The University of Texas, to president of the Austin Gay and Lesbian Chamber of Commerce, to founder of the Austin Pride Foundation, to business owner, to husband. With odds stacked overwhelmingly against me—I had just as much a chance of dying by suicide as I did of rising above my upbringing—how did that happen? I knew there had to be clues in the answer to that question, so I began to dig into the research.

RESILIENT CHILDREN

There's plenty that could go wrong with kids who have upbringings similar to mine. The prevailing research tells us that kids who experience high-stress childhoods are most at risk for both learning impairments and behavioral issues, meaning that they are more likely to have academic and social issues, which will follow them into adulthood—with relationships, their career, and more.[1]

Early research on the topic would refer to me and kids like me as "resilient children," or sometimes "stress-adapted" children, meaning that the environments of our childhood didn't just impair our cognitive and social abilities; rather, our abilities are developmentally adapted or specialized for our environment. Think of it this way: The kid who is focused on an algebra problem and the kid who is focused on how to avoid getting beaten up in the hallway are both employing mental devices that serve them. One has "book smarts" and the other has "street smarts." That's successful intelligence: the ability to work successfully toward the attainment of your goals, within your cultural contexts,[2] and your ability to figure out how to survive in your environment.

One particular way this may manifest is in our ability to focus our attention on one thing or another. A person from a low-risk background—one who grew up able to be singularly focused for long periods of time, never afraid of an unpredictable event interrupting their concentration—may not be able to figure out a problem in an unpredictable environment as effectively as a kid from a high-stress background. The resilient kid from the high-stress background is conditioned to get things done in an unpredictable and sometimes chaotic environment. So, does this make resilient children special? No, it just means that we look at the world a little differently than our low-stress environment peers.

The resilience literature essentially asks one thing, "What does it take to succeed?" This was my question too. Through my research, I learned that successful outcomes have predictable factors, including intelligence and problem-solving skills, hope and optimism, self-control, resourcefulness, and motivation to succeed. While the early research on resilient children suggested they may have some extraordinary skills, more recent research contradicts that assertion.

Resilient children are actually incredibly ordinary—in the best possible way. They don't possess a new superpower; they've got the normal adaptive processes that keep human beings alive—survival. We are *all* able to do the extraordinary if we feel our survival is threatened enough. Even at a young age, I saw my dad and my environment as a threat. I wasn't able to get out of rural Arkansas because I had an above-average ability to be resilient. My ability to recognize the threat of the dangerous circumstances and consequences I grew up around made it possible for me to do what was necessary to survive. Child development researcher Ann Masten from the University of Minnesota called this idea "ordinary magic."[3]

This idea offers an explanation for why some kids stay and some leave. For me, it explains why my mother and brother were able to better tolerate the conditions imposed by my father. My experience was entirely different from theirs. While they may have been discontented, they didn't feel a high enough threat that would cause them to leave, and I eventually did.

I believe the primary threat for me was the danger of being gay. Being gay was so taboo, so socially stigmatized, that the actual threat to my safety and well-being was acutely high. It was greater than the fear of the unknown associated with leaving. By the time I'd left, I had already considered suicide several times. Escaping my life by physically leaving was easy in comparison to escaping through a bullet. But the unknown is scary. In fact, many people will stay in a bad situation until the fear of staying is much greater than the fear of leaving. My survival was threatened, so I did what was necessary to survive: I left.

The instinct to survive, though, doesn't diminish the effects of the experience itself. Reflecting on your childhood can become confusing because it isn't a uniform experience. No one's childhood is *all* bad. My mother often reminds me that while my childhood was less than optimal, there were also some good times. That's a true assessment. But we remember the bad more than the good. Why? Because in order to survive, we had to remember the bad in an attempt to prevent "it" from happening again. Remembering the bad gives us an advantage for detecting its reoccurrence. That remembering turns into a worldview—a survivor's mindset.

THE TWELVE MINDSET METHODS: SURVIVE OR THRIVE?

No problem can be solved from the same consciousness that created it. We must learn to see the world anew.

~ Albert Einstein

Through a six-month, major depressive event as an adult, I realized I wasn't as resilient as I was in childhood. There was something different required of me now, something new. When times got real and got tough, I didn't have the tools I needed to weather the storm. I realized my foundation wasn't firm.

I later came to understand that growing up and getting out of Arkansas had required a survivor's mindset. And even though you can get through life as an adult with such a mindset, that approach failed me at a time when I was at my worst. What I needed as an adult went beyond survival; I needed meaning and purpose in my life. I wanted to feel joy and at peace—part of what I have come to call my personal freedom. Not only did I need to pull myself out of a depression, but I also needed to live for something meaningful. As a kid, I lived to escape. As an adult, what was I now living for?

A survivor's mindset isn't one that leads to personal freedom. It helps you survive; it equips you with the coping mechanisms necessary to make it through the day. A survivor's mindset teaches you how to avoid conflict, squash your emotions, deprive yourself, and keep yourself small. But none of these methods were helping me.

I needed a new mindset, one that empowered me to thrive. I needed a completely different set of skills to help me understand myself and my place in this world. I needed mindset methods that would help me become more agile, reflective, self-aware, and present.

When you thrive, you stand up for yourself; you demand

what you want from your life. You take a stand for who you are and who you want to be. That would have been dangerous for me as a kid. But now, it's the only way I can live fully and create the life I want and deserve.

To create this life, I began an untangling process in which I recognized three categories that I needed to understand about myself:

SELF

the influence my history has on how I show up in the world

STRATEGY

tools to help me better navigate the world and care for myself

SOCIAL

how I connect and relate to other people

Each of these categories had four distinct topics. I started referring to these topics as my 12 Mindset Methods. These mindsets replaced the old ones I had inherited from my upbringing. As I dug deeper into my 12 Mindset Methods, I realized that I had found more than just a way to stave off the depression. These tools became a completely new way to look at my life. These mindsets would help me create a life worth living.

SELF
1. Purpose: a sense of meaning
2. Internal Dialogue: the ongoing conversation in your head
3. Identity: knowing who you are
4. Unitary Functioning: experiencing your whole self

STRATEGY

5. Becoming: striving to live up to your potential

6. Money: worth absent currency

7. Productivity: bringing to each moment that which is necessary

8. Mindfulness: awareness of experience

SOCIAL

9. Help: receiving without resistance

10. Belonging: unconditional acceptance

11. Ambition: advocating for yourself

12. Legacy: living consequentially

The journey from surviving to thriving isn't linear. It's more like waking up one day to find yourself in the middle of the jungle, not knowing where you are or how to get out. This state of being can very well lead you to ask: *Is this it? Is this all there is? This seems hopeless, so why bother?*

When that happens, you need a map. I'm hoping that this book will be a map for you. This is the book I wish someone had handed me when I was asking those tough existential questions and starting my process of breaking and untangling.

The 12 Mindset Methods are not an excuse to blame anyone, not even your parents. But they do require that you understand the influence that your parents had on you. The goal is not to remember and blame; instead, the goal is to understand, accept, and overcome. There comes a time in our lives when we have to acknowledge that we are in control of how we experience our reality. We have to get to a place where we acknowledge that, while our circumstances and upbringing may have influenced who we have been, we are responsible for who we are now. There comes a time when we must accept that responsibility for ourselves and release our parents—either the real ones or the ones we have projected into our world. As long as we continue to see our parents in our current environment, we will continue to see ourselves as a child. If we continue to blame them for our troubles or anticipate them coming to our rescue, we won't experience personal freedom, maturity, or growth. And while we have to take total responsibility for our life's journey, it doesn't mean we have to travel this path alone.

The journey for everyone is different, but what we have in common is the gap that exists between where we are and where we want to be. What's common among us is twofold: the recognition that our lives are less than we intended and our belief that we are capable of more.

So, what keeps us from getting there? What stands in our way? What is in this divide that is holding us back? The following pages will explore this divide and how to navigate it, even during those times when it seems like the destination keeps moving away from you.

Each of the 12 Mindset Methods represents something that has held me back when I wasn't enjoying my life. This is not an exhaustive list, however, and I have confidence that as I grow and age, I will likely continue to add to it.

What my experience has taught me with certainty is that there is no "hacking" your way to a great life. There's no hack for creating a life with meaning and purpose that serves you and others and leads to legacy. You can't take a magic pill, say the magic words, or attend the magic workshop that will turn it all around. You need to put in the work, and this book is an invitation for you to begin (or go deeper!) into this process. As you break and untangle, you'll find the keys to your personal transformation in the darkest, most remote, and hidden corners of yourself.

These methods are not intellectual; they are experiential. You can't just read them, memorize them, and then have your life be filled with sunshine and rainbows for the rest of your days. No, no, no. You have to work at these mindsets daily, hourly—moment by moment—until you're able to fully integrate the parts of you that need processing. You will eventually develop a self-acceptance that is unshakable as you discover the freedom that exists when you are unencumbered by mindsets that have boxed you into a way of life that no longer serves you. This is the path of personal development.

Ultimately, you experience your best life when you are untethered from the past and unattached to the future, living in an ever-present state. I invite you to come back to these lessons as you grow. What you learn from this book on your first reading will be different than what you glean on the second. As you grow, so will your perspective and the context in which you view the lessons in this book. There are no life sentences because life is ever-changing. The frameworks I'm offering you are designed to help you navigate each change without rigidity or doctrine.

Living fully authentic is an everyday effort; it's not something you can check off once on a checklist and be done. The 12 Mindset Methods are ideas that I have to be reminded of every day. With every thought or emotion, I point to one or more of the methods to explore what's really going on with me. They are like indicator lights on a car, reminding you to check your engine, put on your seatbelt, or add wiper fluid.

These 12 Mindset Methods represent areas of my life that are worthy of re-examination as I grow. No one area is stagnant, and none of them can grow or diminish without having an effect on the other areas. The work in one area doesn't happen in isolation; it happens in tandem with the others. Progress isn't linear, because life isn't meant to be experienced that way. Don't let the construct of time determine your progress. There's no destination here, only a journey.

I'm honored to be part of your process. To help us connect, I've created an online companion course for this book on my website. Visit ChadPeevy.com to find the additional resources referenced throughout the book. The chapters that follow will outline in depth each of the 12 Mindset Methods. I'll share my experiences as I break and untangle the process. I've also included self-paced exercises that you can do to help guide your journey.

SELF

the influence my history has on how I show up in the world

PURPOSE

INTERNAL DIALOGUE

IDENTITY

UNITARY FUNCTIONING

PURPOSE
CHAPTER 1

Clarity is a result of our action.

~ Chad Peevy

Much of the circumstances of our lives are thrust upon us—meaning, we don't consciously decide them. We don't choose our parents. We don't choose where we were born. We don't choose our elementary school, our hometown, or our neighborhood. We don't choose our race, our hair color, or our sexual orientation. We don't even get to choose our name. And yet, we try to make sense of our lives through the lens of those experiences. This idea of being thrown into the circumstances of our lives was explored by the German philosopher Martin Heidegger. He called it "thrownness."[1]

If we allow our lives to continue in thrownness, without awareness or interruption, we simply create a life of default, a life where our progress is the result of the last domino that has fallen. A life that is the continuation of the cycle we were born into. Often, the sense of lacking purpose in our lives is the result of living in an unbroken cycle, which perpetuates a life by default wherein the next domino falls without any intention or purpose.

For example, how did you get your job? Did you intentionally seek out a role that would allow you to make the greatest contribution? Did you start your business because you made a conscious decision to follow your passion? Or was it the result of convenience and circumstance? How did you end up in your relationship? Were you conscientious about what you wanted in a partner? What about where you live? Your social circle? How do you parent? What are your political views? Your religious beliefs?

Bringing an awareness to the continuity and perpetuation of our thrownness is an untangling process that I'll refer to in this book as "breaking the cycle." To break the cycle is to summon the courage to do something different than that which has been passed onto you. Buried under the fear required for this process, you will discover something unfamiliar and remarkable: yourself.

To find purpose, clarity, and meaning, you must awaken to the fact that so much of *who* you are is a result of the life you were *thrown* into. You must become clear on the impact of your own thrownness and acknowledge that much of your life is a result of circumstances and convenience. To break the cycle, you have to recognize that you have gone through much of life allowing the next, nearest domino to fall without any thought or consideration.

As kids, our power to make decisions was limited and heavily influenced by our circumstances and others' expectations. For too many of us, those circumstances and expectations we were thrown into were hostile. We experienced cultures brewed in hatred, jealousy, ignorance, and randomness through the lens of our youthful naiveté. We were caught in circumstances that didn't align with our own realities or who we were striving to become. This misalignment created a gap between what we were thrown into and who we knew we could be, leaving us feeling like the "other"—isolated and cut off from an idealized version of ourselves. In an effort to conform to what we believed was right, or what others would find acceptable, we lost ourselves. Without the freedom and safety that would allow us to explore and question our circumstances and thrownness, doubts about our future and distaste for the reality of the here and now got turned inward. Seeking purpose remained secondary to survival and fitting in with what was expected. The resulting consequence is a life that feels devoid of meaning.

When you're trying to please other people, it's hard to get clarity around what you want for yourself. Too many voices swirl around in your head, competing for your attention and, ultimately, your submission. Your mind is always on, guessing what is expected of you at any given moment. As humans, we sabotage our joy by assuming the role of the chameleon, always changing to match our environment. There's no peace in being a constant people-pleaser; it's exhausting. All of your actions are designed to please others in exchange for their love and approval at the expense of loving yourself. This is not a recipe for finding purpose in your own life. In your efforts to be what other people need you to be, you become lost. When you can't hold onto yourself, the greater likelihood is that you'll conform to anything, even if it's painful—emotionally, spiritually, and often physically.

We stay in relationships that are less than ideal in order to please our partner and not create waves. We let the boss treat us badly. We let our kids run all over us. We numb our minds with rotten movies and cable news. Why? Because it is easier to adapt, to conform, to go with the flow. But the consequence of surrendering to our thrownness is a life unlived, unexpressed, and void of purpose. It's up to you now to break this cycle, to take agency, and to *throw* yourself into the life you want.

Breaking your cycle is both liberating and terrifying. It's an awakening that shines a spotlight on the power of your decisions, which determine everything about your life—good and bad. Even in the smallest of behaviors, decisions add up to your entire life's experience. Every decision you make matters. The lack of awareness around what shaped past decisions may have gotten us here, but we have it in us to make decisions that can either keep us where we are or get us where we want to go.

At the moment in which we awaken from thrownness and step into awareness, we begin to see our lives as our own. We awaken to the power we have to make decisions that move us closer to a life filled with purpose, clarity, and meaning.

What is your life's purpose? It's a question that often feels too big to answer. But it need not be overwhelming if we'll just take a step back to look at the idea and remove the pressure on ourselves to come up with the perfect answer.

OUR COMMON PURPOSE

The ideas of purpose, clarity, and meaning are difficult to divorce, but they aren't the same. *Purpose* relates to our life's contribution. *Meaning* relates to the satisfaction we experience when we feel and see that purpose realized. And *clarity* relates to our ability to recognize how our purpose and meaning align in our lives. Clarity of purpose isn't a challenge you must confront. It will appear as a result of your actions and experimentation toward your purpose.

It's not only the knowledge of our purpose that is significant. It's how intentional we are about the manner in which we are living our purpose and the degree to which we feel that our purpose contributes to a life of meaning. When these ideas are in alignment, we are finally able to experience what I call our personal freedom.

When we live with personal freedom, we give ourselves permission to experience our lives fully and authentically—free of the mindsets that have boxed us into patterns and ideas that have limited our expression of ourselves. Freedom is what gives us the tools to handle any circumstance, unencumbered by our past or any outside expectations. Freedom grants us the space to be fully ourselves—free from the judgment of others or of ourselves. Personal freedom is a near-spiritual state in which we feel most alive and connected, creating a feeling of unity toward others and peace within ourselves.

So how do we experience this when the deck seems to be stacked against us? When we face the constraints of our past, biology, expectations, family, and work? All of which seem like bars of the same cage. This question has been asked throughout the ages, and human beings greater than I have attempted to answer it. This is how I make sense of it all.

To experience our personal freedom, we must first understand our life's purpose. This idea used to overwhelm me. If you're feeling a knot in your stomach right now, a tinge in your neck, or a headache coming on, feel free to just sit and take a few deep breaths. I understand the magnitude of this idea. I understand the fear of getting it wrong, the judgment you imagine will come from others, even the guilt of waiting this long to address it. Just remember that these are all bars of a self-constructed prison. With some effort, you can escape the prison bars you stand behind and realize that at this point in time, only you are holding yourself back. By learning and applying the tools I'll be guiding you through in this book, you will feel a freedom and release unlike any other.

To make finding your life purpose less overwhelming, let's break *purpose* down into three parts: universal commonality, personal scope, and duration.

First, we all share a common purpose: to serve one another. We're not alone. None of us exist in a vacuum or as a singularity. We coexist. This idea has been shared across ideological spectrums and through the ages.

You, my brothers and sisters, were called to be free.
But do not use your freedom to indulge the flesh;
rather, serve one another humbly in love.
~ Galatians 5:13 NIV

Our prime purpose in this life is to help others.
And if you can't help them, at least don't hurt them.
~ Dalai Lama

Serve the need of others, and all your own needs will be fulfilled.
Through selfless action, fulfillment is attained.
~ Lao Tzu; from the seventh verse of the Tao Te Ching

Second, purpose can be very limited in scope and still be deeply meaningful. Your contribution can be one of service to others in ways big or small, far-reaching or concentrated. Your purpose may be to raise great kids, or develop the next pandemic vaccine. Perhaps your purpose is to make people laugh. Or maybe it's to send mankind to the moon. We all have a role to play because of our interconnectedness. And because of our connection, your purpose may be a contribution of service to others either directly or indirectly.

Sometimes the way we contribute to one another's life is by working on ourselves—breaking the cycles of our past so they are not repeated in future generations. Your own personal development journey is generous of you to undertake, deeply meaningful, and highly impactful. Taking the time to reflect on your own life and how you show up in the world is in itself a contribution. Don't allow shame, guilt, or fear to diminish the contributions you make to yourself. There will be seasons of your life that require quiet, intentional, and purposeful focus on yourself. Our lives are made up of seasons; some seasons are just for you.

Third, your purpose need not be a life sentence. Our life's purpose is much like the seasons: it changes as time passes. Being self-aware will tell us when it's time for that season to change. And as we become clear in one area of our lives, new areas of growth will present themselves and challenge us to mature and grow into what awaits in the next season. As clarity fluctuates, it hints that something different is required. As you grow, your ability to contribute to this common purpose will also grow. What was learned in the last season will further inform our purpose through which we have deeper impact and glean greater meaning.

The changing of these life seasons is a good thing. They are the nature of this life journey that you're on. Knowing this, the question you can ask yourself is: *What is my purpose for this season of my life?* The season may be a month, a year, or maybe thirty years. When it comes to our life purpose, the traditional idea of time shouldn't be thought of as a marker for success or setbacks. Simply be assured that once you've learned the lessons this current season was meant to teach you, you'll move on to the next.

DISCOVERING THE *HOW VS. WHY* OF PURPOSE

Smart people like to ask *why*. *Why* is a trap.

Children ask why about everything. Their curiosity is healthy; it allows them to make sense of their world. But we are no longer children. Why has it's place, but shouldn't be used to delay or deter us from living and experiencing our purpose. Why is a form of distraction that can go on forever, without resolution. There's always another reason why—another rabbit hole to explore. Eventually, we have to move on from *why* and start asking *how*. We often think, *Why do I feel pulled to help those in need?* Instead, ask yourself, *How can I best help those in need? Why* is great for self-reflection. But *how* puts us in the here and now, leading us toward action, experience, and living our purpose rather than just thinking about it.

Why is a circle of questions that have the potential to never arrive at a meaningful answer. *Why* may leave us stranded in something unresolved, only answering a portion of the question we are really asking: *Who am I, and why am I here?* It's *the* existential question. The question that those who wake up to their own thrownness will ask. The path to answering it is a personal one that should lead you right out of your comfort zone and directly into a confrontation with your life's purpose.

The challenge that requires decision and action is: How will you use your life to contribute to our collective purpose? *Why* is attached to ego because it separates us from the lived experience of our purpose. *How* is attached to outcomes. *How* is the action that brings us into the present.

Ultimately, the how is up to you. When the how is answered, you'll gain more clarity of *who* you are.

It's easy to become overwhelmed with the potential of how. Sometimes it feels like we live in a world of endless possibilities and we're offered unlimited choice. While all those opportunities could seem liberating, without a way of narrowing them down, you can quickly become paralyzed. That paralysis will disguise itself as chaos, anxiety, stagnation, or even boredom, which only further detaches you from putting your purpose into action. For the sake of clarity, we have to learn how to limit and focus our efforts. We do that by focusing on: 1) how one contributes, and 2) where one makes that contribution.

These are your decisions to make. You can't wait for someone to tell you what it is or wait for someone to give you permission to make your contribution. Be your own authority and say, "Permission granted!" Decide what your contribution is in this moment, in this season, without the pressure of believing that whatever you decide carries a life sentence. Summon the courage to move boldly, and allow yourself the grace to be wrong.

Once you know where you can contribute, you must decide what specific action you will take to make your contribution.

EXERCISE

To determine what that action might be, ask yourself a series of questions:

1. What can I teach that would make someone else's life easier?

2. What gift do I have that must be shared with others?

3. Who must I be, what must I say, and where must I go to live as the fully expressed version of myself?

4. What can I contribute that will leave this world a better place?

5. What has the universe been preparing me for?

6. What do I believe about the world and myself that is uncompromising?

7. Who in this world needs what I can give?

How will you know if you've chosen the right action? The only way to find out is to start. Don't let the idea of starting (or starting over) keep you from action. And don't let the future version of you intimidate the person you are today. Of course, there will be a gap between where you start and where you end up. Life is process; it has no destination. It only requires a direction. We see this through our experience of others. If you've you ever read the first works of authors or the early songs of songwriters, you know that the leaps of progress are evidence of their growth. Give yourself that same opportunity for growth.

Meaning is more deeply felt, and purpose is experienced more clearly, when you are in action and contribution mode. What good is the book never read? What good is the song never heard? How delicious is a cake never eaten? We can't learn, be complete, or experience the benefits of our purpose if we hold back. Our growth is stifled when we don't live with personal freedom because growth is an outward motion that is meant to be shared. If you want your life to grow, you must contribute.

PURPOSE IS NOT THE SAME AS HAPPINESS

How often have you heard or even said, "I just want to be happy"? If experiencing happiness is the goal of your life, I'm afraid you're in for a lot of disappointment. Life is full of struggle, as Victor Frankl so eloquently expounded upon in *Man's Search for Meaning*. To experience a meaningful life is to embrace that struggle, to honor that journey, and to experience the wide range of emotions that include, but are not limited to, happiness. We can't identify a flavor as sweet without knowing what sour tastes like. We only know what brightness is because we've experienced darkness. We know what happiness is because we've felt sadness, anger, and fear.

I can do many things that will make me happy. I can eat a cheeseburger, down a chocolate shake, have sex, get drunk, or laugh at a movie. Any of these things would make me happy. But none of these things give my life deep purpose. Purpose transcends base-level emotion.

Pay attention to your emotions, but don't take them too seriously because not every emotion is useful. Emotions are fleeting and unreliable, appearing as a reaction to a world in which we have little to no control. To live a life in pursuit of an emotion will be an empty life, chasing something to fill a hole that must be constantly refilled. Chasing the emotion will not deliver the meaning you seek and is an unworthy use of your life's energy.

On your life's journey, you will experience a spectrum of feelings. But those feelings are like indicator lights on the dashboard; they are not the engine itself. When you begin to live in personal freedom, it means experiencing a full range of emotions, not just the ones that you, or the people around you, find pleasant. To be free is to have the room in this life to be fully you.

In addition to chasing emotional outcomes, we often encounter other roadblocks that would deny us the experience of living our purpose. If you're anything like me, when you recognize that a change is needed in your life, you want that change to occur immediately. But personal development is a journey that progresses at its own pace. Your journey will likely be more like a dirt road than a highway. You'll probably go more slowly than you'd like as you traverse the twists and turns of that bumpy dirt road. And on that dirt road, you'll encounter the three largest roadblocks to discovering your purpose and experiencing your personal freedom: resistance, emotional avoidance, and anxiety.

RESISTING PURPOSE

Action toward your purpose, and even the allure to experience personal freedom, may be met with resistance. Resistance occurs when we interfere with our own progress, launching counterattacks against ourselves that stifle our growth. Without resistance, we flow freely into a life wherein our purpose is clear. Without resistance, we effortlessly and without apology make room for our full selves, living fully and authentically in the face of life's circumstances. But all too often we find that it isn't that easy to just flow and go. We confront ourselves with a range of obstacles, both real and imaginary.

I go to therapy every week, and each time I will resist a different perspective outright. I've paid life coaches and business coaches for feedback and advice, only to immediately discount their perspective when it's offered. We've all been there and done this when asked (of ourselves or by others) to move beyond that which we find comfortable. Any kind of change is difficult, especially when changing that which is your cultural or familial inheritance.

You should expect the voices of your upbringing to haunt you. Doing things the way they've always been done will seem safer than trying something new. You may yearn for the ease of the familiar over the discomfort of growth. You might see a new way as a repudiation of the old so much that you might question your confidence and sense of self. Fear will validate your reasons to stay small more than it will liberate your inhibition.

Resistance is a tool of the ego. It is the ego's effort to maintain itself. And since the ego only wants to prove itself right, regardless of what's actually good for you, it will attempt to convince you to not start anything new. It will tell you maintain your life as it is, to stay comfortable in a state of homeostasis. It will create doubt. Where resistance exists, fear and pride exist too. Fear of rejection, of isolation, of what others might think. Fear of judgment, of expressing yourself, of success.

But growth exists in exploring these fears. On the other side of these fears isn't just growth and the courage to overcome them; there's also love, compassion, and the permission to be the fully expressed version of you. Succumbing to the ego will limit our action toward our purpose and diminish the freedom it will bring.

Our life's purpose is real and definitive of who we are in this moment, but so, too, is our resistance to it. The resistance is as much a part of us as the purpose; therefore you need to know how to process it. You don't have to understand electricity to know that if you flip the light switch, the room lights up. Similarly, you don't have to understand that if you acknowledge your resistance, it loses its grip on you. Don't resist your resistance—explore it. Should that resistance show up, welcome it and learn from it.

Our resistance to the unknown is one of our greatest personal tragedies. On the other side of resistance is unrealized purpose, such as growth, joy, and even greatness. Don't ignore or suppress your resistance; what we resist will persist. Instead, allow yourself the freedom to move through the resistance to discover and become more fully you. What is necessary in the presence of resistance is exactly its opposite: risk, spontaneity, unpredictability, selflessness, vulnerability, and generosity.

EXERCISE

To help you identify your resistance, ask yourself these questions:

1. When I think about living my life's purpose, I am filled with a sense of _____ and also _____ (its opposite).

2. What would have to be true about you if you said yes to living your life's purpose rather than no?

3. What would I say to someone else if I thought they were playing small with their life and not living their potential?

Getting clear on your resistance and how it's showing up allows you to be better equipped to see how you are engaging in emotional avoidance or substitution.

EMOTIONAL AVOIDANCE AND SUBSTITUTION

Another form of resistance, yet a more specific one, is emotional avoidance and substitution. When engaging in this type of resistance, you're not resisting your purpose or the change necessary to live that purpose. You're resisting the emotion you'd either have to give up or experience as a consequence of doing something different. To truly live a life in personal freedom, we have to be willing to feel more. To do something different can feel like so much more than just trying something new; it can feel like a betrayal of tradition. It can feel like an act of self-ostracism. Even the thought of experiencing the emotional turmoil of blazing your own path can cause us to avoid that path altogether.

We constantly self-pacify, opting for the most pleasing emotional state at any given time. This is a form of emotional substitution. We're able to do this because we have a choice when it comes to our emotions. I can choose to be angry, express it, move through it, and let it go. Or I can avoid my anger and allow it to get stuck inside of me. It's my choice. I can choose to be sad for how someone treats me, or I can choose to be mad at them for mistreating me. I can also choose to examine that unfortunate experience, including the sadness, anger, and a wide spectrum of emotional reactions.

Personal freedom doesn't exist in repression or avoidance. It exists as a full expression of yourself. Even when that expression seems negative, unfamiliar, or unsafe, it is necessary. If you don't allow yourself to feel the full range of your emotions, you deny yourself the freedom to do so and will likely end up projecting or transferring those emotions onto the people around you. This is a process that, once started, will set your ego into overdrive on a mission to always prove you right. This effectively blocks our personal freedom and our ability to be in contribution to others. If we can't see those to whom we contribute our life's purpose, absent the ego-stained lens of our life, we cannot fully experience the meaning of our purpose or of our contribution to them. Our purpose and contribution become tainted when the ego gets in the way.

If we don't own all of our emotions, they will tie us up. Anger, fear, grief, resentment, guilt—all of these are bars of the same cage. And when we're caged, we isolate ourselves from others and from our purposeful contribution.

We cannot experience a life of personal freedom if we are afraid to feel. No, not all feelings are useful, but they can be informative. Anxiety is one such feeling, a very unpleasant one that can manifest in all sorts of ways. From shortness of breath, to restlessness, to jitters, anxiety is something I think we would all like to avoid. But what can anxiety teach us?

EXERCISE

Use these journal prompts to help you explore ways in which you may be avoiding or substituting your full emotional range:

1. Are there ways in which you numb your life rather than experiencing a full emotional range? Perhaps through a vice, like cigarettes, alcohol, or weed? A distraction, like TV or grazing for food? Maybe a habit, like being closed off to new people or being quick to judge others? For example: *Rather than confronting my spouse about my anger for something they've done, I go for a walk instead.*

2. I avoid feeling _____ , because there was a time in my life that it was unsafe to do so.

3. I know I would feel better if I didn't hold myself back from expressing myself when I feel _____ .

4. I choose the pacifying emotion rather than the one that would bring me closer to experiencing my personal freedom because _____ .

A LIFE OUT OF ALIGNMENT IS ANXIOUS

The German philosopher Martin Heidegger was known for his work in ontology (the study of existence or being) and challenged us to ask ourselves an important question: If we were to narrate the stories of our life, would they be stories worth telling? Would they instruct or inspire those who observed us? Would we ourselves be inspired? Or are we living small, sticking to the script of a so-called secure job, subjecting ourselves to other people's expectations, hiding behind a busy schedule? Perhaps the only audience that matters in our life has grown bored. Perhaps apathy has set in. We may have tuned out the narration of our own life and substituted it with pills, alcohol, work, stories on TV, sex, or food. Perhaps those remedies are no longer sufficient to numb the pain of our unsatisfied life story.

If you're experiencing boredom with your current life story, and if you're making decisions that don't lead you toward your personal freedom, then you're creating fertile ground for anxiety to thrive. While experiencing the anxiety, it will be difficult or impossible to find clarity or meaning.

Anxiety informs the degree to which we are aligned with our personal freedom. Its presence reveals to you that there's an opportunity for a better story to be told about your life. How do you know if you're experiencing your personal freedom? How anxious are you feeling?

In our culture, we treat anxiety like it's a headache, like a nuisance that we can fix with a pill or some quiet time. Perhaps for some, that is the solution. But that wasn't my experience. There have been times in my life when my mind would race, my skin would crawl, my hands would itch, and my heart would flutter. Desperate for relief, I took the pills. I tried to time-block the unease out of my life. I tried to distract myself. Each remedy brought with it a degree of relief; inevitably, though, the anxiety would return. I even reached a point where I resigned myself to the idea that I would always have anxiety, and I'd simply have to accept it.

Then I began to see anxiety as a tool to help me, instead of a condition needing to be squashed. I started to see it as an alarm clock—buzzing, flashing, and ringing in times of misalignment. I began to notice that when life seemed murky, when anything meaningful was absent and my life's narration didn't match my true self, anxiety was present.

What if anxiety is your mind's way of telling you to wake up? What if anxiety is an indicator of the degree to which your lifestyle is in service of your purpose? What if your anxiety isn't something that you need to rid yourself of but is actually a mechanism by which you are being revealed to yourself? What if your anxiety is actually a gift?

Before I started to change how I looked at my anxiety, one of its side effects was a craving for isolation. I found it hard to be around other people, and their presence intensified my anxious feelings. What I came to realize was that the anxiety was intensified because the presence of others brought my awareness to my life in that moment. I was having an anxious reaction to how I saw myself and my place in the world. Anxiety connects you to the world by making you aware of your place in it. It highlights the gap that exists between who you are and who you know you're meant to be. Your anxiety is revealing that desire to you and inviting you to do something about it.

Anxiety is a feeling of separateness. It causes you to believe that you're separate from your highest self and separate from your purpose. Relief lies in the actions you take and decisions you make about your life right now—and the degree to which they align with the person you are meant to be. Anxiety is a symptom of your mind rejecting the story that your present actions are writing. You can find relief, though, when you take the step of realigning your mindset and writing a new and inspiring story.

OFFER YOURSELF GRACE IN EXPLORATION

The idea of a finding your life's purpose can seem overwhelming. As if these are major decisions that, once made, you're stuck with. I hope that this chapter offered you another perspective. One that gives you permission to show yourself more grace. One that allows you the time and space to experiment, and even be wrong at times.

Life is process, so make room in that process for exploration and change. Being overly critical of yourself and conforming to what you thought was right or expected is what got you here in the first place. You've reached a time in your life when it no longer serves you to spend so much time and energy trying to figure out what others want of you. Life is too short to live for someone else's expectation for you. Too short to live in a boxed-in mindset of someone else's making. Don't let the story of your life be one where you are just waiting around to die—filling your days with a job you hate, going home to an unsatisfying marriage, watching television to numb your emotions, looking for life through your phone screen, and repeating the cycle over again—because you think that's all that you're capable of. That's not a life. You deserve so much more.

The good news is that it doesn't have to be that way. All it takes is a decision to do something about it. You've been given a purpose, something in you that completes the experience of the rest of us. The question is: What is that something? Then, what are you going to do once you discover it? Remember that there's no destination, only a direction. So pick a direction, and grant yourself the grace and space to go.

Since you've picked up this book, I imagine that this is the season for you to spend time and energy untangling yourself, to figure out what you want for your life, to grow. It's going to feel weird at first; it's going to be hard—it definitely was for me. Nonetheless, these ideas need not be overwhelming or inflexible. You are not alone. And the pursuit of your efforts leads to the gift of self-discovery and personal freedom.

I think that too often we forget that this is the one life we get. There are no do-overs. This is it. I'm reminded of the Benjamin Franklin quote: "Some people die at twenty-five and aren't buried until seventy-five." I want to experience all of this life, don't you?

So go, get into action toward your purpose for this season, and know that there are no life sentences. Move graciously through the challenges that life will inevitably throw your way. Be curious about the resistance, but move forward anyway. Feel all the emotions. Take cues from anxiety, but don't be defined or paralyzed by it. Honor the joy, meaning, peace, character, and freedom that you will discover along the journey of this one life you've been gifted.

A mindset of purpose is one that acknowledges your inherent self-worth. Just beware of the detractors, especially the one living in your head. In the next chapter, we'll explore confronting that voice that all too often sabotages your best efforts: your internal dialogue.

INTERNAL DIALOGUE
CHAPTER 2

Surviving is important. Thriving is elegant.

- Maya Angelou

A stock tank is a giant metal bowl used by farmers and ranchers to water livestock. The whole tank is about ten feet across and about two feet deep. One year, my dad decided that it would be a great alternative to a swimming pool, so he put one in our backyard. In the summer, we would all splash around in there to cool off. The edges of this giant metal cow bowl were hot to the touch, and the water was always as warm as a bath, but it was our water oasis. I was about twelve years old on one particularly hot Saturday in June when that stock tank was used as my own personal Jordan River. It was where I was baptized. The week prior, God had revealed to me that I was one of his chosen children; I had been saved.

There wasn't much of mystery around who would show up for my baptism. Membership at our little country church was made up mostly of my extended family. A typical service would pull in around twenty aunts, uncles, cousins, and grandparents, who would sing, pray, listen to a sermon, and then go home. From time to time, there would be special services, as was the case on this day.

The pastor leaned me back into the water as he held his hand over my mouth and nose. "I baptize thee in the name of the Father, the Son, and the Holy Spirit," he proclaimed. He raised me up, and I emerged from the water anew, washed of my sins and reborn in the glory of God.

Almost.

One of my uncles noticed that my whole body didn't go under the water at the same time. My dad wasn't having anything go wrong with this ritual, so he held my legs down while the pastor plunged me under the water for a second time. It was really important that nothing go wrong because this ritual secured my ticket to heaven; we all wanted to make sure that we did this right.

I grew up going to the Sovereign Grace Missionary Baptist Church. I can't speak to all Missionary Baptist churches, but I can speak to this one; it was a fundamentalist Christian organization with more than a few cultlike tendencies. My church professed to believe in the literal meaning of the Bible (as long as it was convenient for them). While literal interpretation of an ancient text that has been translated multiple times over the ages is in itself problematic for thinking people, the part of that religious upbringing that I found most damaging was a doctrine in the Church called predestination.

Predestination hinges on a Calvinist idea that says born-again Christians are predestined for salvation, and their names have been written in the Book of Life before the world began. In other words, Jesus didn't die for everyone—he only died for a few, and those few have already been selected. This means, no matter what good things you do here in this life, none of them will get you into heaven. You can be a murderous, rapist child killer, but as long as your name is in this book, you're in the heaven club. You could be the most philanthropic, kind, and loving person on earth, and if your name isn't in the book—too bad, hell for you.

The Missionary Baptist's brand of thinking at this church also left no room for free will, meaning that people don't have choice in their lives. Church doctrine taught that all things have been pre-determined, and you are merely an empty vessel acting out God's grand script.

There was never an invitation to ask Jesus into your heart like you might hear from a televangelist. You didn't decide to be a Christian; it had already been decided for you. If you are indeed a Christian, then God reveals your salvation to you in his due time. Much of my childhood nights were spent in prayer. My parents, both born-again Christians who had already been saved, would plead with God to save my brother and me.

Salvation was about more than just getting into heaven; it was also acceptance into the tribe—the church tribe, the family tribe. Status of salvation clearly established the insiders and the outsiders. This was a status so elite that even family members who weren't members of our particular church (but attended other Baptist churches) were considered outsiders. Since they didn't subscribe to our particular flavor of Christianity, their faith was lesser than and not true.

When I was around twelve years old, the stuff in my head started hitting the fan. My anxiety was getting more and more intense as I became very aware that I was on the outside of the heaven club, outside of the family tribe. I was beginning to realize that there was something obviously askew about me—something that would disqualify me from walking through the pearly gates.

The week prior to the stock tank Saturday of my baptism was much like any other Saturday. I had spent the day piling brush with my dad. We lived on fifteen acres of woods, and that day he wanted to clear the brush, trim the trees, pull up the stumps, and remove the poison ivy—big tasks for that much land. Every Saturday, and usually during the week, too, you would find us working the land. But on this day, salvation was weighing heavy on my mind.

The pressure to be saved was mounting, partly because I was becoming more aware of the fact that I was different: I was attracted to other boys.

I had known I was different since I was around five years old. I remember feeling different toward the boys at school than I did toward the girls. It wasn't sexual at that age. I think it was just fascination. As I grew up, though, that fascination became something I was ashamed of and knew that I needed to hide. The boys at school, particularly the older ones, must have noticed. By the time I was in middle school, they started calling me words that I didn't understand: *fudge packer, homo, faggot.*

I tried to make sense of what was happening to me at school, avoiding the bullies as best I could. I was navigating my own confusion about what I was experiencing. The real anxiety, though, was what this reality would mean at home. I was freaking out. Fags don't go to heaven. This had been made very clear to me from a really early age. Homosexuals were often the boogey men for the preachers in my church. They were easy targets. Hardened criminals could be redeemed. In fact, one of our pastors had a prison ministry and told stories of the miraculous work of Jesus to save prisoners' souls. But there were never such stories told about homosexuals. Being gay was a sin, one of the greatest sins of all. Gay people were disgusting, vile people, who deserved nothing but an eternity of hellfire and brimstone. The church taught that gay people should all be sent away to a remote island so they couldn't infect the rest of us.

I didn't know that gay people could actually be healthy, contributing members of society. I lived in rural Arkansas, not exactly a gay Mecca. On top of that, there was no healthy queer representation on television at the time—even if there had been, I would never have been allowed to watch it. All I knew about gay people was what I was hearing from the people in my church and the kids at school.

This left me feeling really isolated—and absolutely terrified. If I was gay, being saved wasn't going to be a possibility for me, which meant that I was destined for an eternity in hell. Hell had been described to me as a fiery hot, sulfur-smelling wasteland where the worst of the worst were sent after death—a final destination with no potential for redemption. At home I feared being found out and being abandoned. What the kids at school were putting me through was miserable, but it was nothing compared to the shame I was condemning myself to. The truth of my sexuality had far-reaching, traumatic, and eternal consequences.

As my dad and I cleared and piled brush, I asked him questions about salvation, letting him know how important it was to me. I don't think my parents knew what to do on their own, or how to answer my questions, so they called our pastor to come to our house to pray with me. I spent the rest of that afternoon kneeling beside my parents' bed, crying and begging God to accept me. *Please, God, reveal to me that I, too, am one of your children. Please, just love me. Please, pick me.*

Then, it happened: the elusive and mysterious mystic experience that I had heard about all of my life. I felt a wave wash over me. I was saved. Jesus had swooped in, filled my heart with his mercy, and accepted me into his Kingdom. I looked up from the bed and my tears of fear had miraculously turned to tears of joy.

At least that's what I thought at the time.

Looking back, I realize that the feeling was likely what I would now refer to as my first runner's high—a release of endorphins that sometimes happens during aerobic exercise. I've had many endorphin releases in the years since that had nothing to do with anything religious or spiritual. Each time they happen, I always chuckle and say hello to Jesus. But in that moment, I had worked myself up into such a frenzy that my brain released endorphins to lower my stress and anxiety. It felt so amazing to me that I thought it had to be the presence of the divine.

We were all so relieved. I had been accepted into the heaven club! I was now a full participant in the church, accepted as an equal in the family, and spared from eternal damnation.

All the while, I was growing up, maturing, and developing sexually. My brush with Jesus and my stock-tank baptism hadn't washed my gayness away. The kids at school didn't let up on the bullying, unfortunately, and it was becoming clear that both my mom and dad had their suspicions. It was time for something to ease their concern and prove that I wasn't what they thought. I had to make it clear that I was part of the heaven club and a real member of the tribe.

After stock-tank Saturday, I leaned into my faith more and more as a way to be accepted and feel included. For much of my teenage years, my sexual coming of age, I dived deeper and deeper into the teachings of the Missionary Baptist Church.

I heard terrible things said about gay people, and when I was fifteen years old, I started parroting these hateful ideas from the pulpit of the church. I got it in my head that, because I was so damaged, the only way to repair myself was to go deeper into these beliefs taught by the people from whom I desperately wanted to feel love and belonging. I decided that the best way for me to prove myself would be to dedicate my life to serving God as a minister of his Word.

I bought into my church's beliefs—hook, line, and sinker. I still believed God hated fags, and if God loved me, then there was no way that I could be one—it wouldn't be possible.

Without question, and in direct opposition to what I was experiencing, I adopted their beliefs whole cloth. I would spend my Saturday nights studying the Book of Leviticus, and on Sundays I would deliver a message to the church on the horrible condition of the homosexual.

I never made it through one of those sermons without sobbing. Behind the wooden pulpit of my small country church, addressing twenty members of my extended family, I would stand there, saying horrible things about gay people, crying my eyes out because I knew that I was talking about myself. I was this evil thing that I had always heard about, a disgusting homosexual. I would grab the sides of the pulpit and dig my fingernails into the wood underneath, trying to hold back the tears.

I adopted their beliefs because it was the safest course of action for me. If I was saved, and especially if I was going to be a preacher, then there was no way that God would exclude me from his private club. In order to fit in and to be loved, I accepted this belief system. I was willing to betray myself in exchange for the love and approval of others.

ON BELIEF ORIGINS

There's always a conversation going on inside of us. It comes from the unrelenting little voice in our head that's always present. It's the voice that won't turn off when you're trying to go to sleep. It tells you how amazing you are or how fat you looked today. It says what you really think about your friend's new house. It tells you whether you're worthy of love or not. Every waking moment of your life, that little voice has something to say; it's a little chatterbox, our internal dialogue.

We are born with this loquacious little companion. It starts out innocently enough, but as we grow up, it gets programmed and influenced by our environment.

The little chatterbox is very gullible. When you're growing up, it'll believe just about anything you tell it. It's also very stubborn. Once it adopts a belief, it's really hard to replace it with a new one. Every new idea it encounters has to compete with an old one. Those old beliefs are familiar, and familiar feels good. Most new ideas are rejected outright, usually for no better reason than the old belief was there first. Being right feels too good, and admitting we were wrong can be painful.

Growing up in a fundamentalist Christian church, I was taught to believe many things that weren't congruent with my own life experience. I was taken to church every Sunday morning, Sunday night, and Wednesday night while being taught a set of ideas that did an enormous amount of damage.

I inherited a belief system that contributed greatly to my unhappiness. And yet, I did more than adopt this belief system; I perpetuated it. At least three times a week, the beliefs I carried around were validated. I was being told that my beliefs were right, and who I secretly am is wrong. I was taught that homosexuals go to hell and that the thoughts I was experiencing were sins. It was an untenable position. I wasn't choosing my sexuality, but I desperately needed the love and support of the people who condemned my experience. This tension between my confirmation bias and my reality was tearing my mind apart.

The programming of my own internal dialogue had become my enemy. It was saying things that were beyond dangerous, even deadly, as I was no stranger to suicidal thoughts. At one point, I even had a gun in my hand for that purpose. I understand how awful it can feel to believe that the only escape is the ultimate one.

There's no greater influence on the magnitude of your personal freedom than the conversation going on in your own head. The work of challenging your beliefs and reprogramming that internal dialogue so that it supports you instead of sabotaging you is the most important work of your life.

It took me many years of challenging that belief system to get to a place where I wasn't beating myself up for being me—whether that was from the shame of being gay or having a more liberal leaning than my family and the people I had grown up around. Traces of that internalized homophobia still exist in my little chatterbox to this day, but I continue to do the work and walk my own journey of self-acceptance.

It would be easier to go through life without ever taking the time to reflect on our recurring thoughts, actions, or beliefs. It would be more convenient to continue on, stuck in the familiar. Many people do. But convenience and comfort oftentimes hide the pathway of growth. Some of the most difficult questions we can ask ourselves are those like: *Where did this thought come from? Why do I think that? Is this something that I truly believe? Was this thought passed on to me by someone else? Does that thought align with my own experience?* These are simple but essential questions that a person who wants to thrive and experience their personal freedom must often ask. These questions, left unanswered, allow for fertilization of the cycle we were born into and the perpetuation of those flawed ideas and beliefs.

It's not just religious beliefs that program our chatterbox, but all the beliefs that we pick up as we move through life. Breaking the cycle of those inherited beliefs and untangling the gaps between our beliefs and our reality is the work that will lead an internal dialogue that is more supportive of your personal freedom.

BEATS

Carol Dweck, PhD, author and professor at Stanford, proposed a theoretical framework called BEAT, which is an acronym that represents the idea that Beliefs lead to Emotions that lead to Action Tendencies.[1] Professor Dweck's work explores the ideas of personality and essentially asks: *Are we born with our personalities, or are they developed with our experiences?*

Professor Dweck suggests that we experience a background and foreground in our lives. The information that we gather about our world and how it meets our needs impacts not just our perception of the world in the present, but also how we see and operate in the world in the future. The beliefs and emotions, she suggests, are the background, and our personality traits are the visible foreground and resulting manifestation of those action tendencies.

Put more simply, your beliefs lead to your emotions, which lead to your actions. We experience the outcomes of those actions and recognize their results in the form of life outcomes. Those outcomes that we like become our habits. Those we don't like we come to identify as problems.

Let's reverse it. The problem I'm having is a result of my actions. I engage in those actions because they feel good; they feel good to me because they confirm a belief that I hold about the world and myself.

Professor Dweck's work helped me begin my journey of better understanding my internal chatterbox. I began to see how my beliefs were influencing my life. What I was left with was something that might look like figure 2.1.

Figure 2.1

Our beliefs become alive through our emotions. When our beliefs are expressed, we feel the related emotions behind them. We experience familiar and soothing emotions when we encounter things that reinforce our beliefs. We feel less familiar and uncomfortable emotions when we are forced to encounter things that challenge or contradict our beliefs.

Our desire for familiar or pacifying emotions leads us to actions, or avoidance of action. Even if those actions are in conflict with our best interests, we will act on them anyway if they bring us the desired emotional outcome.

Emotions exist behind all of our behaviors. Here are some of the examples I've recognized in my life: I don't go to the gym because I believe people are judging me when I'm there. It makes me sad and scared to be judged by others. I'm not going to start that business, because I don't believe people will actually pay me for the value I can deliver. Deep down, I'm afraid of failing. I attack people who aren't like me because their life or message requires me to call my beliefs into question. I do this because I'm afraid of being wrong.

Sabotaging beliefs don't just make us avoid behaviors that are good for us; they also cause us to engage in actions that we know aren't good for us. We've all done something that we knew wasn't the right thing to do, but we did it anyway: eating the pie you know you shouldn't, buying shoes we can't afford, hitting the snooze button when we should get up. Those actions, as obviously undesirable as they may be, serve to satisfy some part of us. They reinforce the internal dialogue that we have about ourselves. It's Thanksgiving, so I might as well eat another slice. Those shoes will get me lots of compliments and make my friends jealous. I don't really deserve a better life anyway, so why not sleep a little longer; it won't make any difference.

If an action reinforces your beliefs and feels good, it becomes a habit. Once instilled, you will repeat the behavior to satisfy yourself. An action that doesn't feel good won't lead to a desire to repeat it. The outcomes we experience, whether good or bad, are the result of this predictable pattern in your life.

Your beliefs are the foundation of your ongoing internal dialogue. The chatter in your head that goes on all day is a conversation rooted in your beliefs. Change those beliefs, and you change that conversation. When we untangle those beliefs without judgment and with compassion and grace toward ourselves, we can change our life experience. You can make room for new beliefs and ideas that support who you actually are, not the person someone else expected you to be or the person you believed was necessary to win someone else's love. When you can do that, you will begin to behave in ways that reinforce those new beliefs, have biases toward them, and look for things in the world that reinforce them.

An evaluation of your beliefs will require you to question the source of the beliefs you've modeled. Who or what are your beliefs being molded by? TV? Kids from middle school? Unsuccessful people? Your hillbilly uncle? Fundamentalist religious nuts from your childhood? Beliefs cling to you; they are like knickknacks that you hoard over time. We adopt them, often without actual consideration. They collect and clutter your mind until you make the decision to evaluate which ones are worth keeping and which ones have to go.

If you're unhappy with your life, a careful evaluation of your beliefs may reveal that your ongoing internal dialogue is rife with beliefs that undercut your opportunity to thrive. Are you carrying around beliefs that support or sabotage you? Negative beliefs are cancerous, self-fulfilling prophecies; they breed negativity in your life. Change what you believe about yourself and establish an internal dialogue that supports you. Eventually, those beliefs will lead to emotions and actions that then lead to the results you want for your life.

Personal growth and development is about creating new and desired ways of thinking, feeling, and behaving. That process begins with an examination of the beliefs that inform your ongoing internal conversation—looking at your problems as being the consequences of a flawed system of beliefs. It requires that you intentionally take actions that are uncomfortable, challenge your beliefs, and force a new conversation with yourself. Once you get into this kind of action, see that change is possible, and try on a new belief, your emotions will come into a satisfying alignment with your reality, allowing for real and lasting change.

A LIMITED EMOTIONAL RANGE

Limited beliefs are the result of a limited emotional range.

~ Chad Peevy

I grew up hearing stories about my dad's past: his temper, his mean streak, his athletic prowess, and his reputation for fighting and being a bully. Unfortunately for me, he didn't change much when he became a father.

My dad was the fourth of five children; he became the baby of the family when his two-year-old little brother died from a fever. I think that tragedy afforded him attention as a child that he wasn't ready to give up as an adult. Even once he was married and had kids of his own, his mother continued to coddle him. He had an insatiable appetite for attention, especially from his mother and my mom. When I came along, he wasn't ready to give that attention up to a sensitive little kid who was nothing like him. So, with my mom, my granny, and my granddaddy (his parents) doting over me . . . let's just say I was doomed.

I was a good kid, a quiet boy who didn't cause any mischief, very gentle and sensitive—a momma's boy at home and a teacher's pet at school. Aside from both being momma's boys, the only thing my dad and I have in common is our looks. If I didn't look so much like him, I'm sure there would have been a lot of curiosity about what my mom was doing nine months before I was born, because I didn't resemble him in any other way.

My mother made it clear that she loved me more than she loved him. For as long as I can remember, she had already become disillusioned with his charming hillbilly act. She fawned over me like I'm sure he wished she would have over him. But he was a mean and abusive drunk throughout my early childhood, the early years of their marriage.

My mom married my dad when she was nineteen. When she was twenty years old, she had me. She was the third child of her family. Her older brother was their father's favorite, and her older sister enjoyed being their mother's favorite. Growing up with the knowledge that her siblings were favored over her, my mom was left with issues that she has spent a lifetime struggling with. I saw the consequences of that unapologetic favoritism in her relationship with my father and in how she raised my brother and me. When I came along, I was hers and hers alone; she wouldn't have to compete with anyone for my love and attention. In me, she finally had the love she had always craved.

I'm sure that marrying my dad was, in many ways, a rebellion; it was her escape, coupled with youthful naiveté. My dad was nothing like my mom's family. Don't get me wrong; they were crazy in their own way, like all families. But I always felt like they tried to do the right thing, even if it was often misinformed or misguided. Unfortunately for my mother, her rebellion ultimately backfired in ways she couldn't have imagined.

It was also clear to me from a young age that my dad didn't much care for me. I was never interested in the same things that he liked—things that "the boys" do. I hated hunting and fishing; he lived and breathed those hobbies. He wanted me to be outside all the time; I wanted to help my mom cook. He took pride in his calloused hands; I wanted to have smooth hands. I was undoubtedly a disappointment to him.

The disappointment eventually turned to embarrassment, which quickly evolved to hatred. After all, I was a kid he would have bullied in school. I was getting attention from my granny and my mom (his mother and wife), and he didn't like it. I was his firstborn son and was failing miserably to live up to his expectations. It was a dangerous environment for someone like me to be under the same roof as someone like him.

As a young kid, I became an expert at keeping myself small and hidden. I didn't talk much. I kept my head down and stayed off his radar as much as possible. When he would get drunk or bored, I would find myself in his sights, the target of his cruelty. As a child, I endured brutal and frequent beatings. Not just spankings—beatings. But once my brother was born, I think my dad saw that as an opportunity to have the son he always wanted. That's when the heavy drinking stopped, but the beatings didn't.

As I got older, he would often say to people, "We never even know Chad is on the place," which meant that I was so quiet he would forget that I existed. Yeah, of course I was quiet. I was scared out of my mind that if I got his attention, he would make my life a living hell. My only refuge was to stay small, to go unseen and unheard. As an adult, I came to understand that my dad was a sadist.

He would find any reason he could to beat my ass. Any reason and sometimes no reason at all. If I even looked at him wrong, he would come at me. I can remember the bruises I endured as a young kid. Most of the time his belt was his weapon of choice. But when he was feeling creative, he would use a switch—what us country folk call a small tree branch or stick. And when he was feeling particularly cruel, he would make me go find my own switch for him to beat me with.

Older wood, the small branches that can be found on the ground around the foot of a tree, is usually brittle. Brittle wood will break when you hit something with it. When this exercise in cruelty began, this was my chosen torture device. But when the stick would break, I would have to go find another switch that wouldn't break. That meant finding a small, green piece of wood. Green wood, fresh from the tree, has more give. It won't break and flies faster through the air. It also stings like crazy. I still have the scars on my back to prove it.

What has stuck with me, though, isn't the trauma of the

beatings as much as the psychological warfare he unleashed on me. What did the most damage was when he wouldn't beat me at the time of the alleged infraction; instead, he would wait.

And he would wait.

Not today.

Tomorrow would come and go.

Not today.

The anxiety that caused me was a lot for a little kid to take. The physical beatings themselves were brutal, but the waiting for him to actually do it was the real abuse.

Sometimes a week, sometimes two, and sometimes more would go by. But when he saw me being happy, enjoying myself, living out my childhood, he'd look at me and say, "Don't I owe you one?"

My smile would immediately disappear. Any joy I was experiencing drained from me. I would take my beating. The pain would sting, often bruise, and sometimes scar. As he beat my body, he was doing something actually much worse. He was pummeling my mind with the anxiety, depression, sadness, distrust, and fear that I would be left with for years to come.

Fear was my dad's forte. He had learned his fear tactics from a master: his father. His own childhood was full of abuse. He spent his life afraid of his father; even as an adult, when my granddaddy was old and brittle, my dad was still afraid of him. His father programmed fear into him, and he programmed that fear into me. He would often say to me, as his father had said to him, "No matter how big you get son-ee-boy, I'll always be able to take you. If you ever mess with your old man, I'll kill you." Having heard this from the time he could walk, I imagine he believed it until his father's death. I certainly still believe it. I suppose that's something else we had in common: we were both beneficiaries of an inherited cycle of trauma, abuse, and fear passed down from one generation to the next.

Fear limited my emotional range. I couldn't express other emotions out of the fear of physical retribution. With his fits of rage and the actual beatings, he would remind me of his physical power over me. He might squeeze my leg, leaving bruises. Chase me with a chainsaw. Kill my dogs for no reason. There was never peace on that mountain. He would always find a way to torment me, to instill fear in me. It's no surprise that, later in life, fear would eventually become my dominant emotion.

There are a lot of false lessons that I learned from the abuse my dad inflicted on me. Aside from the absence of a father figure who loved me and whom I could trust, one of those lessons was that being happy meant that bad things would soon follow. Another lesson was that only his anger was allowed, my anger would not be allowed and would be punished.

I guess you could say that he programmed happiness out of me as a child—or at least he tried to. I learned that happiness was dangerous because it lowered my guard. It exposed the joy I feared my dad would rob me of. Eventually, I learned that being happy at all was just a prerequisite to misery. Therefore, I stopped trying to be happy. I stopped trying to find things to do that made me happy. I stopped smiling. I stopped giving the appearance that things were going well. I told myself that things couldn't get too good or the world would come crashing down on me. I can't be too successful, or someone will come and knock me down a peg or two. I can't be confident in myself, in my abilities, or in my talents.

If I am, someone (my dad or someone in the world who reminds me of him) will take this confidence from me.

As a survival mechanism, I began to hide my happiness. I hid it so much that I lost it as a default emotion. It's not gone—I can find it when I'm purposeful about looking for it—but it's an exercise, not a happenstance. Even when I'm able to find it, I'm always afraid of the other shoe dropping. I'm always on the lookout for a traumatic end to the absence of happiness, and I seek the certainty and safety that comes with fear—even if that means making up something imaginary to be afraid of.

When our range of emotional expression is limited, the emotions that we can express become the default. You're always feeling something, and if you're uncomfortable with that feeling, you'll default to what you know. For me, the safest emotion was fear; it became my default.

If you are to learn how to live your life with personal freedom, you have to first discover, identify, and understand your emotions—fear in particular. Learn how fear is showing up in your life, and look for ways that it has both served and sabotaged you. Recognize that the internal dialogue you are having with yourself is being dominated by chronic fear.

Fear is complex. On the one hand, it's necessary for survival and essential to your fight-or-flight response. On the other hand, a life dominated by fear is a life half-lived. The effects of chronic fear have serious consequences. It can lead to digestive issues and heart problems, weaken your immune system, decrease fertility, and even shorten your lifespan. Fear can impair your ability to form long-term memories. It can cause you to live in a state of heightened anxiety that makes the world look scary—and your memories confirm that bias. It can cause an interruption in your brain that doesn't allow you to regulate your emotions, it negatively impacts your decision-making, and it leaves you vulnerable to actions considered inappropriate.[2]

Fear is an unrealistic assessment of a perceived risk. Actions based in fear not only hold you back from a life fully lived, but those actions can also be dangerous.[3] According to the Las Vegas Convention and Visitor Authority, in the year following 9/11, incoming flights were down 6.5 percent while motor vehicle arrivals were up 7.3 percent during the same time.[4] Even though statistics show that driving is more dangerous, thousands of people made a decision (based in fear) that actually put their lives in greater danger. Studies have shown that when a person feels like they have more control, as they would if driving their own car, they feel safer.[5] So, it stands to reason that chronic fear would cause a person to seek out as much control over their other emotions as possible. They regulate when it's not safe to be happy, angry, or even sad, hiding their emotions out of fear of what might happen if they express them.

Why does this matter? When you allow your unjustified fear to limit your life—when fear shows up in your actions, or lack of action—it keeps you from living a fully expressed life. Put simply, fear limits you from being fully you. Rarely are good decisions based in fear. Fear causes three negative results: it keeps you quiet; it causes you to take necessary action too slowly and harmful action too quickly; and it keeps you quiet, small, and paralyzed. If our beliefs do play a role in manufacturing our emotions, then our limiting beliefs about ourselves and what is possible for us are the result of a limited emotional range.

I can remember while growing up in those days, I really wanted to show another emotion. But I knew that if I did, how dangerous that would be. So I held it all in.

I recall how I often found myself looking in the mirror, red faced, tears streaming, trying to convince myself that my time there had an expiration date, hoping that either my dad would die or I would leave home. Either way, I knew one day I would finally escape. The rage engulfed my body, and I would shake as I looked at myself, giving myself permission only to express myself in thought and not out loud because I couldn't risk him hearing me. I would clench my teeth and scream into my hands or pillow.

I didn't realize then that I wasn't crying because I was sad. I was crying because I was so mad. I deserved a loving father, a mother who would protect me, and happiness. If I had expressed this anger as a child, my dad would have responded with violence. When I would cry and express sadness, he would turn to me and say, "Dry it up, or I'll give you something to cry about." What I needed to express as a kid was anger.

Without an appropriate outlet, anger can be extremely damaging,[6] impacting our minds as well as our bodies. The father of psychoanalysis, Sigmund Freud, referred to depression as anger turned inward. When we feel anger, our bodies release stress hormones, increase our heart rate and blood pressure, and raise our blood sugar levels. Too much anger can cause heart attack or stroke, and studies have shown a connection between anger and heart disease. People with a lot of anger are more likely to suffer more frequently from the common cold, the flu, asthma, and skin diseases.

By slowing down and taking the time to understand that your emotional range and dominant emotion matters, the awareness of the limits will help you recognize the opportunity for expansion. Bringing awareness to the idea that you might unknowingly be acting from a dominant emotion will allow you to explore and expand a wider range of your emotions. The awareness itself will create an opportunity to make better decisions and take the best course of action in spite of that dominant emotion.

Fear limited my range of emotions. But the same could be said for someone who grew up in a family where everyone was required to be happy all the time. Or maybe a parent was sad all the time, and that dominant emotion got passed down. Maybe your family didn't avoid anger; therefore anger became the dominant emotion. Any limitation or suppressing of the emotional range will limit the human experience.

Limited beliefs are the result of a limited emotional range. Expand your emotional range, get in touch with the feelings behind the beliefs, and give room for nonsabotaging beliefs to form. If you find that your life has been defined by fear, find ways to explore it to see if those fears are still rational.

Every one of my therapy sessions includes the question, "How does that feel?" I despised this cliché question for years, but let's consider it for a moment. *How does that feel?* For a long time, I didn't know the answer. It was hard for me to find the language to attach to the feelings.

When I have a hard time coming up with an answer, my therapist offers more guidance and gives me prompts: "Do you feel happy, sad, mad, or scared?"

It seems so elementary, so simple. It's like a kindergarten grading system: happy face or sad face. But there's power in the simplicity. You may not understand the range of your emotions, because the expression of those emotions as a child was dangerous for you. Slow down enough to explore the emotional range by exploring the most accessible emotion, as well as other possibilities. For example, if I recognize that I'm scared, is it possible that I'm also angry or maybe sad?

Through years of therapy, I realized that sadness and fear were easier for me to identify because I'd been able to express them more easily, at least internally. Sadness and fear were easier for me to hide; I was able to express them without disrupting others or bringing attention to myself. Those two emotions were most comfortable for me, so that's where I stayed—to the point that I had conditioned myself (or perhaps been conditioned) to stay small, quiet, sad, and scared.

I repressed feelings of happiness and turned my anger inward. Those emotions are more outward-facing emotions that beg to be expressed in a healthy way in order to feel them fully. These feelings were dangerous for me growing up, so I didn't allow for them as much as I needed to.

Paying attention to my fear of my father is no longer serving me. If there's one thing I've learned along the way, it's that on the other side of fear and anger is freedom. Fear will rob you of your greatness; it will cheat you of your full potential.

As adults, we have an opportunity to break the cycle of our own emotional limitations. We have a chance to nurture ourselves and those we love in a new cycle that welcomes and seeks to understand the full range of our emotions.

CHATTERBOX GETS STUCK ON REPEAT

One of the more obvious effects of a limited emotional range happens when the internal dialogue gets stuck on repeat. If we're unable to process our full range of feelings, it's as if our dominant emotion gets stuck, and we begin to create beliefs that will reinforce that feeling. For me, that recurring loop was fear. My survivor mindset told me that it was fear that kept me safe from harm, so the belief informed the emotion, then the emotion began creating beliefs that would support and perpetuate the emotion.

To survive, we have to be aware of what could threaten us. When looking at a situation, someone with a survivor mindset is immediately going to consider all the ways that situation could harm them, then take precautionary measures to mitigate damage to themselves.

When the scanning for the threats gets caught in a loop, it's like a record player that starts to skip on the same spot on the record. Buddhists have a word for this type of thought spiral: pa-pañca (pa-PUN-cha), loosely translated to mean "proliferation." This idea of getting stuck on a potential negative outcome is what I call the obsessive loop.

You may be thinking that this sounds like worrying.[7] I've certainly had my share of worries, but the obsessive loop is like worrying on steroids. It's like a drumbeat in your head that never goes away. It's there during your waking and sleeping hours. You dream about the object of your obsession, and you wake up thinking about it. It's even there when you're in conversation with other people. You can hear them, but their words are drowned out by the volume of chatter in your own head. It's always there; overthinking becomes your mind's constant companion.

When I enter an obsessive loop, it's my most guarded and secluded place. I'm able to shut reality out, when it's reality that I need the most. I don't think about any of the goings on of my day-to-day life. I get stuck thinking about the artificial dilemma I've created in my head. I've found myself caught in loops, asking: *Do I have cancer? Is he going to leave me? Is this business going to fail? Am I going to go broke? Am I going to be homeless?*

This loop creates a type of panic. When I'm in this state, I feel my breath shorten and my heart beat with aggravation. I feel my skin crawl. This state of alertness, being attuned to the threat, is what served me for so long. It allowed me to stay focused on what could go wrong because, for so many years, that wasn't an alternate universe of fear that I had created in my head; it was a real fear of my dad and a need to survive his abuse.

My obsessive loop is kind of like a passionate bad fit (a disconnect between what is needed versus what is delivered that can lead to a part of our personality that anticipates being denied that which is needed).[8] Another way to think about a passionate bad fit is that you return to a feeling that "hurts so good." A feeling that, while not positive, reinforces the familiar. When you're craving familiarity and certainty, it may be the hurt that satisfies that need.

Why does this happen? Clearly there's a purpose. Here are the three main reasons I believe this phenomenon, this obsessive loop, happens in my life: it's a distraction, it's familiar, and it's a regression to an illusion of love and belonging. These reasons can serve a purpose, even if the outcomes are not particularly desirable. Let me go into further detail on these three reasons.

First, the loop is a distraction. It has allowed a very active mind to find something to remain focused on. My imagination can run wild while I avoid reality, even though reality is almost always better than the imaginary disaster that I've created in my head. This alternate universe that I've designed and created around fear is a place in my head that does not support my ability to thrive. That obsession might be a person or relationship, my appearance, or a health issue. While this loop is ongoing, there's no room for anything else in my head (namely reality) because I've created a threat crisis that needs my most immediate attention. The loop becomes my retreat.

When you find yourself in this state, you would be better

served to look past the object of the obsession and look for the obsessive thinking itself; that will help you snap back to reality. That means literally saying to yourself, *I'm in an obsessive loop. I'm going to stop this and make my way back to what is real.* It helps to see whatever crisis you've created in black-and-white. For example, if it's a financial obsession, go look at your numbers—they don't lie. If it's a health obsession, go to the doctor and find out for certain what, if anything, is going on with you. Get as grounded as possible in reality.

Second, the obsessive loop shows up because it's familiar. The fear that exists in this obsessive state of mind hurts me and has held me back, but it's familiar. And familiar often feels better than the unknown. The unknown is dangerous and painful. Familiarity is disguised as a sense of control.

And third, the obsessive loop is a regression to an illusion of love and belonging. A regression that I allow to feel closer to those who were supposed to love and protect me.[9] I know this can be a hard idea to accept. But if you've ever experienced this, I'm inviting you to consider whether you hold yourself back, or maybe even sabotage yourself, in the hopes that the person who was supposed to love and protect you when you were a child will come to your rescue now. Part of the obsessive loop is this cruel denial. The obsessive loop allows us to imagine the painful scenario that requires this person to help us, but the help never arrives. They aren't coming to the rescue. It's up to us to find another way to complete the obsessive loop.

Obsessive loops show their ugly heads at weird times. I've found that mine typically show up when I want to feel connected to my family. On certain holidays and other special days, I miss them; I want to feel connected to them. And the only way I feel connected is through emotional suffering. It's what I know.

When you find yourself caught in one of these obsessive loops, it's important to stop and acknowledge it. The awareness of it is the pathway out of it. It is then that you can feel your way out of it and into healthier emotional territory.

Our brains are like heat-seeking missiles. They are constantly searching to make connections, to reinforce existing connections, to make easy connections between one thought and another. The chatterbox living in our head just wants to be fed the familiar, self-reassuring beliefs and will seek out the emotions and actions that do just that.

So how does one break that cycle and begin to untangle an existing belief system? Here are a few ideas that have helped me. First, introduce your internal dialogue to a system of logic and reason. Second, tell your brain to start looking for something else. And third, give the heat-seeking missiles in your mind a new heat to seek.

STOICISM / CBT

If you've been in therapy, you've likely experienced some form of Cognitive Behavioral Therapy (CBT). CBT, a typically short-term and problem-focused methodology, is widely used among thera-pists, psychologists, social workers, and counselors to identify and quickly achieve a specific goal of working through a person's emo-tional distress. It's important because one of the original thinkers behind CBT, Albert Ellis, made it quite clear that he believed this was a process that a person can start on their own and realize its benefit. We can use the ideas from this method to help ourselves.

Much of modern-day CBT is rooted in Stoic philosophy.[10]

In fact, Ellis primarily attributed his ABC approach to Stoic philosophy, particularly Epictetus and Marcus Aurelius. The ABC approach says that an Activating Event + our Beliefs = our Consequences.

This approach isn't too dissimilar from Dweck's BEAT model discussed earlier. What is central to both Ellis and Dweck's models is that our beliefs play an overwhelming role in our life's outcomes. Our perception of things that happen to us informs our beliefs and therefore influences how we see our life's outcomes. For example, if we have a minor car accident, we could come away with the idea that the accident was a result of a series of minor mistakes. Or we could get really angry, see ourselves as a victim, and be left with an idea that everyone else is a bad driver.

Stoic philosophy can also help us become aware of the influence of our beliefs on life's outcomes. Stoicism introduces logic and reason into our belief systems to allow us to better frame those beliefs that are illogical.

> *Men are disturbed not by the things which happen,*
> *but by their opinions about the things.*
>
> *~ Epictetus*

According to Ellis, there are three main irrational beliefs that lead our minds astray when we attempt to make sense of things that happen to us in our lives:

1. *The belief that we must be successful.* Failure is a part of life; perhaps our most valuable lessons are learned in failure. When we adopt the irrational belief that we must be successful in all things, we are denying ourselves the real value of any experience (positive or negative), one where expectations dictate the journey.

This kind of thinking limits the range of potential positive outcomes that might be outside of our expectations. If we hold an irrational belief that we must be successful, life will be full of disappointment and only be seen in binary terms: pass or fail, black or white. Such a rigid way of looking at the world doesn't leave much room for growth. The butterfly doesn't go directly from caterpillar to butterfly; there's a process. We're better off approaching life with the recognition that our attachment to our expectations limits our life's experience.

2.   *The belief that others must treat us well.* To go through life believing that everyone has to treat you fairly is limiting. Is it reasonable to have a *desire* for people to like you? Of course. Is it reasonable to hold in your mind a *demand* that others like you? No. If in my mind I demand that others like me, then it would require me to conform to what I believe they would expect of me. When I have to become something else in exchange for another person's love and approval, it isn't just an irrational belief, it's also a roadblock to personal freedom. I don't hold in my mind a *demand* that others like me; instead, I seek the personal freedom to fully be and express myself regardless of how I'm treated.

3.   *The belief that the conditions under which we live must be agreeable to us.* Perhaps you've found yourself in a situation in which the circumstances didn't match what you had expected. This happens to everyone, but trouble comes when you believe that it shouldn't ever happen to you. Sometimes circumstances

can't be controlled. When you're intolerant to the circumstances, the beliefs that form will most certainly taint how you view your life. Instead, seek to freely express yourself regardless of the conditions.

These irrational beliefs, Ellis proposes, are the basis for the misery that shows up in our life—whether that be anger, depression, anxiety, or other manifestations. He suggests that instead of thinking of irrational *musts*, we approach our lives with a more rational set of *preferences*.

But be aware that inflexible preferences can cause misery just the same. A more supportive mindset is one that says, "While I might prefer one thing over the other, I'm not attached to either." Attachment to the preference itself can be the limitation.

This is the intersection of CBT and Stoicism. When life throws lemons at you, will you adopt a mindset of making lemonade, or get pissed off about the lemons or the person throwing the lemons? Will you get angry that you allowed yourself to be hit by the lemons, or that the universe created lemons in the first place?

When it rains, will you be mad at the rain, cursing the thunder and screaming at the lightning? Or will you grab an umbrella and go about your day? Will you put on a raincoat or make different plans?

Stoicism offers a roadmap for how to respond to life's events. It provides the tools for how to respond in the moment. If you *can* do something about it, you *should*. If you can't do anything about it, then you should let it go.

We often hear, "It is what it is." This isn't a flippant colloquialism; it's a modern-day interpretation of Stoic philosophy. Most people spend their lives refusing to accept reality and live their lives ruled less by reason and more by their emotions—perhaps even by a dominant emotion that needs to be resolved. We see people throwing temper tantrums, wallowing in cognitive disturbance, leaving them prone to anxiety, depression, and anger. Most people form their beliefs and then apply those beliefs and the emotions attached to them to every part of their lives—overgeneralizing their limited experiences to their life's reality. Not every problem is resolved with anger, or tears, or by retreating.

Stoicism tells us just the opposite. It's a practice of looking objectively at each circumstance we are presented with and then proceeding with reason.

> *To look for the fig in winter is a madman's act.*
>
> *~ Marcus Aurelius*

Stoicism helps remind me of what's important in my life and what isn't. It gives me ideas about how to preserve my mental energy for the endeavors that are worthy and have the potential to be influenced by my efforts. This isn't a suppression of emotion; it's about experiencing a range of diverse emotions.

Stoicism is for those who are active in their pursuit of a great life. It's an emotional practice that should be thought of like a physical practice, such as lifting weights or doing cardio. Stoicism is a way of life that requires active engagement.

EXERCISE

To help you untangle ways that dominant emotions and irrational beliefs show up for you, take your journal and write your reflections on the following questions:

1. Think about the last time you encountered a situation that didn't go your way, resulting in a state of depression, anger, or anxiety. Did you respond with a dominant emotion? If so, name that emotion.

2. Which of the irrational beliefs outlined in this section most applies to your response? Did you assume that you should have been successful? That you should have been treated well by others? Or that the conditions should have been perfect? Write down the beliefs that most accurately fit your circumstance.

3. Reflect on how you might react to that situation if it were to happen now, without thinking of your preferred outcome. Write our your reaction.

4. Spend a few minutes journaling how that would impact your feelings afterward and how anyone else might have be impacted differently because of your adjusted response.

EXPAND YOUR CHATTERBOX VOCABULARY

My chatterbox was always looking to confirm my most negative and paranoid beliefs about other people and myself. This self-sabotage was simply a consequence of its limited vocabulary.

There were three ways that I learned to expand my chatterbox vocabulary. The first was to start intentionally looking for the good. The second was to reroute negative thoughts with three simple words (but what if?). And the third was to change my environment.

1. LOOK FOR THE GOOD.

My story is one of long-endured trauma. When that's the case, it can be hard to stay in an optimistic mindset. When you have a survivor's mindset, you find it difficult to look for the good, much less find it. If you do happen to find it, even briefly, it's almost a reflex to immediately discount the good and bring yourself back to the more familiar feeling of what we might rationalize as a less than ideal version of reality.

After years of working on this, I understood that the reality was that I was addicted to feeling bad about myself. By making myself feel unworthy, I had some control over those unpleasant feelings. If I allowed myself to experience happiness, my dad would come along and take that away; he had all the control. Somewhere along the way, I learned that it was better for me to cause my own unhappiness because that seemed safer.

A survivor's mindset trains itself to always be on the lookout for the bad in order to survive. But to thrive, to teach the chatterbox some new vocabulary, we have to learn to look for the good. In his book *Learned Optimism*, Martin Seligman offers an exercise that I have found helpful to put this idea into practice. Place a notebook and pen next to your bed. Each night, before you go to sleep, write down three good things that happened that day and why they were good. Do this every night.

This simple exercise will train your mind to start looking for the good throughout your day. If you're alive and breathing, you can certainly find three good things that happened to you today. It may be the fact that you're still breathing. It may be that you're going to bed with a roof over your head. I'm writing this book during the pandemic of 2020, so nearly every day I write that I'm grateful for my health. Yes, some days will force you to be more basic with your gratitude, but that's the point. The chatterbox has a vocabulary based in criticism and complaining, so bringing awareness to the good in your day teaches it new words. Even when things seem really horrible, there's always some good to be found if you look for it.

2. FOLLOW UP FEARFUL THOUGHTS WITH "BUT WHAT IF . . . ?"

The chatterbox has a tendency to be dramatic. When it seems like the world is on fire and the sky is falling, simply stop and ask yourself this simple question: "But what if . . . ?" (Follow this by stating a positive potential outcome.)

The trick is to get quicker at recalling those three words. First, accept that it's going to take time for the mindset you've had all these years to make way for the new one you're adopting. So, instead of beating yourself up for having a skeptical thought, just learn to add these three words onto the end. It might go something like this:

> ► Someone calls or approaches you to have a conversation.
> ► Your initial thought is that they want to criticize or scold you for something; your head fills with dread and catastrophic thoughts.

▶ Your higher self intervenes and says, *"But what if they don't have negative intentions? What if they are coming over here to compliment me?"*

Adding "but what if?" to your internal dialogue will help bring you a sense of calm and rationality. It will reign in a tendency to catastrophize or skew to the negative potential of life's outcomes. It will help you engage in life more freely because you're opening your life up to more rewarding results rather than avoiding your worst imaginations.

3. CHANGE YOUR ENVIRONMENT.

After years of expecting the worst, my personality developed a prickly outer shell. Like a porcupine, I had an exterior that protected me from being hurt. It was another survival mechanism. As I started to recognize this, I was beginning to understand that personal development isn't just an internal game; it's an external one as well. We have to work on how we show up in the world and also be conscious of our surroundings.

Over time, I came to the realization that I am not actually a porcupine. I am, in fact, human. I was really excited and wanted to share the news!

I joined a friend for coffee and shared this revelation, explaining my relief that I no longer had to put on this cynical, pessimistic mask.

To my surprise, she laughed and said, "You are the most pessimistic person I know." I was devastated. How could she say that? Didn't she realize that I had done all this work on myself? That I was only hiding behind this mask to protect myself?

At that moment, I realized that I had attracted other porcupines into my life, people who were just as prickly as I was, if not more. This friend was an unapologetic porcupine. And furthermore, she was quite happy with her sharp quills.

I'll be the first to tell you: Creating this change, both internal and external, is tough. It's so much easier to be around other cynical people, to bitch about the way things are so that you don't get your hopes up and get let down. It's easier to be arrogant and not be the first to speak to people because they may not speak back. It's easier to expect the worst because if the worst happens, you don't get hurt. But this is all irrational thinking. It's also not the only mask that people put on. Some put on a mask of fake happiness, of sadness, of victim, of protector, and so on.

Removing that mask requires putting the idea of personal freedom into practice. You have to *practice* personal freedom, just like you would practice the piano—it's a skill that has to be developed by doing the work you'll find in this book and elsewhere on your journey.

By now, you know that there is power in familiarity. This is true of the people we spend time around. We seek out people who allow us to feel the familiar. If you're on a personal development journey, those familiar surroundings may become untenable. There's a good chance you'll discover that you, too, have surrounded yourself with porcupines. But practicing personal freedom may require a change in your environment. Changing your environment can be as simple as introducing something new into it, even if it's just the idea of dropping your protective shell. I'm not suggesting you break up with all your friends, or others from your past, as everyone is on their own journey and taking it at their own pace. And even if their journey isn't the same as yours, you can see your time with them as practice. Practice looking at your circumstances through a new lens. People who are further along on the journey can act as your role models. As you'll see in chapter 13, I encourage you to put yourself in situations with other people who see the good in you, in other people, and in the world.

What you'll find when you change your environment is that people who are thriving, who are living their personal freedom (people who were never porcupines or who are recovering) don't want to be around porcupines. You can't be your old porcupine self around them—thankfully, they won't tolerate it. While a few might give you the gift of being direct, letting you know when you exhibit porcupine behavior, most won't. Instead, they just won't allow you into their environment. Let them know about your journey, and ask for their grace and honesty. With continued practice and support, change is possible.

AFFIRMING QUESTIONS

The chatterbox is unwieldy and has an extremely short attention span. As you work to reject your old beliefs and install new ones, we can use that sort of attention span to our advantage by asking affirming questions.

We live in an age of affirmations. If affirmations help you align your mindset, you should practice them; a purposeful affirmation is certainly better than negative thoughts by default.

If you're not well-practiced in affirmations, it can be challenging to get started. Sometimes our autopilot thoughts are so ingrained that they've cut deeps trails in our minds. New affirmations can feel so foreign that they're simply unbelievable.

Our brains are constantly searching to make connections that will tie ideas together, associations that reinforce existing connections, in order to make easy connections between one thought and another. While affirmations can disrupt these connections, I believe affirming questions are a more effective way. Here are some examples:

Instead of: *I have loving relationships with all the people in my life.*
Try: *How can I create a life full of love and joy?*

Instead of: *People love being my friend.*
Try: *How can I make other people find joy in spending time with me?*

Instead of: *I am rich, famous, and successful.*
Try: *How do I get all of my needs abundantly met?*

This is a simple method; instead of stating affirmations, you ask yourself affirming questions. You give your brain intellectual catnip to ponder and create a series of new synaptic connections that satisfy the questions without having to introduce affirmative thoughts that you may taint with skepticism. This method uses the nature of your mind in your favor instead of trying to force a square peg into a round hole. Affirming questions tell your brain what heat to seek.

UNDERSTANDING LEADS TO CHANGE

If you find yourself unsatisfied with your life, and if you're anything like me, you'll want to change it all and change it fast. I'll look for the most convenient life hack to make it all better. But looking for a life hack is like putting a Band-Aid on a gunshot wound. Hacks may help in the short term, but they don't lead to lasting change.

What you believe about yourself and the world has been reinforced nonstop by the most powerful person in your life—you—based on the way you were programmed by the people you relied on for survival as a kid. I want to remind you that this process of untangling isn't one of assigning blame. This isn't about blaming your parents for the way your life turned out, but it is a process of understanding how you were parented. That's where so much of our programming comes from, so it would be naïve to ignore it. This understanding will offer you clues as to why you do the things you do—essentially waking you up to your own beliefs, emotions, behaviors, and their consequences. When you understand, you can change.

One of the most challenging and most courageous acts of our lives is to question all of our beliefs and change our internal dialogue—to reprogram that internal dialogue. A therapist, a coach, a spouse, a mentor, a friend, or a school of philosophy can help you recognize your patterns and help you move closer to personal freedom. But even with help, these changes will not happen overnight. The best any of us can do is to bring awareness to that conversation in our head and begin the work of untangling the sabotaging thoughts that inform this experience we call life.

IDENTITY
CHAPTER 3

We are not who our senses tell us we are.
We are an infinite being.
We do not get what we want; we get who we are.

–Les Brown

More than 70,000 people cheered as I strutted to the center of the football field at Donald W. Reynolds Razorback Stadium. Alone on the painted grass of an empty football field, I felt the wind slightly catch the feathers in my hat and the stadium lights dance off the sequins across my chest. The roar of the crowd sent waves of adrenaline through my body.

A reporter had just interviewed me to be featured in my hometown newspaper. In just a few days, everyone back home would see my picture in the paper and read about my climb to the top of the marching band ranks.

Out of the corner of my eye I could see Brian, my fellow

drum major and best friend. In marching band, I had friends—a best friend even! I belonged somewhere, my childhood dreams finally realized.

The university experience was amazing in so many ways, but school days were simply recovery time for the next home football game. The excitement and anticipation I felt inside would intensify as the weekdays passed and Saturday drew near.

To say I was addicted to my identity as drum major wouldn't properly convey the magnitude. Being drum major wasn't a job, a role, a position, or a title. Drum major was who I was, full stop.

I took a giant breath and blew the whistle, giving the command for more than three hundred of my fellow band members to pour onto the field. This was heaven, and I was God.

"Ladies and gentlemen, now taking the field, the University of Arkansas Razorback Marching Band! The band is under the field direction of Drum Major Chad Peevy from Alma, Arkansas . . ."

Then it all went away.

My dad was a barefoot kicker on his high school football team, a game for which I had no interest. High school football games were the place to be on a Friday night in rural Arkansas. From the time I was old enough to go, my dad would take me to these games. My disinterest in the game, though, didn't tamper my enthusiasm for this Friday night ritual.

It was halftime that I loved. Once the football players got out of the way, the field was made available for its true and intended purpose. My eyes would gaze in wonder at the uniforms, the sparkles, the big hats, the color, the sound. I had no idea what the band was doing, or what exactly I was watching. All I knew was that it was loud and flashy, yet orderly and structured. I thought it was the coolest thing I had ever seen, and I knew that somehow, someday, I just had to be part of it. Despite the flashy color guards and instrumental solos, the real object of my affection was the drum major.

I had no idea what the drum major was doing. But it didn't matter to me. I was going to do that, no matter what it took. I didn't know how, but one day I would be the one standing up there on that podium. Standing in front of all these people, unapologetically fully expressed, that guy was the manifestation of total freedom for my young mind.

At home, I was trained to stay small, watch my mannerisms, go unseen and unheard. But here was this kid at a football game being cheered on for standing in the front of a marching band, waving his arms and doing anything but staying small. Expressing himself through his movement and flash wasn't just acceptable, it was expected. I saw an opportunity for an outlet, and I had to have it.

When I was old enough to sign up for middle school band, my mom took me to the orientation. This would be my first trip into the band's inner sanctum. I remember the band room's high ceilings, the grungy carpet, and the instruments stacked up on painted wooden shelves along the wall. The room was considerably less glamorous than what I had seen on the football field, but that didn't diminish my resolve. Shiny instruments that I recognized from halftime were lined up on long tables set up around the room. That night, kids and their parents would meet with the instrument salespeople and purchase or rent the instrument they would one day carry into the Friday night halftime show.

My mother and I must have looked like we were lost at the flea market, because the instrument salespeople ushered us away from their tables over to the band director, Mr. Greenwood. He was an effeminate man by Arkansas standards; he was young, had a trendy haircut, and wore tight clothes. Before this night, I knew him by reputation only, since all the kids made fun of him. They called him the same names my bullies called me. I didn't realize it at the time, but that night was the first time I came face-to-face with a gay person, someone like me. Without saying anything, simply by displaying kindness and patience, he showed me that people like me had a place in band.

After explaining to me that I couldn't even audition to be drum major for another two years, he got me set up with a baritone, my third-choice instrument, behind French horn and trombone. Because I was confused as to why I couldn't just be drum major full time and not bother with an instrument, Mr. Greenwood went on to explain that I needed to spend two years learning my instrument before I would have the opportunity to be in marching band. After that, I would spend one semester in marching band and one semester in concert band each year. I had no interest in concert band. It was all about blending and fitting in, and I had enough of that in my life already. But with my eyes on the prize, I reluctantly lugged that horn around and practiced just enough to stay in band, waiting for my rise to the podium.

Band would end up playing a major role in my life. The baritone I begrudgingly played eventually landed me a marching band scholarship at the University of Arkansas. I declared as a music education major with the intent of being a band director, since I thought it would be the closest thing to becoming a professional drum major. Band offered me more than just an extracurricular activity; it gave me an escape route from home, a way to safely express myself, and an identity.

I was fixated on being drum major; it helped me understand the world and my place in it. I didn't know who I was without that position. Even the years that I wasn't eligible to be drum major, I saw myself as the drum major in waiting.

Band is where I found friends. It turned out to be a pretty gay-friendly environment (if not friendly, at least not unbearably hostile). It gave me a sanctuary to fit in at school. I had found my people, my tribe. Plus, the more success I had at being the drum major, the more reinforced that identity became publicly. Not only did I define my life that way, other people related to me and attached that identity to me as well. It didn't hurt that my parents approved of me being in band and being the leader of the group. Everyone knew me as drum major, and that recognition made me feel valued.

When my first year of eligibility to audition for drum major at the U of A came around, I got it. I was ecstatic, a culmination of years of hard work was now being recognized beyond my small hometown. Each year, drum majors had to reaudition with everyone else. So my second eligible year, I showed up to the audition wearing my special shirt that had "DRUM MAJOR" embroidered on the front, certain of the outcome. But when the results were posted, I didn't get it.

More than just embarrassed and disappointed, I was gutted of my identity. I was so fixated on my role, my title, my position, that when I got the news, I absolutely lost it. It was an ugly cry and sickness in my stomach that overtook me. The role I dreamed of playing as a boy, the position I worked to earn, the title that defined my life . . . was gone. If I wasn't the drum major, who was I?

I wasn't equipped with the emotional tools to cope, and so I did all sort of things to manage my mind. That night, I drank a bottle of white brandy, probably because that's all I had in my dorm room. The next day, I started making calls to other universities to see if I could audition there. I even used my key to the band offices to look at all the audition forms, certain there had been a mistake in score calculations. These were not my finest or most dignified days.

Eventually, I calmed down and committed to finishing my degree at Arkansas. I continued on the music education path as a way to salvage some part of that identity. The absence of the drum major role had left me lost and without a compass, so I just kept going down that most familiar path.

After graduation, I was accepted to The University of Texas at Austin's master's program for music and human learning. During that time, I realized that band wasn't a lifelong career path for me. Rather, it was an escape route for me. It gave me a safe place and a sense of belonging as a misfit kid. Band gave me an environment to grow, experience some amazing things, and meet some great people. Even though I wasn't calling it as such at the time, I recognized that the season of band had passed in my life. It had served its purpose for me, and I was grateful. Band allowed me to leave Arkansas and move to a place that I love and have called home ever since. There, I met my husband, started my businesses, and discovered more of myself. I'm grateful that I eventually let go of my drum major identity, and with that, my attachment to band. By letting that season pass, I gave my life room for something new: a new season.

Sometimes we become so attached to the idea of an identity that we lose sight of who we really are. We don't usually notice this is happening until that part of our identity is threatened or taken away from us. At this point, we become consumed with defending and protecting that identity. In our defense, we grasp to that identity even tighter, only to create more problems and incongruence. Band taught me these lessons about my identity; for you, it may be motherhood, a career, sports, a marriage, or something else.

My attachment to an identity, especially one that helped me

define myself and my place in the world, also allowed me to ignore what I was hiding behind that identity. I had to face more than the loss itself. I had to confront what it meant for me to hold onto it. Why was I hiding behind that identity? What was it covering up? What was it allowing me to express that I didn't feel free to express otherwise?

Down the road, I had to come to terms with the fact that I was so dependent and attached to my identity as drum major that, when I lost it, I immediately went looking for a new one. In fact, immediately after losing that audition, I was actively and unknowingly creating a new identity: victim. I wanted to blame the new band director, the student who took my spot, homophobia, my parents, and myself. But replacing my old identity with victimhood, while convenient and in many ways satisfying, wasn't going to help me.

Lacking self-awareness, I latched onto the identity of victim, a most dangerous identity. By adopting this identity, I was freely giving away my freedom and power to other people. I was allowing myself to be defined by what other people thought of me, and I was caging myself into an existence that I can only characterize as miserable. To be clear, I wasn't victimized by someone else; I had victimized myself. And, in doing so, I was unwittingly undermining myself. I was allowing this new identity to replace the previous one that I had assumed as a little kid. But neither of these would serve me.

Turns out the victim identity was familiar to me. I was the victim of an abusive father, victim of a rough childhood, victim of my bullies, and on and on. Again, let me be clear: I'm not excusing any perpetrators' bad behavior. And I'm not saying that we can't take some time to process and even feel our way through those bad things that have happened to us. What I *am* saying is that we have a say in whether we allow our circumstances to define us.

You can choose to see your past circumstances as having prepared you for your life as it is in this moment, or you can see yourself as a victim of them. My hope for you is that, through all of the work you do to better understand yourself, you can relinquish any trace of your identity associated with victimhood. Ultimately, I had to realize that blame would not free me. I had to realize that, though I may not have chosen the circumstances, I could choose how to see and define my experience. Personal freedom exists outside an identity shackled by a victim mindset.

What we fail to realize in that moment of threat or loss is that thing, that identity, is artificial. It's just an idea. That thing isn't who we really are; it's just a gift that allowed us to express who we were at that moment of our lives. When we aren't attached to an identity, that freedom gives us room to experience more life—more flexibility, less judgment, fewer expectations imposed on ourselves or by others. The ideas we develop about who we are have a way of sticking and acting as a way to validate us. But an attachment to our identity is a roadblock to our personal freedom.

Facing the loss of an identity, or allowing ourselves to free ourselves from one, can be a gift that brings us closer to who we really are. A gift that can allow us to see ourselves without an artificial identity obstructing the view. If we can accept that gift, it's an opportunity for us to discover our true selves and make significant and meaningful changes in our lives that will draw us closer to what we want.

WHAT IS "IDENTITY" ANYWAY?

Your identity is a collection of stories that you have come to accept as your truth. As you were growing up, the people in your life had ideas about who you were and who they wanted you to be. From the information you received from these people, and based on your experiences, you made up stories that define who you are and how you want others to see you. These stories, and how you interpreted them, have become your worldview. They defined your place in your world, how you relate to others, and how they relate to you. Simply put: What you thought, you have become. And because of the way your mind works, these beliefs are reinforced; they permeate and perpetuate.

There's an old Indian parable, *The Blind Men and the Elephant*, about a group of blind men who come upon an elephant. One of the men walks up to the elephant, touches it, and begins to describe the tusk. One man describes the tail, and another describes the side of the elephant. Each man describes his reality based on a small part of the animal. All of the men are accurate and telling the truth, but each man is also experiencing the same animal in completely different ways—ways that are unbelievable to the other men. They argue over what is truth, unaware that they're all telling the truth, just from different perspectives. And furthermore, they're unaware that all of those perspectives were available to them should they decide to reframe their experience.

Your identity, how you've come to see your place in the world, has formed in much the same way. You've experienced just a small part of the world and, in fact, of yourself. But your frame of reference is based on your limited experiences.

Coming into this awareness about your life, you come face-to-face with your potential. If the way you think about the world is how you experience the world, reason follows that your thoughts, based on your limited experiences, produced your current circumstances. Imagine being the man in the parable who was at the ass-end of that elephant. If he just stayed there, he would miss out on the majesty of this marvelous animal. Taking responsibility for how you currently experience the world opens the opportunity and freedom to expand that experience.

If your thoughts produced your life as it is right now, then your thoughts can produce something else. Don't allow yourself to get stuck with the ass-end of the elephant.

Don't confuse who you are with what you've done. Who are you? Not who people think you should be. Not who you used to be. Not your function or role in something or someone else's life. Who are you, really? At your core, who are you?

It's a question you have to ask because who you believe you are is who you will behave as. This will dictate your habits, form your environment, determine your happiness, and, ultimately, your personal freedom. Even if absent any awareness of it, you have chosen who you are. But with awareness you can change your choices. Remember, there are no life sentences. Who will you choose to become?

When you're not true to yourself, you're not living your authentic life. Some part of you will sense that this misalignment exists and will express itself: that's anxiety. Anxiety is the untenable gap between who you're behaving as and who you really are.

For me, there are many contributing factors to my anxiety, but it's highest when my identity is out of alignment. When I hold back and don't say what I need to say, I feel that anxiety. I feel it when I don't behave in ways that uphold who I really am and when I allow fear to hold me back. The fearful me isn't the true me; he has forgotten who he is, believing untrue stories he's telling himself.

Your identity is a collection of stories that you have come to accept as your truth. Which stories will you tell yourself?

MANIFEST IDENTITY FIXATION

I don't think that my experience when I lost my drum major role was all that unusual. Think of the high school star quarterback who never moves on from his days of glory. The PTO mom who has no sense of herself outside of the role. The workaholic who's so fixated on the work that they have no sense of themselves outside of it.

Personal freedom is recognizing that no matter the season, we'll show up fully as the person we've worked so hard to become. It means fully expressing who we are and who we're becoming. It's not limited by role, title, or position. What makes us who we are is bigger than can be contained by a singular manifestation of these attributes.

The kids will grow up. The job will go away. The business will have ups and downs. Your days as an aspiring solo musician, the next NFL draft pick, or Olympic athlete may have passed. But that doesn't define you; it's just the season you're living through. Who you are is bigger than any of those roles.

I refer to this phenomenon of fixation on the role as "manifest identity fixation." We fixate on the role and not on our attributes that make us great at that role. When under this spell, we don't see ourselves; we only see the medium through which we express who we are.

I got fixated on becoming a drum major, not the attributes that made me a good drum major: leadership skills, communication skills, performance skills, and confidence. I fixated on the manifest expression of who I was, not who I am. This manifest identity fixation limits our perspective. It limits the scope of what's possible for our lives. It keeps us in that job, that marriage, that mindset. It tells you that how you've chosen to express yourself defines you are. This mindset keeps us small and confined; it blocks the confidence that comes with our personal freedom.

Identity is directly tied to your confidence. When you don't have a handle on your identity, it's easy to forget who you are. It's easy to get lost and walk around as if you were a shell of a human being—or worse, a chameleon. It leaves you without a core. When you remember exactly who you are, what you've been through, how you've overcome difficult odds, how you've helped so many people, and how you've contributed to your community (your industry, your family), those are good days. Those are the days when it feels like nothing can stop you because you know that no matter what comes along, you can handle it. That's living in confidence and personal freedom.

Taking away my drum major role didn't diminish who I am; it simply required that I search for a new medium for expression. Your role isn't who you are; you're so much more than that. Actively look for who you are within those manifestations. In them, you'll not just find confidence; you'll also find yourself.

FREEDOM FROM IDENTITY

True freedom exists when we are free from any attachment to our manifest identity. This attachment limits our lives and sets boundaries for what we see as possible for ourselves. When we're unaware of our attachment, we can't be released from its constraint. If we limit our view of self, we will seek out things that reinforce this narrow self-expression and avoid anything that might challenge or expand it. We will defend and maintain it instead of allowing for growth and maturation.

This will cause you to miss out on the experience that you actually crave—your personal freedom. This is the life experience you deserve, the essence of life. But if you continue to defend your position at the ass-end of that elephant, you'll stay stuck there.

Accepting yourself for who you are is your only true identity. All other ideas of identity are a fantasy. For the blind men in the story, experiencing color would be a fantasy. But the men had everything they needed to have *their* full experience of the elephant. They were able to move around; they had their senses of touch, smell, and hearing; and they were able to use language to discuss their findings. They had everything they needed to move on to a new experience and satisfy all the senses that were available to them.

You, too, have everything you need. There's no need for a fantasy version of you that stays hidden by a manifest identity. You don't need anything other than what you already have to realize your own potential. All you need to do is give yourself permission to experience more—as you. Allow yourself freedom from any attachment, expectations, or limitations connected to your manifest identity.

You don't need a massive transformation to become something else; you're already enough. What you need is to realize the full potential of who you are so your true self can be revealed. The more you resist who you really are, the more anxiety you will experience, and the less freedom you will know in this life.

As you move toward freedom, keep in mind that your identity is different from your personality. Your identity is how you see yourself; your personality is how others experience that identity. It's as if we stand between the two. In one direction, we look inward and see ourselves for who we really are. In the other direction, we project to the world what we want others to experience of us. Our personality is always a mask, unlike our identity, which only comes with the option of a mask if we allow it.

We get to choose what we want others to see. We can have their experience be the result of our emotional reaction to the world, or we can be intentional about what we allow others to see. We can allow others to see the good, true, and permanent identity that is authentic. Or we can hide behind a manifestation that is volatile, contingent, illusory, and temporary.

Real freedom comes from knowing who you are, not what you do or what you've done. Releasing yourself from a manifest identity doesn't turn you into a different person; instead, it express-es who you are and who you have been all along.

WRITE A STORY ABOUT YOURSELF WORTH BELIEVING

Getting to the core of who you are will require some thoughtful and honest reflection. Many people go through life as a person that other people expect them to be. This isn't personal freedom. Comfortable? Perhaps. Full of anxiety? Absolutely. Certainly not a life lived to the fullest.

By getting underneath your manifestation of self and getting to the core, you have the opportunity to create your own profile in courage. Knowing what you stand for, what you represent, and what you believe in will make your life's story worth writing.

EXERCISE

To help you begin to break and untangle your ideas of identity, spend some time journaling the answer to each of these questions:

1.   Right now, I'm expressing who I am through _____ (job, title, role, etc.).

2.   The reason that I'm so good at _____ (answer to question 1) is that I am _____.

3.   If _____(answer to question 1) were stripped away from me, I would be okay because I know that I am _____.

4.   I know that I am worthy of my dreams because I am _____.

5.   I can confidently enter into any season of my life because I know that I am _____.

If identity is an area you know would offer you an opportunity for growth, come back to these answers regularly. Remind yourself of those parts of you that make you smile and your heart swell.

ALLOW THE RIGHT PEOPLE TO CONTRIBUTE TO THE STORY OF YOU

It's hard to see yourself in the picture from behind the camera. Who can you get to help you see clearly? Our identities are made up of stories we tell ourselves and stories that others have told us. It's wise, and necessary, to seek the counsel of those people in your life who see the best in you. Their guidance can tremendously impact the outcomes in your life and can help you realize the potential you are blind to in yourself.

There are a number of ways that you can get this kind of perspective: friends, spouse, kids, students, therapist, coach, colleagues. This can be a tough process if you're not used to it, so here are some ideas to help you get started:

First, start to listen to the gifts that the supportive people in your life are offering you. When they say nice things about you, practice hearing, pausing, and accepting a compliment. Accept their gift without apology or qualifiers. In other words, don't discount what they're saying to you. If they say you look nice, don't immediately brush off the compliment by saying that you bought your outfit on sale, or you've had it forever and hardly ever wear it. Just say thank you. Don't deny the person paying you a compliment the chance to give you this gift. They wanted to give it, so be a good recipient.

Second, after you begin to allow yourself to receive kind words from others, begin to ask for feedback that will help you see yourself from their perspective. Start to build up your repertoire of supportive and affirming stories about yourself. It's actually really easy to do this. You can even use this book as an excuse. Have a conversation and ask your trusted people something like:

Hey, I've been doing some personal development work, and I'm reading a book that says I should seek feedback from people in my life who can offer me some perspective. I thought of you. Can I ask you some questions? What do you see as my greatest strength? What do you know you can always count on with me? Can you think of a time that I've let you down? If so, could you share that experience with me?

What's an opportunity for growth that you think I may be blind to or have ignored? If I wasn't (identity: ex. drum major of the band) would we still be friends? What do you see in me beyond that role?

When you do this, don't diminish their feedback by deflecting. Just say thank you and let them know how much you appreciate their generosity. Then, be prepared to return the favor for them. Thoughtful and reflective people like to know what you think of them, especially when you open up the space for this kind of vulnerable dialogue. Be kind, honest, generous, and direct with your feedback. This honesty will bring you closer together, give you more perspective on how you're showing up in the world, and provide you with another story to inform your identity.

CREATE REMINDERS FOR YOURSELF

As you work to get to know yourself better and develop a firmer grip on your own identity, it's likely that you'll have days where you forget. Fear will show its ugly head, and doubt will make its way into your internal dialogue. Falling out of your routine for one reason or another can cause you to lose perspective. Knowing that this will inevitably happen, it's important to set up some reminders for yourself.

I have clients who set an alarm on their phone that goes off once a day, every day. They label the alarm with three words as a reminder of who they are. Common words include: *kind, thoughtful, generous, loving, compassionate, joyous, happy, satisfied, leader, open, confident, free.* When setting your alarms, choose the words that speak most to you.

Another way to set up reminders for yourself is to simply write down what you're learning about yourself in your journal.

Document the stories that support the identity you want to define you—stories of your own as well as stories that your most supportive allies have given you. Write down the things that you choose to believe and want to be reminded of during times of uncertainty. I do this in a few ways: 1) I have a note on my phone. 2) I have a "happy box" of cards and letters that people have sent me. 3) I keep a folder of positive feedback in my email inbox.

Don't forget that you can ask the people who care about you to remind you as well. If you're having the blues, it's okay to tell them that you're having a hard day. Allow them in these moments to do for you what you're having a hard time doing for yourself— reminding you of who you are.

CREATE THE SPACE TO BE YOU

You aren't just your kid's mom, your spouse's husband, your company's founder, your community's leader. You have an identity that is being expressed through your roles for this season of your life. But these roles don't define you; they're an expression of you. When you break the idea that you are only defined by the role and untangle who it is behind the role, you'll create the space to be more of yourself. Give yourself the gift of truly getting to know yourself.

This section is intended to inspire, not instruct. I am not a medical doctor, psychiatrist, social worker, counselor, or therapist. I'm just a fellow traveler who discovered what works for me, and I'd like to share that with you. What works for me may or may not be appropriate for you, so you should consult your physician before making any change in your nutrition, medication, or exercise routine.

UNITARY FUNCTIONING
CHAPTER 4

We often measure wellbeing as happiness or satisfaction with life. The search for happiness is often confused with the pursuit of pleasure, but wellbeing is about more than living 'the good life'; it is about having meaning in life, about fulfilling our potential and feeling that our lives are worthwhile.

~R. Eckersley

"Where does it hurt?" This is a perfectly appropriate question for a doctor to ask a child who had come in to see him. Dr. Smith was a kind man with brown hair, a mustache, rosy cheeks, and round features. He was one of just a few doctors in my hometown.

My legs, too short still for my feet to reach the ground, dangled from the patient's table, which was covered in a long, thin strip of paper. The room smelled like most of the treatment rooms I've been in—rubbing alcohol. Dr. Smith sat on a short stool that allowed him to wheel around the room. My mother sat in a chair in the corner.

"It just hurts all over," I said, unable to pinpoint the exact place that was causing me pain.

My young mind didn't have the vocabulary to adequately communicate where I was hurting. Unaware of the difference between physical and emotional pain, and unaware that one can cause the other, I was unable to communicate how or what I was feeling.

He checked all the normal places: looked in my ears, gazed up my nose, listened to my heart and lungs, pressed around on my stomach. As he poked and prodded, he asked, "Does it hurt when I do this?" He turned to my mother and asked, "What have you noticed? Any changes in routine or with his diet? Anything going on at school?"

"No, nothing that I know of," she answered.

These visits weren't unusual for me, and the outcome was almost always the same. "I can't find anything wrong with him. Maybe he's got a bug. It'll pass, " he reported. Then, my mother would thank him, and we would leave his office no closer to an answer as to why I wasn't feeling well.

I would be back at school the same day.

I don't remember the doctor ever asking if anything was going on at home. Perhaps he was afraid of the answer. It was a small town, and my father had a reputation.

Several years later, when I was in high school, Dr. Smith supplied me with samples of anti-depression and anti-anxiety medication. I preferred it that way, because there was no record of samples being given. I was young when this started, but even back then I was aware of the social stigma of taking medication for any type of mental condition.

The pain I felt as a kid wasn't made up. It wasn't something I was lying about just so I could get out of going to school. It was real. The source of that pain has taken years to discover, and it's no less real than if it were a tumor.

Where does it hurt? What a great question. A simple question with a range of answers that aren't so simple.

Where does it hurt? It hurts all over the place.

For me, depression comes on like a wave in the ocean. It's distant at first, but I can see a small swell on the horizon.

I like to surf when I get the chance. When surfing, like in life, you're floating along on your board, enjoying the water, and soaking up the sun most of the time. But when you have depressive tendencies, like when you're surfing, you're always looking for what's coming next.

Sometimes those waves are small—not even big enough to ride—so you just lie there and let them gently pass beneath you. But other times that wave is doozy, and you know you're going to ride it. So you pop up, get your balance, and coast toward the shore.

When depression hits me, mixed with anxiety, it hits me like the water when I lose my balance on the surfboard. It's messy, it hurts, and because my surroundings are unrelenting, it feels like I'm going to drown.

No, really, it feels like I'm going to drown. My breath is shallow. I feel the shock of the fall in my bones. My chest tightens and hurts. My limbs feel numb, and the anxiety makes my skin crawl. I often feel a sensation that makes me think that if I could just throw up, I would feel better . . . and I hate throwing up.

I've experienced what I now recognize as depression and anxiety, to one degree or another, for as long as I can remember. I'm always surprised by the physical feelings that accompany the emotional feelings every time I get weighed down. It's almost as if my body is at war with my out-of-control mind, which is the real battlefield of my life.

My trips to the doctor's office didn't stop when I was a kid. I kept going back, continuing to plead with doctors to make me feel better. My conversations with Dr. Smith had given me the vocabulary to ask other doctors for sample medication when I left Arkansas. They were more than happy to comply with my requests.

I was a young man, growing up gay in Arkansas with a sadistic father and an ill-equipped mother. I was living in fear every day of being found out, of being rejected, of going to hell. I was being traumatized. No pill was going to fix that.

In retrospect, what I really needed was an education about how to express my emotions in a healthy and safe way. I needed a physical education, a nutrition plan, role models and mentors. I needed a supportive peer group. I needed to feel safe and be heard. None of these things were available to me.

And while they wouldn't have "fixed" me either, they would have at least given me the tools to cope with my circumstances in a way that supported my current and future development. A set of mind, body, and spirit "thriving" skills would have given me an opportunity to grow, develop, and mature through the process instead of simply being numbed to the experience. Being numbed by the medication prevented me from addressing my underlying issues, forcing me to address them down the road. I was forced to confront my childhood issues alongside the issues that came along with young adulthood. My ability to navigate through young adulthood was stunted by the circumstances of my upbringing. I had a significant lack of life skills.

For as long as I can remember, I have carried with me what I call my "dark passenger."[1] My depression has been a passenger on this life journey with me, a part of me that has to be managed at all times. While it's a part of me that I wish didn't exist, I can't deny the major role it has played in my life.

I'm not a person who condemns medications that help so many people living with anxiety and depression. Nor do I condemn the people who take them. I can only speak to my experience—one that could have been improved first, by better parenting; second, by teachers and administrators in an education system who weren't afraid of speaking up for me; and third, by professionals who might have directed me toward psychology and not pharmacology.

It took me years to realize that, while I certainly have battles with depression and anxiety, I don't suffer from chronic mental illness. It wasn't the depression or anxiety that needed to be treated; those were the symptoms of my life experience. I needed to learn how to live with and manage them when they show up. What I suffer from, even still, is what we all suffer from, and that is the human condition.[2] My attempts to fix that issue were, wrongly and prematurely, with antidepressants and benzodiazepines. I needed a different kind of healing. I needed to understand the connection between my mind, body, and spirit—what I call unitary functioning.

Let me be clear once more: I'm not a doctor. I can only speak to my own experience. For me, antidepressants were not the appropriate remedy. For you, they may be, and that's absolutely no one's business but yours. I am in no way suggesting that anyone should stop taking their medication; I took antidepressants for several years. What I am suggesting is that we are an overmedicated, "quick-fix" society—too often willing to settle for a better day than a better life. Too often willing to just get by than to do the hard work of really living a great life experience.

Along my journey, I learned that for me, taking a pill was like a Band-Aid; it wasn't the appropriate long-term solution to the underlying issues that needed to be healed. I finally realized that if I wanted to live a fully expressed life, I had to seek out new ways to heal. I had to learn a new way of living, along with the skills that I needed to thrive and experience my own personal freedom.

It's never too late to get this type of education; it's a lifelong learning process. It's a healing education that can lead to relief from the pain of our past. For me, and for so many others, that pain is manifest in the form of anxiety and depression. Statistically, you or someone you love is living with depression and anxiety. By sharing my journey to manage the pain and by sharing the strategies I've found that help me, perhaps it will give you some perspective on your own journey or equip you to help a loved one.

OUR MIND, BODY, AND SPIRITUAL SYSTEMS ARE CONNECTED

When I was a kid and would go to the doctor complaining, he couldn't find anything wrong with my body. The reason he wasn't able to diagnose a physical problem didn't become clear to me for a while. What I came to understand is that we have a three-way connection that is constantly transmitting information back and forth between systems: the connection of the mind, body, and spirit.

Research has exhaustively shown that your mind is directly affected by your body.[3] Exercise has been proven to reduce anxiety and depression.[4] Studies have shown that physical activity can have psychological benefits as both a treatment and preventative measure against mild to moderate emotional illness.[5]

While there exists a landmine of contradictions in the language that discerns between spirituality[6] and religion, the research overwhelmingly shows that there's a connection between spirituality and our overall well-being. Spirituality affords our life's journey a meaningful, thriving, and fully expressed experience when not abused or perverted for a maligned agenda.

The connection between mind, body, and spirit doesn't just enable the positive opportunities for increased well-being; it also transmits the negative when they are ignored, abused, or mis-aligned. I've found that if I am feeling a high degree of mental stress, my hands itch. If I'm not exercising regularly, I'll start to feel blue. If I'm not connecting with others, I feel adrift, lonely, and lost. If I'm not mindful of my spirituality, I can feel isolated and uncertain of my purpose. One system is always impacting the others, and ultimately our overall life experience.

Realize that if you're not feeling emotionally or physically strong and vital in the way you would like, you have these three systems to consider. Explore systematic causality, or how one impacts another. Don't think of your mind, body, and spirit as separate systems but rather as an interconnected human experience generator.

TAKE CARE OF YOUR BODY

As a band nerd growing up, my natural enemy was the athletics department. Therefore, I despised all things related to a gym, court, or locker room. But during my college years, I began to put together that if I could get my heart rate up a bit, my mind would respond. And the effects of the physical activity lasted beyond my time at the gym. I found that physical activity improved my mental well-being. Was that because of the chemical reactions that the activity caused in my body or because it provided a change of pace and scenery? Perhaps both. What was undeniable, though, was that I felt different; the exercise helped.

When considering how physical health contributes to experiencing personal freedom, think about the areas of rest, nutrition, exercise, and energy. If you don't have your health, if you don't have the energy to make it through the day, it's simply impossible to be at your best. Forget the idea of living fully —you just won't feel like it. So, while you may prefer the cheeseburger and shake, eating healthy foods and taking care of your body are essential to good mental well-being and your pursuit to be the best version of yourself. As you put together your own plan, consult with your physician and consider how each of those parts will play a role in your well-being.

When I first started making the connection between mind and body, my plan was really simple: eat better and exercise. I would do cardio four to five times per week and lift weights two to three times per week. I learned how to eat better by following the nutrition plan provided by my gym. It was cheap, if not free. It was all I had, and it was a major improvement over what I had been doing. Eating healthfully and exercising were somewhat foreign to me, since a major part of my diet growing up was flavored instant oatmeal, Little Debbie Snack Cakes, pizza, soda, pie, McDonald's, Taco Bell, and a steady supply of Southern comfort food. If my '80's kid diet sounds familiar to you, and you didn't grow up in an environment where nutrition and exercise was a priority, don't worry—these are all things you can learn. There is a deep breadth of resources out there to help you live a great, healthy, long life.

Taking care of your body, specifically with what you put in your body, has an immense impact on your life experience. Studies have shown that nutrition plans consisting of whole, unprocessed foods (fruits, veggies, fish) protect against depressive symptoms, whereas processed foods, sweets, fried foods, high-fat dairy, and refined cereals all make us vulnerable to depression.[7] The quality of our nutritional habits has an impact on how we feel.[8] This is important to remember when you're feeling down. If you try to soothe yourself with junk food, that may only make it worse. Many studies have explored the benefits of a Mediterranean-style diet, which includes plant-based foods, vegetables, fresh and dried fruit, whole-grain cereals, nuts, and legumes—all of which are important for good mental health.⁹

When it comes to my physical journey, I always make the decision to level it up. I make the conscious choice not to go to a gym full of people who look like me. I'm not the guy with the six-pack abs, but I go to a gym full of those guys. The difference motivates me because I look at the gym as a physical and an aspirational activity. Even if it's only a 10 percent marginal difference between them and me, that little bit motivates and encourages me to work a little harder. Do I sometimes feel intimidated? Yes. Have I seen myself grow as a result of my environment? Yes. This approach works for me. Whether it's a gym, an intermural sports league, or long walks, I encourage you to find what works for you for better physical health.

When I was in my mid-thirties, one of my mentors challenged me to have the healthiest year of my life. Not one to back down from a challenge, I started down the path to better health. It was on that path that I discovered functional medicine and Dr. Phillip Oubre, my functional medicine doctor.

Functional medicine doctors are licensed medical doctors who can do anything you might expect a conventional physician to do. My doctor describes functional medicine as an approach that seeks to find the root cause of your symptom; instead of just treating the symptom, a functional medicine practitioner will keep looking for the root cause of that symptom until they find it.

What I like about functional medicine is the individualized plan. My doctor was able to evaluate my blood work and genetic testing results and get me on a long-term wellness plan that was tailored to my specific needs. When I first met with Dr. Oubre, the appointment lasted about three hours. He did an exhaustive life history interview and reviewed blood work and genetic testing that he had ordered prior to our meeting.

One of the downers about working with a functional medicine doctor is that they aren't big fans of some of my favorite things: sugar, gluten, and dairy. Dr. Oubre has insisted that those be cut from my diet. And with great reluctance, I have considerably cut them out. Little Debbie and I finally had to end our lifelong relationship. But the results have been spectacular: diminished allergy problems, fewer digestive issues, and feeling better physically and mentally.

No matter where you are physically, taking your physiology to the next level will make you feel better more quickly than you might expect.

You only get one body. Whatever is waiting for you at your next level, you're going to need a healthy body to get you there. When you feel better, you live better!

Through this process, I also learned that I had neglected the importance of rest. You shouldn't feel tired all the time. You shouldn't have to take stimulants to function. Take the time to rest. Would you rather function at 50 percent, twelve hours a day? Or would you rather function at 100 percent, eight hours a day? Resting means being intentional about recharging your mind, body, and spirit.

The idea of spirit was one that caught me off guard.

PICK YOUR OWN JOURNEY TO GOD

We are not human beings having a spiritual experience.
We are spiritual beings having a human experience.

– Pierre Teilhard de Chardin

When you grow up in a fundamentalist environment like I did, it can be tempting to simply turn your back on all things spiritual. For years, I had nothing but contempt for any conversation that even remotely included the idea of spirituality. During my childhood, an organization of so-called "faithful" people had perverted ideas of spirituality for their hateful, racist, bigoted, and misogynistic purposes. When I was a young adult, in an effort to get George W. Bush reelected, the Republican party hijacked faith to propagate a message of hate toward gay people who wanted to be married. I've had experiences throughout my life where a so-called religious person wanted me marginalized, denied basic human rights, denied the right to love whom I choose, and even wanted me dead. These people have been cruel not only to me but others like me. They have marginalized us and cast us as villains in life's plot. As a result, I often felt as if my spirituality had been hijacked by religious terrorists.

These types of so-called "holy" attacks, launched toward the most vulnerable and least-understood parts of the human experience, can serve to further blind us to the nature and needs of our spirit, turning us away from exploring a part of who we are and one of our most basic and essential needs. Neglecting the spiritual self is neglecting the whole self. You cannot experience personal freedom when the spirit is neglected.

It took me many years to come to a place of openness toward the idea of spirituality. In my life, it had always been coopted to excuse bad behavior; at first, I only saw it as the language of a group that I needed to belong to in order to survive. Later, I rejected it wholesale, unable to distinguish spirituality from a religion that wasn't meant for people like me. And yet, all the while, I felt as though some part of me was missing, incomplete, or malnourished. Because of past experiences, I will freely admit that I have an enormous resistance to all things religious or religion-adjacent; I'm full of skepticism toward any church or organized religion. Nonetheless, I am resolved to fully experience my own spirituality. I refuse to cede my spirituality to those who would hijack that part of my human experience. It is not theirs to take.

I don't subscribe to any religion, and the words I use for "God" are fluid at best. But in my mind, there is undoubtedly a spiritual element of the human condition that demands to be satisfied. It is in the spirit that we are fulfilled, find meaning, feel at peace, discover, and live our purpose.

For too many of us, religion isolated and (directly and indirectly) harmed us. It's a universal human experience to ask existential questions, perhaps even more so when you feel different from what you see reflected in the pulpit or in the pews. On our journey, we must learn to differentiate our past experiences and religious terrorism and take responsibility for this part of ourselves. There's a difference between your spirit (connection to and place in the universe), God (how we relate to the spirit), and religion (a codification of ideas that offer a group or organization's common explanation of spirituality and God).

To deny your spirituality is to deny a part of yourself. That denial is no different than if you cut off your own leg; your spirituality is a part that makes your experience whole.

We can't throw away spirituality simply because religious practice has perverted its purity. In reality, those of us with or without faith are all ultimately asking the same questions: What is the meaning of my life? How did I get here? Who am I? What is the meaning of love, loss, and death? These are spiritual questions worthy of our consideration. Our search to answer them allows us to better understand our place in the world and make decisions about what we make of the human experience, individually and collectively. The answers determine how well we treat other people, other forms of life, our planet, and ourselves.

I'm particularly fond of how developmental psychologist Howard Gardner spoke about spirituality;[10] he referred to it as a form of "existential intelligence,"[11] essentially the pursuit of understanding and making sense of the world so that you can make decisions about how you exist in it. Later in his career, Gardner referred to it as "philosophical intelligence," expanding the definition to include those matters that concern the spiritual, moral, emotional, transcendental, cosmic, and religious. In both terms is the idea that there's a human need to connect with something larger than yourself. This simple idea captures, for me, the essence of what it means to be spiritual. The trouble comes when we become entrenched in our attachment to what we believe that larger "something" is, how it's expressed, and how we connect with it. This tends to constrict our opportunity for imagination, evolution, or dynamism. When we define spirituality personally (as our connection to something greater than ourselves rather than institutionally), it becomes accessible to even the most scientifically minded. The connection is up to us to determine.

On your own time, and through the means and language with which you are most comfortable, you deserve to experience your spiritual connection to the universe. Your spirituality is a part of you, and it's equally as important as your mental, physical, and emotional well-being.

Just like you may need a therapist to help with your mind or emotions, or a personal trainer or nutritionist to help with your body, you may need help along your spiritual journey. I've learned over the years that not all people of faith are like the people that I grew up with or those who have aligned with political movements to further their hateful views. There are good people in good churches who lead with love. Organized religion can serve an important purpose. These religions can offer guides, who have dedicated their lives to spiritual exploration, to help a person explore their spirituality. There are communities of people who are on a similar journey of spiritual exploration. Must you participate in church to explore your spirituality? Absolutely not. You do not need religion (especially not religions that have become an extension of a political movement) to dictate the means and methods of your spiritual experience. And most importantly, your choice to have or not have religion in your life doesn't make you any less than anyone else. Spirituality is not a singular path by which you must experience that part of your humanity. Be infinitely curious, seek your own answers, and discover what works for you.

Whether your vehicle to God is a solo practice or a community of like-minded people, don't deny yourself the journey. Not all religious organizations are bad; in fact, some are quite good. But there's no requirement that you have to subscribe to anyone else's way of thinking about your own journey to your spirituality. My own belief is that it matters little, if at all, to whom or to what you pray. Whether the target of your prayer be God, Allah, the Universe, or your highest self, it's the intention of your prayer that matters. The intended recipient matters only to the degree to which it brings you closer to your spiritual actualization.

There are also spiritual teachers or advisors who can guide you on this journey, without the dogma of religion. Your guide may describe themself as a pastor, priest, monk, lama, nun, shaman, guru, spiritual advisor, coach, or imam. Find what works for you now and experience the joy in this season of exploration. Discover what's most comfortable for you, without the stigma you may have

grown up with. And never forget that there are no life sentences—even in spiritual exploration. When you're ready, or have new
questions that need fresh answers, you'll feel led to do something
different and explore your spirituality from another perspective.

The search for answers to existential questions becomes more
important to us the more isolated we feel. *Who am I? Why am I
here? What is my purpose?* These are questions that are not just theoretical exercises in thought; they are, in fact, deeply and personally
meaningful. They speak not just to our collective human experience, but they also speak directly to us as people: Why am *I* here?
What is *my* purpose?

Far too many have sought and not found answers to these
questions that satisfied their curiosity. We've been given limited
places to turn to for answers to questions about who we are. We
have negated our spirit because of the religious hijacking of spirituality. And, blocked from our spirituality, we are forced to find
answers outside of ourselves through material and superficial medi-
ums of external validation that will never adequately feed that part
of us that we recognize as our spirit.

Being open to our spirituality allows us to connect with
the people around us and also connect deeper to ourselves. Allow yourself to experience awareness of your own struggle to seek
understanding. Allow yourself to feel a moment of oneness with
your partner. To feel the unconditional love of a pet. Walk barefoot in the grass and feel at one with the earth.[12] Allow yourself to
be carried away and moved to tears by music. These are spiritual
moments for me that connect me to something deeper. Don't deny
yourself these moments of connection, of love, of compassion, of
gratitude.

Do not deny your spirit. No one—not a church, a religion,
or a guru—has all the answers for the questions you will ask.
Nonetheless . . .

Seek—and know that you may never get answers to the questions you ask, only clues to guide your path and illuminate your next step.

Seek—and know that any clarity gained will only create room for more questions.

Seek—and know that spiritual satisfaction lies in the journey itself.

Seek—and grant yourself permission to explore your spirituality with a sense of personal freedom.

Do not deny yourself a spiritual journey.

CREATE YOUR PERSONAL CARE PLAN

When you aren't intentional about your life, chaos has a way of showing up. Taking care of yourself and, specifically, considering the care of your mind, body, and spirit requires intentionality and practice. If you've made it this far in life, you likely know from experience that there are things that work for you and things that don't when it comes to your operating as your best self. If you're not aware of what those things are, start paying attention. Notice how you feel after a good night's sleep versus staying up late, after eating late at night, after drinking, after exercising, or not. The things you learn about yourself from maintaining this level of awareness will inform your personal care plan. As you create this plan, explore the ways that it can bring together the things that satisfy your mind, body, and spirit.

To create your personal care plan, start by listing the things that you know you need to do to take care of yourself on an hourly, daily, weekly, monthly, quarterly, and annual basis.

Here's an example:

ANNUAL SELF-CARE

▶ Take a vacation

▶ Spend at least two full days planning and visualizing what I want my year to look like

QUARTERLY SELF-CARE

▶ Take a mini trip (drive somewhere and stay overnight)

▶ Take the time to visualize and plan what I want for the next quarter

MONTHLY SELF-CARE

▶ Get a massage

▶ Take the time to visualize and plan what I want for the next month

WEEKLY SELF-CARE

▶ Financial check-in

▶ Do something social; connect with someone I love

▶ Read a book

▶ Plan a date night

▶ Take a B-12 shot

▶ Take the time to visualize and plan what I want for the next week

▶ Bike ride (allows me to connect mind, body, and spirit at once)

DAILY SELF-CARE

▶ Workout—at least thirty minutes of cardio or weight training

▶ Morning Routine:

- Meditate
- Exercise
- Walk the dog
- Take supplements
- Breakfast
- Check in with my husband
- Read a book that interests me
- Take the time to visualize and plan what I want for tomorrow

HOURLY SELF-CARE

▶ Take a break for at least ten minutes
▶ Change my focus and attention
▶ Get some fresh air
▶ Drink some water
▶ Pet my dog

Fill-in-the-blank personal care plans are available in the online companion course for this book at ChadPeevy.com/book

MAKE THIS YOUR HEALTHIEST YEAR EVER

Imagine yourself having energy all day long. Imagine the rush of feeling physically powerful throughout your day and the pride you'll have for making good decisions about your health. Imagine the impact that the changes you make for your health and well-being will have on your family! Why wait? Start the healthiest year of your life right now.

Here are some ideas to get you started:

- ▶ Start moving. Even if it's just thirty minutes a day . . . move!
- ▶ Level up your physical exercise experience.
- ▶ Make an appointment with a functional medicine doctor (and go). Go through their process and let them develop a personal health plan for you.
- ▶ Make an appointment with a nutritionist (and go). Our bodies don't react to different foods the same way. Let them help you figure out what works best for you.
- ▶ Level up your rest. Plan and prepare for it. No screens or work at least one hour before bed. Get seven to eight hours of quality sleep on a good pillow, mattress, and sheets. Take your rest as seriously as you take the rest of your life.
- ▶ Explore activities that bring mind, body, and spirit together for you. Become intentional about making them a part of your personal care plan.

If you need additional resources, a more budget-friendly solution, or help finding a functional medicine practitioner, I've provided additional resources for you in the companion part of this course found at: ChadPeevy.com/book

ENLIST OTHERS TO HELP YOU

When I find myself out of alignment in mind, body, and spirit, it's not just me who suffers. Depression and anxiety also impact the people around me. I have an incredible husband who accepts me for all of me. Even when he can't relate to how I'm feeling, he demonstrates compassion toward me. But he doesn't always know what to do. There are likely people around you who want to help you but don't know how. I hope you'll share these ideas with them. This is what I've shared with Pasha to help him understand me better when I'm having dark days:

> ▶ **Don't stop asking:** I know it's frustrating to ask me questions when in return I give one-word answers, but it's not personal. Please keep asking.
> ▶ **Be with me:** I don't want to be alone, even if I say I do. You don't have to do anything; just being near me is usually enough.
> ▶ **Pause:** Let's press pause on topics that you know cause me stress on a good day; those things can wait. If they can't wait, I trust you to make good decisions without me.
> ▶ **It's okay for you to be happy:** Be joyful and express your happiness. Your joy is contagious.
> ▶ **Please be patient with me**: This will pass. And thank you for loving me through it; I know that can be hard to do.

It's important to enroll those you love in your journey—not just some of it, all of it. I'm always taken aback in my work by just how much we expect other people to read our minds. When we leave what we need up to chance, we shouldn't expect more than a chance of getting it. Have the courage to be direct and explicit about what you need to be supported on your journey. We'll look more at asking for help in a later chapter. Until then, enlist others to help you by sharing these ideas and your own for what you need when you're feeling the symptoms of your mind, body, and spirit becoming misaligned.

TAKE ANOTHER STEP

Put your physical being in a place that allows your spirit to be revealed and your mind to be refreshed. The human experience isn't siloed into the elements of our being, but rather made whole by the joining of our mind, body, and spirit.

This connection is worthy of our exploration and necessary for experiencing our personal freedom. To deny any part of that integrated connection is to deny the whole of ourselves.

It takes a lot of courage to acknowledge the power you have over this experience. It's much easier to blame, play victim, and avoid than it is to search, find limited and short-lived solutions, search again, fail, and then try all over again. As you demonstrate your resilience and continue on your path, remember that your life's path is unique to you. Allow your course of exploration to go down the forgotten and mysterious alleys that have the potential to bring you joy, excitement, and, ultimately, that much-craved sense of aliveness.

It's never too late to take another step on your journey. A step that opens up another part of you, maybe even a part that has been denied or neglected. It's never too late to ask yourself where it hurts and seek the healing power that exists in the connection of mind, body, and spirit.

STRATEGY

*tools to help me better navigate
the world and care for myself*

BECOMING

MONEY

MINDFULNESS

PRODUCTIVITY

BECOMING
CHAPTER 5

A bird sitting on a tree is never afraid of the branch breaking
because its trust is not on the branch but on its own wings.

~ Charlie Wardle

When I question my therapist's process and the purpose of our weekly sessions, he often responds with something about helping me get more out of life. I find myself thinking about that idea and what it means to me. What is this "more" that I'm after? I have a roof over my head, food to eat, and a loving husband. What more do I need?

I've come to realize that more is essentially more life, or aliveness. I've also come realize that getting more is a process. A process that can be easily derailed by comfort, fear, doubt, depression, anxiety, isolation, and all the other means by which we sabotage ourselves. A process that must be engaged beyond the four walls of the therapist's office.

Throughout this book are ideas for how to break and untangle an inheritance of toxic mindsets. This requires becoming aware of the limitations that exist in my life—those ways of thinking that are blocking my potential for more life. Limitations that include many of the survival mechanisms that served me in the past. Even before I knew what *more* meant for me, I knew I had to reject that toxic inheritance.

I don't believe our purpose here is to just survive our past and coast to the grave once we're on the other side of survival. The experiences we survive prepare us for the more meaningful ones that will follow. You discover that meaning through your service to others through your gifts, by becoming the full potential that is within you. There's so much more to be experienced and shared in this life. The question is: Will you allow yourself to step into your own process of becoming?

The idea of becoming was a lesson that Pasha and I were forced to embrace early in our relationship—both individually and as a couple. We both came to our relationship without a safety net. If things went wrong, we didn't have anyone to fall back on for help. Our parents weren't going to bail us out because they were unable and/or unwilling. We also became aware that we wouldn't be able to fall back on our traditional education to get what we wanted from life. Our degrees had prepared us for something narrower than the wide range of experiences we wanted from life. We knew that we were on our own. We knew that our success or our failure was completely on us. So, we had to work really hard and step into a mindset of becoming that which we wanted from life. It wasn't going to come from anywhere else.

We wanted as complete and full a life as possible—circumstances and background be damned. We understood that in those areas of life where we wanted more, it was up to us to get it. We knew that we loved each other and wanted to make our relationship work. We also knew that each of us would need to adopt a mindset of becoming a better partner to the other. We both exercised the grace necessary to allow the other person to become that which would give us both more in our relationship. Together, we made a decision to embrace our becoming as individuals and as a couple.

The process of becoming relies on your acknowledgment that there's a gap in your life. Becoming requires an acknowledgment that there are things you want to get and experience in life that you don't yet have the tools to receive. A mindset that sees the bridge to be crossed that spans between where you are, and where you want to be. This process requires that you recognize that the person you want to become is someone within your power to create. It's not happenstance that you step into the person you are meant to be; it's through a process. A process that will go on for the rest of your life.

One of life's great awakenings is that no one is going to swoop in and save you; this life is what you make of it. There comes a time when we must accept the fact that there are great teachers from whom we can learn—but no saviors. We are the savior we've been looking for.

Figuring out and exploring what more could be out there for you requires a mindset of becoming. This mindset rejects stagnation or giving up. It embraces the idea that it's up to me to become what I want. It realizes that the greatest joy in life lies in the struggle to get more out of life. It embraces the gift of learning and its benefits. When I embrace my becoming, I'm not limited by who I was, who I was expected to be, how I'm seen, or even how I see myself. I'm in the process of becoming.

If you find yourself wanting more, consider that your grit, resilience, determination, and dedication to your own becoming must match the life you want.

The process of becoming isn't just in our individual untangling or in our relationships, but also in our work. Our journey in this life is made more complete and more meaningful when we serve others. For most of us, it's through our work that we serve. I've learned that the more skilled I've become in my work, the more useful I am to others. Being in a position to be of service to others not only helps them, but it also brings a sense of meaning to our own lives. Don't we all want to experience deeper meaning?

In your process of becoming, you may need to learn the strategies required to market yourself, your career, or your business. You may have to learn how to speak in public, manage your money, or sell yourself or a product. It's just as likely that you will need to develop skills of the personal variety that influence your work too. You may need to learn how to be a better team player or team leader, how to listen to others, or how to make better use of your time.

I know that personal and professional development can seem like a real drag. It's not an exciting, quick-fix, magic recipe that will immediately turn your life around. Nonetheless, the importance can't be overstated. These are the long-haul, incremental life lessons that will develop and ultimately allow you to realize your potential. Your personal and professional skills are yours; they can't be taken away.

PERSONAL AND PROFESSIONAL DEVELOPMENT

There are two tracks on the journey of becoming: one is getting to know yourself through a process of self-discovery (personal development); the other is a process of deepening the skills of the service through which you will contribute to the world (professional development).

The fact that you're reading this book tells me that you're someone who is interested in and on the path of personal growth and discovery. I honor you for that vulnerability and openness, and I'm grateful that our paths have crossed. While personal development may be what brought you to this book, I want to encourage you to also consider your professional development.

Professional development can be a vehicle for realizing outcomes of your personal development. Think of it like this: Let's imagine that my purpose is to help people get into great physical shape. I get a job as a personal trainer at the local gym. After a year of working at the gym, none of my clients have achieved their goals. None are in any better shape than when they started training with me. None have lost any weight. In fact, my clients miss about 50 percent of their sessions with me. I doubt that I would find a lot of personal meaning in my work if those were my professional results. To experience more meaning in this part of my life, I would need to deepen my professional skills. I would need to dive deeper into human motivation theory, nutrition, kinesiology, and all the other areas of learning that could help me better serve the people I want to help.

Professional development is a selfless act; it's through your professional development that you learn how to best use your personal gifts to serve those who need you and will sustain you on your life's path.

Like many things in life, through your service of others, you will yield personal benefit. How? Professional development helps you:

- ▶ create greater opportunity for yourself;
- ▶ bring clarity to your life's meaning;
- ▶ build your confidence;
- ▶ leave behind a legacy that has the structure and resources to sustain;

▶ increase your self-worth and net worth;

▶ let go of your own ego through your service to others; and

▶ identify and avoid the ruts of life.

Being great at something is how we distinguish ourselves. It's how we come into our own sense of self and separate from our upbringing. It's a healthy step on our path of differentiation from our roots.

Throw yourself into all parts of yourself. Fall in love with your ability to know yourself, and do something good with that awareness. Be great at what you do. There's no better investment.

Deep professional skills will bring you a sense of calm and safety in moments of fear and uncertainty. When faced with the unknown, put yourself through exercises, like listing all the ways you could make an income and survive if everything else failed. Put the fear and certainty in black-and-white. That list will uncover more square feet of your own safety net—one that you have created and stitched together. Your skills and abilities become your safety net, assurance, and confidence to travel down a path of greater becoming.

Right now, you have the unparalleled ability to develop your skills more than any other time in human history. The knowledge available to you is near unlimited, from online training and education platforms to your public library. Your ability to cultivate deep skills will allow you to create a greater life for yourself and those you love. Whether you want to be a doctor, lawyer, engineer, author, graphic designer, or politician, the resources to develop the skills you need to be successful are out there.

The skills you develop will play a major role in the quality of your life. There's beauty in the fact that the development of those skills is completely within your control. You get to decide the direction you'll go and how deeply you will develop those skills. Your purpose is to serve; the level at which you are able serve is what will ultimately bring you lifelong satisfaction. No matter what you decide to become, be the very best version of yourself within your profession. What you do will play a minor role in determining your happiness; *how* you do it will mean so much more.

DECISIONS

A decision is a conclusion based on everything you believe about yourself.

~ A Course in Miracles

Your decisions, whether or not you're aware of them, are what got you where you are today. The decision to pay attention in school or the decision to goof off. The decision to go to college or to go straight into the workforce. To allow yourself to have professional mentors or go it alone. None are necessarily right or wrong, but they all contribute to where you find yourself, for better or worse. And, just as all of those decisions have determined where you are today, the decisions you make today will create the life you have tomorrow.

Along your path of development, you'll be presented with an enormous amount of ideas, advice, rules, laws, and routines. It can all be really overwhelming. There will be days when you're tempted to ignore it all and pretend like a better way forward isn't there for you. Days when you'll be tempted to fall back into comforting and familiar behaviors. Days when the idea of intentionally engaging in challenging behaviors seems like engaging in acts of cruelty. Days when you spend time comparing your progress to that of others and wonder why you're even trying.

These, too, are decisions. Instead of comparing yourself to others, trying to do it all at once, or changing your entire life in a day, adopt one simple method for making progress in your own becoming. Make one good decision at a time. That's all. As each moment comes along throughout your day, make the choice that allows you to take one small step in the right direction. You don't have to make all the right decisions all at the same time. Just make the next right decision.

Delaying decisions that will move you forward and into your own becoming is a defense of the status quo. When you don't decide, you are, in fact, deciding to keep things the way they are. The Latin origin of the word decision is *decisionem*, which means "to cut off." On your journey of development, you have to cut off anything that doesn't serve you. Cut off things that don't offer you a map to where you want to go, or trigger the tendency to compare yourself. Cut off the doubt and limiting beliefs that are holding you back; cut off the confusion from overwhelm. Progress is a process of elimination. The process of becoming is one of being decisive.

THERE IS NO DESTINATION, ONLY A DIRECTION

The mindset of becoming leaves room for growth and encourages you to embrace the journey—to see the beauty in life's path, not its destination. There is no destination, only a direction and a constant state of becoming. The only real destination is death.

The idea of becoming can be especially challenging, since we live in a culture that is addicted to the destination. Perhaps that's because the journey can be, and oftentimes is, unpleasant.

The journey is where the real work happens; it's where we discover the struggle and strife, the hardships and setbacks. It's where we confront emotions that we would rather stuff back into the darkest corners of our mind. The journey of becoming is where we truly examine what we're made of and leave ourselves open to criticism that reveals our opportunities for growth.

The journey is where we learn. We learn about ourselves, our character, our fortitude, and our tenacity. We learn how well we've surrounded ourselves with people who encourage and support our growth. We discover the difference we're making and the impact we're having. The journey is where we express ourselves, where we connect with our humanity and share our joy and love with others. We learn how successfully we've broken the cycle of inherited mindsets.

Becoming simply means that you are striving to be better today than you were yesterday. Are you consciously and intentionally working to become a better version of you? Or are you settling for a life partially lived? Will you find joy in a constant state of becoming, or will you settle for where you've landed?

Becoming anything is a process and a practice. The remainder of this chapter will give you exercises to help you enhance or begin that process and practice.

GOING DEEPER INTO YOUR BECOMING

This exercise will help you discover the opportunities that exist for you to grow.

EXERCISE

Take out your journal and make a list of all of your current skills. Create a column for both your personal and professional skills. Here are some prompts to help you:

PERSONAL:

1. My friends would say that my greatest "friend" skill is my ability to . . .

2. The people closest to me (mom, spouse, kids, friends) would say that I'm a good person because . . .

3. People fall in love with me because of my . . .

4. I love that the people I love see me as someone who . . .

PROFESSIONAL:

1. When my back is against the wall, I'm someone who will . . .

2. When given a challenge, I'm the person who . . .

3. My boss/employees would say that I'm the person they come to for . . .

4. The thing I can do better than anyone in my business is . . .

Now think about the person you're becoming. Write in your journal how old this visualized version of youself is and describe your qualities.

> ▸ When I look at the _____ year-old version of myself, I see someone who . . .

Now write down the personal and professional skills that version of you has. Here are some prompts to help you:

PERSONAL:

1. Describe how that person interacts with and treats other people.

2. Describe the relationship that person has with their family.

3. Describe how that person sees and talks about themself.

4. Describe the personal qualities you most admire and respect about them.

PROFESSIONAL:

1. Describe how that person is seen in their industry.

2. Describe the contributions that person has made to their industry.

3. Describe what you most admire and respect about what that person has achieved in their career.

4. Describe the impact that person is making for the greater good within their profession.

CRAFT YOUR PERSONAL CURRICULUM

Think back on your experience in school. Your teachers provided a plan for your education—a sequence of lessons, concepts, and ideas that built one on top of the other. You learned how to count before you learned how to add and subtract. You learned your ABCs before you learned how to read or write. In school, you had professionals who created a curriculum that would serve you once you left the classroom.

As an adult, it's up to you to create that curriculum for yourself. To determine which lessons, ideas, and concepts you want to explore. To determine what's necessary for you to learn in order to be prepared for the life you want. It's time for you to create your life's curriculum.

As you think about and begin to put together that curriculum, remember that you are capable of learning new things. Remember the first time you looked at an algebra problem? For me, it might as well have been in Martian language. But with time, study, and, most importantly, help, I eventually got the hang of it.

On your journey of development, you're going to be faced with ideas that seem incomprehensible at first glance. Show yourself some grace, have faith in yourself, and remember that you eventually learned how to walk, how to read, how to write, and how to count. You're very capable of learning new things. Just stick with it, give it some time, and ask for help.

EXERCISE

In the previous section, you were asked to describe where you are personally and professionally and who you would like to become. Now, list the skills that would be necessary for you to develop to become that person. To keep this simple, start with the three most obvious skills that come to mind and list them in order of priority:

1. _____

2. _____

3. _____

What makes this path of becoming all the more powerful isn't just that you get to pick the areas in which you want to develop, but you also get to pick your teachers. The next step is to do an online search for the people in the world who are talking about and teaching the skills that you just wrote down. Personally, I like to start by researching people who have written books on the topics that I want to develop. In fact, you can see my entire library at ChadPeevy.com/library.

There are people in the world who have mastered and teach the skills that you need to develop. To your benefit, those people are uploading videos, writing books, teaching classes, offering coaching or consulting, and hosting seminars that you can access. Start following those people and consuming their content. While you're at it, unfollow those who don't support your journey.

Here are some ideas to get you started:

▶ Seek out opportunities for development offered by your employer.

▶ Sign up for classes at your community college.

▶ Audit a course at the nearest university.

▶ Sign up for online courses on the topics you care about.

▶ Find local groups who meet in person who share your interest; if there isn't one, create it.

▶ Hire a coach.

▶ Join a mastermind.

▶ Teach the topic you want to know more about; there's no faster way to learn than to teach.

▶ Read books.

▶ Watch videos.

▶ Attend conferences and workshops.

Take the first one and go deepen your skills in that area. Take those lessons and dive into the next one you would like to explore.

This is the process of crafting your own life's curriculum. Most of us are no longer in a system that will curate our development for us; it's up to us to do that. It's up to us to determine the lessons, and it's up to us to determine whether we've learned enough to move on to the next class.

In my own life, I've found that I will go deep into something, think on it for a while, talk to others about it to hear their ideas, and then move on. It's also very common for me to come back to these lessons later. It's not unusual for me to reread a book a year or two after having read it the first time. When I do, I always pick up on something that I didn't catch the first time. It's as if the lessons I learned the first time have had some time to settle, and the second time around I'm able to go deeper with the teacher/author.

Take your skill development seriously. Those skills, which can be developed at any age or stage, are your gateway to discovering more meaning in your life and accessing a higher level of service that will create a deeper meaning of purpose.

PLAY

As seriously as you take your life's curriculum, it is equally important to play. Play creates a space for us where making mistakes is safe and expected. There's less pressure to be perfect, and the stakes of making a mortgage or rent payment aren't on the line.

A state of constant pressure to perform at your best at everything all the time lends itself to burnout and setting unrealistic expectations. And while it's essential to take time away from being "on," play provides value for when you're back at it. Research suggests that engaging in play, whether related to a problem-solving task or not, yields benefit to problem-solving ability.[1]

Here's my challenge for you: Go do something that you're terrible at. Something that you know that you'll more than likely be the worst person in the room at whatever the activity is. It could be yoga, racquetball, singing, soccer, pottery—it doesn't matter. Go find something.

Why do I think this is important for you? Challenging yourself to take on activities that force you to operate with a beginner's mind interrupts your normal thought pattern and allows you to function at a higher level. In a sense, engaging in an activity that you suck at charges your batteries to take on the other areas of your life.

Different seasons of my life have given me the opportunity to try a lot of different things. I've joined a bowling league, taken ballroom dancing lessons, skied, and even done CrossFit. Keep in mind that these aren't activities that I went into with a mindset dedicated to mastery. I went into them with the hope of getting a taste of something different. To give myself the opportunity to activate another part of my brain. To get out of my routine thought process and into something I'm not accustomed to. It's a distraction from life's routine. We all need healthy and positive distractions in our lives.

What can you do this week that will force you to interrupt your routine pattern? What is your form of play for this season of your life?

FLY

No matter what circumstances, environment, or genetics created in my life, no one could ever take away my intelligence, my degrees, my resourcefulness, my work ethic, or any of the skills I have chosen to develop. All of those skills are mine. In my view, there is no greater investment of your time, money, or resources.

I know that personal or professional development can seem mundane and boring, but for me, there was a time when that's all that I had to hold on to. At times when it felt like everyone and everything else was letting me down, I could always count on myself to exercise my mind, to read, to explore, to learn, to lean into my own becoming.

Becoming is a means by which you take responsibility and ownership for yourself. Like the quote that opened this chapter, becoming is how we come to depend on our own wings rather than the branch on which we stand. Allow your process of becoming to bring you joy and give you the courage to spread your wings and fly.

MONEY
CHAPTER 6

The only thing I have to release in order to get what I want is my story about why I can't have it.

~ Source unknown

When Pasha and I first got together, we were two complete messes, fumbling our way through life, in economic circumstances that were foreign to us.

Pasha had just earned his doctorate in violin performance at the University of Texas, wrapping up nine years of higher education. In the early days of his private studio, Pasha couldn't keep more than two students at a time. As soon as he would get a third student, one of the original two would leave. He had a hard time building up enough students to create any kind of reliable income, so in addition to teaching, he was playing weddings, subbing with the symphony, and doing whatever he could to earn a living playing violin.

I was just finishing up with Austin Pride. Along with my founding board members, I had started the Austin Pride Foundation. The parade, the festival, the 5K run, the interfaith service, the block party, the concerts, the big gay garage sale—they were all in my rearview mirror. I was also just finishing up my term as president of the Austin Gay and Lesbian Chamber of Commerce. Overall, I was tired, but I thought I was doing okay for myself.

I didn't know it then, but a recession was about to catch up to the Austin economy and turn my world upside down. It had already hit other parts of the country, but I was too young, too inexperienced in business, and too distracted by all the volunteer work I was doing to realize what was going on.

At the time, I owned a marketing firm in the real estate industry. But during the recession, people stopped buying houses, and real estate agents couldn't afford their own bills—they certainly didn't have the money to pay for my marketing services anymore. I had five employees, and I was responsible for their livelihoods. Letting people go because I no longer had the money to pay them was humiliating and devastating. I felt bad for them. I felt bad for myself. I just felt really bad overall. Then my car was repossessed.

One morning Pasha looked at me and said, "Babe, we have twenty-three cents in the bank." Let's be clear, he was talking about his account—mine was probably in the negative.

During those days we ate a lot of Progresso soup with American cheese singles and saltine crackers. And when I say a lot, I mean sometimes twice a day. For two people who don't cook, that was the cheapest and most filling meal we could come up with.

There were a lot of people suffering during the Great Recession from 2007–2009. Though we had lost a lot, Pasha and I both acknowledge we were fortunate to have had a roof over our heads because many people lost theirs.

In the years since, the circumstances of our lives have changed dramatically. Now, we're fortunate to live in a luxury condo, drive a luxury car, and take luxury vacations. We have each created multiple six-figure incomes for several consecutive years. We aren't super-rich by any means, but we are light-years away from where we were.

STOP and pay attention to the thoughts that have popped into your head since you started reading this chapter.

When you read about Pasha's and my financial journey, you had a reaction. You made a judgment—good or bad, positive or negative. You might have said to yourself something like . . .

What a bragger! Or . . .
I can't believe he just shared that! Or . . .
What kind of idiot loses his business? Or . . .
I don't care about any money stuff. It's none of my business. Or . . .
Good for them. I'm so happy for them.

You could have had these or any number of other reactions. I don't care what it was, because your reaction isn't about me—it is all about you and your relationship with money. So, be brutally honest with yourself about what thoughts my words brought up for you.

Whatever that reaction was, take note of it. Take out your journal and write down the feelings you just had.

What did you feel in your body, and what did you say in your mind when I told you that Pasha and I were struggling and broke. What did you feel when you read that I now live a luxury life?

Your reaction is important. It's something we'll explore more as we get deeper into this chapter. But for now, just note what that reaction was and record it.

Pasha and I were at a Mexican restaurant with a couple of friends. We had shared with them some of our relationship stories—particularly about what our lives were like when we first started dating, how we were mostly poor and struggling.

Our friend looked at me and asked, "What turned things around for you guys? How did you go from where you were to where you are now?"

Without putting any thought into the answer, I said, "We just worked really hard."

I had no idea just how offensive that answer can be.

She shot back at me (as she should've), "Chad, a lot of people work really hard and never get ahead."

After that conversation, I began to really think about what had changed things for Pasha and me over the years. How did we go from relying on the kindness of others to get a good meal to a life of abundance?

We didn't go to work for big companies with fancy new jobs.

We didn't inherit any money.

We didn't win the lottery.

We do work hard, but she's right—a lot of people work really hard.

So, what was it?

The search for that answer became clearer as I started examining how we both came to think about money and our relationship with it: our money mindset.

Money mindset isn't about getting rich. It's not something to work on only if you want to be a millionaire. It's for everyone. This chapter doesn't reveal a get-rich-quick secret. I'm not going to tell you any insider stock information—I don't have any. But what I'm going to share could very well change your life and your relationship with money.

For years, my mood and my life satisfaction were often measured by the number of dollars in my bank account. There was a direct correlation between my money and my mood. Exploring your money mindset isn't just about dollars and cents. For me, it was about feeling better—about my life and myself. There's no reason a bank account should determine happiness and well-being, nor should it impact how you treat other people. What I'm going to share with you in the pages to come changed my life; a healthy money mindset can change your life too.

At the end of this chapter, I'll invite you to begin the process of breaking and untangling your inherited money mindset so that you can begin to write a new one. To help you through the process, I'll share parts of my money mindset inheritance with you. In the next few pages, you'll read bits and pieces of memories and impressions that helped me understand my relationship with money as an adult. It may seem fragmented and contradictory—perhaps it won't make any sense to you. That's okay. In fact, it's the point of the exercise. What I want to do is bring awareness to all that has been inherited so that the untangling of those inconstancies and nonsense can be seen through adult eyes and a new mindset can have space to develop.

MY MONEY STORY

When I was a kid, money wasn't something we talked a lot about in our family. We were a lower middle-class family in rural Arkansas. We didn't have a lot, but we weren't worried about where our next meal would come from either (if that worry existed for my parents, my brother and I never knew about it). My financial concerns as a kid were mostly passive in nature.

My parents both worked full-time; they worked hourly jobs and got a paycheck every two weeks. Both of my parents had hustle. They maintained steady employment throughout my childhood. They weren't afraid of work, and I'm grateful for the work ethic they demonstrated.

Like so many people, though, I didn't learn financial literacy from my parents. Nonetheless, through their actions and attitudes, they taught me lesson after lesson about money.[1]

DAD'S MONEY

My dad was a classic dabbler. He never really mastered any one thing, but he had varied interests and would try anything from motorcycles, to boats, to carpentry, to taxidermy. Sometimes there was money involved, but usually there was more money being spent than earned. It was clear to me, from a young age, that his money was for him, not the whole family. There were really no limits, constraints, or concerns for others as it related to his spending. I saw my dad buying himself boats, guns, hunting and fishing gear—toys for boys, basically.

He guarded his money and any information about his income. He had a jar above the refrigerator where he kept his pay stubs. That jar was off limits to me. So was his wallet. He kept cash in his wallet, which typically sat on top of the microwave (my parents didn't have a credit card until I was in high school). The wallet was within reach, but I wasn't allowed to touch it, and he never gave me money.

MOM'S MONEY

My mother, the consummate hustler, would work her full-time job all day long, and almost always had a money-making side hustle. She usually took to the multilevel marketing products. Any money I needed as a kid came from my mother: lunch money, field trip money, yearbook money, money to go to the city pool.

The way she spent money also had an impact. My mom is really quite beautiful. She always looked good and bought clothes that complemented her. The way she looks and dresses has always been important to her. Even so, I don't ever remember my mom buying anything at full retail price. In fact, we spent many weekends shopping for her at secondhand thrift stores, where she bought nearly all of her clothes.

My mom provided for my brother and me. She took care of us, and she sacrificed for us—that's how I experienced her money. It was a stark contrast to how I experienced my dad. For my mom, as soon as money came in, it went right back out . . . to us.

MONEY IN THEIR MARRIAGE

There were times growing up when my mom would muster up the courage to leave my dad after he had done something bad enough that she was *finally* going to leave him. She would pack up my brother and me and drive us the four miles to her mother's house. Sometimes these fits of courage would last an afternoon, sometimes a few days. There's plenty that I remember, but what stands out the most is what would get my mom back home with my dad. He would always show up with jewelry or something else that he bought to woo her, and we would pack back up and go home. His form of an apology was to buy her something, and her form of forgiveness was to accept that gift. I can remember, even as a kid, having the conversation about us leaving home for good. My mom told me on more than one occasion that it would just be too difficult financially for us to leave. My young mind understood that her message meant that his money held us hostage. Money was the thing that lured her back and kept her compliant when things got tough.

MONEY AT SCHOOL

The public schools I attended were truly a hodgepodge of different financial realities. I went to school with kids who lived in poverty and kids whose parents were well off. I always believed that I fit somewhere in the middle.

My earliest memory about money comes from when I was in elementary school. My best friend's parents had divorced, so Josh and his sister were being raised by their single mom. Because of their new reality and decreased household income, Josh was eligible to receive free lunches at school. I remember him telling me about it excitedly.

I thought he was so cool, and I so desperately wanted to fit in and be like him. At that age, I didn't understand what financial hardships a family had to experience to qualify for that program. But I did understand that he no longer had to live with his dad. I wanted that, too, and I suppose I was jealous. This free lunch thing sounded really amazing.

So, I went home one day to ask if I could get free lunches, too, perhaps aware that if I were less of a financial burden, my mom and I could leave. My dad was enthusiastic about the idea of me getting free lunches, so he encouraged my mom to check if I would qualify (his motives were clearly different from mine). But my mom discovered that their combined income exceeded the eligibility requirements, and it wouldn't be possible.

UNTANGLING MY MONEY MINDSET

I'm grateful for the perspective that rural Arkansas public school gave me. I'm grateful that I never missed a meal growing up and that my parents were able to provide for me. But the message I got about money when I was growing up was complicated. From the way that money was used for Dad's fun but was a source of stress for Mom, to the way money was secret and off limits, to money being the thing that held me hostage but also had the potential to be my liberator. What money represented to my young mind was complex. Without realizing it, my parents were writing my money mindset for me, which I have continued to carry with me. Right or wrong, the memories and impressions that I picked up from those experiences have shaped my understanding about money and the role I have allowed it to play in my life. These memories influenced every part of my relationship with money—the way I earn, save, give, avoid, borrow, overspend, and more. As an adult, my job now is to unpack those narratives, bring awareness to them, and connect the dots between what I saw as a kid and how that showed up for me as an adult. Doing so allows for a more informed and mature understanding that can explain current attitudes, behavior, and habits, and give me the opportunity to change future behavior. Let me share what I mean by connecting some of the dots from my money story with how they showed up for me as an adult.

There was a quiet nobility to my friend in being eligible enough to qualify for free lunches. I so desperately wanted to fit in and be like him, but my young mind didn't have enough information or maturity to really process the entirety of the situation. And then, my dad gave me the message that he approved. I later realized that memory played a big role in creating an income ceiling for me. A ceiling that allowed me to be comfortable—to fit in with my peers but not stand out too much. My young mind got the idea that making too much money would make me an outsider—and since I spent my life feeling like an outsider, continuing to feel like one was exactly what I was trying to avoid.

Then there was the memory of my dad's wallet being off limits and his pay stubs secret. Here are a few of the ideas that his attitude and behavior around money taught me:

- ▶ My money is my money; it's for me and not for the family.
- ▶ The money I have is for my happiness alone.
- ▶ If you need money, ask your mother.
- ▶ Money is secretive and mysterious.
- ▶ Money keeps us together.
- ▶ Money is always just out of reach.

The first time I noticed the effects of this inheritance was in my business. As an entrepreneur, I've often been in the position to ask for the sale, to ask for money in exchange for services. By working through my money mindset, I realized that I asked men for the sale quite differently than I asked women.

I wanted men to work with me. I have many male clients, but I had a harder time asking them to pay me. Sometimes I even worked really hard to impress them and make them happy before asking for money for my services, if I asked at all.

With women, I had no problem and no hesitation asking for the sale. I could be very clear about what I would do and how much they would pay.

Through my own money mindset work, I realized that the way my parents handled money taught me that money comes from women, not men. Even in business, I was constantly recreating the relationship I had with my dad. In a way, I was setting my male clients up to deprive me while I worked to gain their approval, near perfectly echoing the relationship I had with my dad and money growing up.

With my mom, I discovered that I have mostly rebelled against what she taught me about money. My mom used the excuse with me that money kept us with my dad, which was dangerous for me as a kid. And even though I believe that her actual money habits were healthier than those of my dad's—she was a better money manager—I rebelled against her money mindset. It shouldn't be a surprise that I married someone who mirrors my mother's money mindset.

Bringing my awareness to what I experienced as my parent's relationship with money has allowed me to begin making changes to my own money mindset. Instead of unconsciously mirroring or rebelling, I can allow that awareness to bring objectivity and maturity to more fully develop a money mindset that serves instead of sabotages me.

These cause-and-effect memories and circumstances weren't apparent to me until I began the intentional work of untangling my money mindset. I had to become more aware of my money memories to break the cycle of a money mindset that no longer served me. We're so young when these memories form, and we're working with such limited knowledge about a complicated concept. The trouble is that we enter adulthood still carrying around these ideas about money that aren't serving us. We avoid money, ignore our bank accounts, get into debt, overspend, or adopt a "feast or famine" mindset that's simply not reflective of our current realities. We develop an unhealthy relationship with money because we continue to approach it with the perspective from those old, imperfect memories and incomplete impressions. Our work in this chapter is to untangle those memories to help you start to gain some perspective around your relationship with money.

I've spent years breaking down my money story, trying to understand it. All the while, I've been writing a new story with new and more helpful information. My experience has been one of breaking down my money mindset and building it back up. But this journey hasn't been like laying a foundation and building a new house one brick at a time. This mindset method journey has been a process more closely resembling that of remodeling a house, where the structure has to remain standing, but I go through it room by room, taking out what I don't want, replacing it with something new, and then moving to the next room and starting all over again. All to say, building a money mindset requires a methodical and (in my experience) long journey. I've found this journey to be eye-opening, painful, infuriating, and yet quite fun, liberating, and even profitable.

THE PURPOSE AND POWER OF MONEY

> *Money is like an iron ring we put through our nose.*
> *It is now leading us around wherever it wants.*
> *We just forgot that we are the ones who designed it.*
>
> *~ Mark Kinney*

Before we get to our money mindset, there are macroeconomic issues worthy of our collective evaluation. There's no doubt that income inequality here in the United States has reached an immoral level. We need to change the fact that our criminal justice system favors those with more money. We need to change the disparity of employee and executive compensation. We need to change the earnings gap that exists between men and women. All of these macroeconomic issues warrant our attention, if not outrage. I applaud those on the frontlines of that ideological battlefield who push all of us to think about how we can more fairly earn, compensate, and tax.

For the purposes of this chapter, I'll focus on the microeconomic landscape—the relationship that each of us has with money individually. The macro issues are important, but regardless of the progress made on those issues, there are micro issues that impact each of us profoundly, persistently, and pervasively. When untangling our money mindset, we have to divorce these ideas of the macro and micro. What we see reported about the economy on the news isn't necessarily our personal reality. What that leaves us with, then, has to begin with our understanding of the purpose and power of money in our lives.

Money doesn't have a personality or attitude. It's neither good nor bad, right nor wrong. It has no gender, no race, no political affiliation, no religion. Money only has the power that we give it. And we give it a lot of power.

Money is a tool made of nothing more than fancy paper, a piece of metal, or a blip on a computer screen. You could say the same about a roll of toilet paper, a key, or a cat video. And yet, we assign money an enormous amount of value and agency. We allow it to determine things like where we live, who we marry, how many kids we'll have (or if we'll have kids at all), what we eat, how we spend our time, our education, what we do for a living, even how we allow people to treat us. All of these things can be traced back to the value we, as individuals, place on it and ultimately the relationship we have with it.

Short a massive revolution or zombie apocalypse, there's really no escaping the important role that money plays in our lives, whether you have a little or a lot. Whether it's something that you want more of or feel like you have too much of, money is an inescapable part of all of our lives, which is why we need to have as healthy a relationship with it as we can.

And just like we have to learn how to think about a healthy lifestyle and put it into practice so that we don't fall prey to disease, we also have to learn how to think about healthy habits around money and put them into practice.

A healthy money mindset isn't about having more; it's about a relationship with money that allows for greater personal freedom. Let me be clear: having a lot of money doesn't make someone a better person. Trust me, I know lots of rich jerks. I also know rich people who are extremely kind and generous. I know poor people who are jerks, too, and others who are kind and generous. Money doesn't make someone a jerk or kind; it amplifies who they already are.

Money serves two purposes in our lives: one practical and one principled. Practically, money allows us to acquire things like food, clothing, and shelter. It allows us to satisfy the most basic needs for ourselves and for those who rely on us. The principled purpose allows us to express who we are and what we value. In other words, money doesn't determine your value; it's a medium through which you can express your values. Money allows you to create the life you want and support the people and causes that you care about. It's not about self-worth; it's about self-expression. To understand how we express ourselves through money, we need to understand the importance of where it comes from, the attitude by which we receive it, and what we do with it once we have it.

THE SOURCE OF MONEY

Imagine standing in the middle of a stream of water. The water may be coming to you quickly or slowly. It may be up to your ankles or up to your waist. Either way, it's flowing toward you.

The source of the water matters, right? If it's flowing from a clean source, it is welcomed, appreciated, and enjoyed. You can play in it, drink it, or store it away for future use. But if it's flowing from a toxic source, it can make you sick. You resist the flow of water coming to you because it's unsatisfying, repugnant, unwanted.

As the water moves past you, you're able to interrupt and direct it.

Just like water flows, so does money. Whether you have a lot or a little, does the flow from source to spending align with your values? Does the source of your money bring you joy and reflect your values? When money comes into your life, how do you manage it, and what's your relationship with it? And once money leaves you, is it flowing to a place in alignment with your values? When thinking about your money mindset, three conditions matter: source, relationship, and stewardship.

A healthy money mindset is one that understands and appreciates that money is meant to flow, beginning with the source. The source is important, because money carries with it the energy and intent from which it came.

Are you happy with the source of your money? Do you have a job where your contributions are meaningful and recognized as such? Do you serve clients that appreciate and honor what you do for them? Do you have a business that you're proud of? I'm a capitalist through and through, and I'm unapologetic about it, but I admit that chasing money just for the money can be lonely and devoid of purpose.

Whether the source of your money is your business, your job, or your trust fund, does the source give you a sense of meaning and purpose for your life? Too many people are working in jobs they hate for people they hate even more. Too many people have businesses whose only purpose is to make money, absent any mission or contribution that is important to them. Some people live on trust funds that rob them of their opportunity to find meaning in contribution and for that contribution to be recognized financially.

Doesn't it feel good to work with people that you really like? Doesn't it feel good to help them get what they want and for them to pay you what you're worth? When the source is out of alignment with your purpose, it feels more like you're having to fight for every dollar or work really hard for your money. When your purpose is in alignment with the source of your money, you simply allow the flow and receive. Mindset is to money what wind is to a sail; find the alignment, catch the wind.

RECEIVING MONEY

When money comes into your life, it can elicit a range of emotions and start a cascade of thought. For one reason or another, you might feel guilt or shame that, consciously or unconsciously, leads to you get rid of that money as soon as you can. Maybe you become scared of something, and that fear leads you to save money to the point of hoarding. That same fear may lead you to get rid of that money because you're afraid of someone taking it from you. Maybe you get really excited about that money and you want to show it off, so you buy shiny things that you later regret.

The money mindset you've inherited will influence your reaction to the money you receive. We'll explore your reaction in the exercises below, but first I want to offer you an opportunity to slow down and gain some clarity around how you react when you receive. What are the thoughts, feelings, and beliefs you have when money comes to you?

Bringing awareness to how you feel when money comes into your life can help you develop a money mindset that supports your financial health. Those initial thoughts and beliefs about receiving money will determine the actions that follow. Remember, our beliefs and emotions lead to actions—and this same idea is true when it comes to money.

Bring someone to mind and imagine that person just handed you a hundred dollars. Take a second to breathe and reflect on the thoughts and feelings that you're experiencing right now.

Are you happy or excited? Skeptical of the source? Feeling guilty because someone you love could use it more than you? Immediately thinking about what you're going to buy yourself? Afraid that someone might take it from you? Feeling like you owe something to the person who handed you that money? Angry that they didn't hand you more?

The feelings created when that money comes into your life can act as a replacement for some other pain, pleasure, or trauma tangled up in your inherited money mindset. When money comes into your life, it may trigger a memory or belief that you've stored away. If you're living with an underdeveloped money mindset, receiving money may lead you to take actions that satisfy the emotions and confirm the beliefs you're holding about money.

There are two states of receiving that support a healthy money mindset: gratitude and sufficiency.

When you receive money, does your mind go toward gratitude? When you get paid, do you feel gratitude or resentment? Anxiety or excitement? Our minds are like heat-seeking missiles. So when you express gratitude, you're telling your mind what heat to seek. Gratitude is catnip for the universe. Gratitude makes it clear what you want, and your brain will seek ways to make more satisfying connections that reaffirm that sense of gratitude. Meaning that when you become intentional about expressing positive emotion in response to desired actions, your brain will seek out opportunities to recreate that experience. When the source of your money is in alignment with who you are, every dollar that flows to you is a gift. Whether a lot of money or a just a little, there is no minimum or maximum, it's important to express gratitude.

Being passive or indifferent is to see money come in and dismiss it as expected, owed, or due. It's a passive way to look at the flow that is absent any energetic feedback loop; if money is an energetic flow, then gratitude helps complete that loop.

Too often, we are so worried about that dollar leaving us that we never really appreciate that it has flowed into our lives. Pause when that money comes in and say thank you for every dollar and the person or organization that sent it your way. Each dollar carries intent and energy from its source. So take a minute to appreciate that source.

The second state that supports a healthy money mindset is sufficiency. When you receive money, are you in a state of sufficiency or lack? One of my own struggles, and one that I have found that other entrepreneurs share, is the tendency to allow my bank account balance to dictate my mood and outlook on life. When the bank account gets low, we question our own value. When the back account hits a number we find acceptable, those feelings of value improve. This is a sign of an underdeveloped money mindset.

It's important, when developing our money mindset, to establish sufficiency, a sense of "enough-ness." Enough isn't a number; it's a mindset. It's how we think about our life and our circumstances, regardless of our bank account balance. Because even when money is short, you are sufficient. I've experienced times in my life when I've had a lot. I've also had very little, but I've always had enough. Enough time, enough skills, enough love, enough support, enough resourcefulness, enough drive and ambition. I've got enough. It's up to you to discover your own state of "enough." It's there that you'll find a healthy money mindset, one that supports your overall well-being and goals for financial health.

The inverse of a sufficient money mindset is lack. What's interesting to me is that the idea of lack can be present even when there's an abundance of money. Lack is a mindset, one where we wake up and say we didn't get enough sleep, we complain that we don't get enough vacation time, we aren't having enough sex, we don't have enough friends, we aren't productive enough, or we're not successful enough. We're so busy looking at what isn't there that we forget what is abundantly present.

Remember, your brain is a heat-seeking missile; when you focus on the lack, bringing energy and attention to what isn't there, your mind will look to create more of it. Allowing yourself to focus on the lack creates a dangerous loop, since lack is a bucket that can never be filled. No matter how much you have, there can always be lack if you look for it. Even when times are financially tough, we have to create a mindset that appreciates the money that *is* there, focusing our attention on its presence, not on the lack. The money that isn't there isn't yours. The money that is there is yours. So express gratitude for what you have instead of becoming angry or anxious about something that doesn't exist.

Think of a shepherd tending his sheep. What would happen if he put all of his focus on the sheep that aren't in his flock, upset that he doesn't have more sheep? He stews in anger and complains about the sheep in his fold. How long do you think it would take before the wolves would overtake his herd or the sheep that are there wander into the wilderness?

When money finds you, is it finding a mindset of gratitude and sufficiency? If so, your stewardship will bring you joy and meaning.

STEWARDSHIP

When I was growing up, both of my grannies would give me cash for my birthday. I looked forward to it every year. One granny gave me twenty dollars, and the other gave me ten. The amounts never changed over the years, and this practice went on well into my early twenties. Every year, the same rituals graced me; one would mail me a card with a check in it, the other would hand me cash. Both gestures meant the world to me. To this day, it brings a tear to my eye to think about it. It would be easy to look at those amounts and dismiss them as small, but those gifts were more than just cash. That cash carried with it mountains of love. The intent with which it was given was the real gift. To me, those gifts were examples of the purest form of money source and stewardship.

When money comes into your life, you become a steward of that money—you're responsible for those dollars. Stewardship is different than spending, though spending is a form of stewardship. Stewardship includes investing, philanthropy, saving, and spending. Effective stewardship is a responsibility that requires awareness of how you will direct the money you've received. Stewardship means that you've become the source. Those dollars will carry your intent, your energy, and your values as they flow through and from you.

No matter how much we have or don't have, money allows us to make a difference. It gives voice to our values. And we can make a great difference with what we have through our intent and energy.

A healthy relationship with money is one that brings awareness to the entire sequence of the flow, from the source, to the receiving, to the stewardship. It requires that you ask yourself: *I have this money for the moment. How do I use it for the highest good?* A healthy money mindset is one of allocation, not accumulation.

There are too many folks waiting to make a difference with their money because they don't understand this idea. They're waiting to fulfill their philanthropic ambitions because they're embarrassed that the amount isn't as much as they think it should be. This is a sign of an underdeveloped money mindset. A healthy money mindset recognizes the intent, the energy, and the love behind any gift of any size. There is no gift too small. You can choose to make a difference with what you have or choose to make no difference at all. You will be known for your gifts, not your gains.

This same idea also applies to our spending. A healthy money mindset brings awareness to the energy of the money we spend. Are we spending our money on products and services from companies that share our values and amplify our voices through our patronage? If you want to make the world a better place, support the businesses that share your vision for that world. Think twice before you taint your own flow of money by denying it to a company that charges more and aligns with your values and instead, offering it to a company that has lower price but compromises your values. When your stewardship is out of alignment with your values, you are tainting the flow. Be a good steward with what you have, and what you have will expand.

Awareness of how money flows in and out of our lives can't be ignored if we are to have a healthy money mindset. A positive relationship with money supports its practical and principled use in our lives. Money acts as a mirror; how we utilize it is a reflection of what we value and how much we value ourselves.

WRITING YOUR MONEY STORY

> *When a person acts without knowledge of*
> *what he thinks, feels, needs or wants,*
> *he does not yet have the option of*
> *choosing to act differently.*
>
> ~ *Clark Moustakas*

Remember earlier when I asked you to write down your reactions at the beginning of this chapter? These reactions are part of your money mindset. By doing the work of untangling your money mindset, you'll begin to connect the dots of your memories about money with your attitude, behavior, and habits with money today.

And when you do, you'll begin to understand why you might pay your bills late, why you avoid your student loan payments, why you don't ask for what you're worth, why you can never seem to get ahead, why you never spend any money on yourself, why you don't give to charity, why money seems to go out as quickly as it comes in, why you always seem to only have just enough.

The answers to these questions and more will be discovered in your money mindset.

You may find that you're carrying around shame, embarrassment, or a grudge. Maybe you're modeling bad behavior or just believing things that simply aren't true for you anymore.

Even if you're well-off financially, I encourage you to do this work. Some of the most powerful feedback I get from my well-off private students is that, though they thought they had a great relationship with money, this exercise brought them awareness of what money mindset they are passing along to their children and even their employees. Your money mindset isn't self-contained— just like yours was passed on to you, you are helping to write the money mindsets of the significant people in your life.

When I do live training with big groups, there's an exercise that I almost always do. It's a transformational exercise that I'd like to guide you through.

To get started, go to the online companion course for this book found at ChadPeevy.com/book. This is my gift to you. I hope that, by unpacking your own money mindset, you'll begin to see once again how your programming, the stories you've been told or have continued to tell yourself, have been made manifest in your life. And once you've identified that programming, you can begin the process of replacing it so that it serves you now and doesn't sabotage you. I'm also including a self-paced version of the exercise here in the pages to follow.

You'll want to give yourself at least one hour for the set of reflections to finish out this chapter. Don't feel like you have to do it all at once; break the exercises up into sessions that allow you go deep with each question. It's better to give yourself the time to reflect on each question rather than rushing through.

EXERCISE

Find a comfortable, quiet space to begin. Take out your journal and something to write with. You may want to turn on some music to help you focus.

Remember, you can find a guided version of this exercise where I walk you through the process at ChadPeevy.com/book

PART 1:
EXPLORING YOUR EXISTING RELATIONSHIP WITH MONEY

For each of the words below, write in your journal what memories come up for you when you speak the word aloud, what feelings you have, and any beliefs that come to you mind. To clarify:

<u>Memories</u>: any stories that pop into your head when you see or say the word

<u>Feelings</u>: stick with the basics: happy, mad, sad, or scared

<u>Beliefs</u>: any rules, quotes, or memes that you've adopted around that word or idea. For example: *It is easier for a camel to pass through the eye of a needle than it is for a rich man to enter into the Kingdom of God.*

- ► Earning
- ► Spending
- ► Saving
- ► Giving

- ▸ Borrowing
- ▸ Loaning
- ▸ Receiving
- ▸ People who are rich
- ▸ People who are poor
- ▸ People who are middle class

PART 2:
EXAMINING YOUR MONEY PAST

Journal your reaction to each of the following questions. Push yourself to spend at least three minutes on each question, though longer is better.

- ▸ What did you learn about money in your family?
- ▸ How have you echoed or rebelled against the money mindset your mother passed on to you?
- ▸ How have you echoed or rebelled against the money mindset your father passed on to you?
- ▸ How did the significant people in your life make you feel about money?
- ▸ What did your religion or culture teach you about money?
- ▸ How have your ups and downs with money impacted you?
- ▸ Has money ever brought you shame or embarrassment?
- ▸ Has money ever brought you joy and happiness?

PART 3:
CONNECT THE DOTS AND UNTANGLE THE
CONNECTING THREADS

Journal your reaction to each of the following questions. Push yourself to spend at least three minutes on each question, though longer is better.

- ► How are you holding on to your past through your relationship with money?
- ► How are you allowing money to keep you chained to dysfunctional relationships?
- ► What is showing up in your relationship with money today that you can connect back to your money mindset? In what ways have you echoed or rebelled?
- ► Is your money past affecting your relationships today?
- ► What in your money mindset do you need to let go of?
- ► What in your money mindset needs your forgiveness?

IT'S OKAY TO GO SLOW

Take a deep breath. What you just did took a lot of courage. Give yourself credit for facing and examining your relationship with money. This is deep work, and I honor you for putting in the effort. It's work that you will likely continue for years to come. Your existing money mindset wasn't formed in an instant; it was created and reinforced over years of your life. What began as a memory turned into a way of looking at something that turned into a habit—a habit with money, which is present in your life every day. Give yourself the grace to go slow, to be patient with yourself, and to be compassionate with what you have uncovered. It's okay if you don't know how to change what you've discovered; the awareness is enough for you to say no to an old mindset, even if you don't know what should replace it yet. Doing this work is creating change and breaking the cycle of an inherited money mindset.

I know that for me and the many students I've guided through this exercise, there are immediate revelations and then long-term work to do. I first did the work on my own money mindset with the help of Bari Tessler's book, *The Art of Money*, in 2016. Since then, I've carried a handwritten copy in my backpack of the notes I took when reading it. The inherited money mindset is deeply ingrained in us. In many cultures, including the one I grew up in, talking about money was considered taboo. When you don't talk about and work through something, it doesn't get a chance to evolve or mature. I tell you this in hopes that you'll be easy with yourself as you do this work; it's really deep and challenging stuff. Honor yourself for making the effort, show yourself compassion for trying something different, and grant yourself forgiveness for past mistakes.

Disclaimer: I am not a medical professional. What I'm going to share with you here is simply a reflection of how I have experienced and managed my depression and anxiety, and how I understand them. Consult your health care provider before making any changes to your mental health plan or treatment.

MINDFULNESS
CHAPTER 7

If you want to understand your mind, sit down and observe it.

- Anagarika Munidra

I'm no stranger to depression or anxiety; both have been a part of my life experience since childhood. Fourth grade may actually be when I had my first encounter with depression (though I certainly didn't know it as depression at that age). And though I wouldn't characterize depression this way now, what I remember then is feeling a sense of perpetual sadness.

It was in fourth grade when I realized that I was different—different in a way that would be seen as unacceptable. Until then, my effeminate mannerisms could have been passed off as those of a little kid, but around the fourth grade, reactions seemed to change. All of a sudden, that little kid was to act a certain way, be a certain way, talk a certain way, and like certain things. That same year, my best friend's brother died; while hunting, he accidentally shot himself in the leg and bled out. I was also seeing changes in my dad's behavior about that time—my little brother had been born just two years before, and my dad really took a special interest in him. Dad started drinking less and was around more often. That whole season of my young life had been particularly traumatic. I was nine and ten years old, dealing with things that were larger than my young mind could really handle.

It had become clear to my mom and my teachers that something wasn't quite right with me. Even though I spent much of elementary school in regular appointments with the school counselor, I knew not to share too much. We would never have talked about our home life with the likes of a schoolteacher or counselor; they were outsiders and were looked upon with suspicion. I often wonder if they all knew what was happening to me. Did they know about the abuse at home? Did they know that I was gay? Did they know that I had no idea what gay even meant and that I was struggling to understand what I was feeling?

Unsure or in denial about what was going on with me, my mother, teacher, and school counselor decided that it must have been the academic pressure that was getting to me. My school district assigned our classes from first to fifth grade based on our academic performance and aptitude. So as little kids, we were very aware of our ranking and which class we were in. I was in the "top class" with all the "smart kids" or "gifted and talented" kids. Other students would be classified as being in the "second class," "third class," and so on. Our class all moved through the elementary grades together in these segregated silos, so it was common for kids in the top class to befriend other top-class kids.

My mother, teacher, and school counselor decided that, going into the fifth grade, I would be dropped to the second class. But I only knew the kids in the top class—kids that I had been with since first grade. So when they dropped me down to second class the following year, I found myself with kids I didn't really know. I was an outcast. The second-class kids were smart enough to know they were in the second class, and they didn't exactly welcome a top-class refugee who had fallen from grace in the academic hierarchy.

My process of untangling required me to explore my depression and anxiety so that I could learn how to better manage them. I get asked a lot, and I wonder myself, if the depression and anxiety will ever completely go away. My honest answer is that I don't know. For me, they haven't yet. What I can tell you though is that I've found strategies that help me live with them in a way that doesn't overwhelm my life. I've learned ways of living that mitigate their recurrence, and I utilize coping tools for when they do show up. In the past, they may have overcome me for days, weeks, and even months at a time. But now, I've been able to find ways that make the recurrences shorter and less frequent.

In this chapter, I'll share with you my mindfulness journey, which helps me live with my depression and anxiety, rather than suffer from them.

THE THREE SELVES

There are three versions of us present in our lives all the time: our past, present, and future selves. They are often in conflict with one another. If you've ever been faced with a decision in your life and thought to yourself, *On the one hand I think* this, *on the other hand I think* that, you've experienced this type of internal conflict. A practice in mindfulness allows us to balance the past and future selves in a way that brings us peace and solitude in the present self and ultimately resolve internal friction.

I've come to see my depression as a state that occurs when the past self encroaches on the present self. When the present self is overcome by unresolved feelings from the past, I experience what I know as depression. The memories I can access trace back to that period around fourth grade. Then, it would have been unsafe for me at home to express my anger about my new expectations, my confusion and anger around my feeling of being different, my anger about what was happening at school. Freud referred to depression as rage turned inward, and I had a lot to be mad about. The short-term survivor skill was to hold onto the anger, be mad at myself, and beat myself up for not living up to expectations. That skill protected me at the time, but it had long-term consequences. For me, depression is a toxic mix of anger, boredom, resentment, guilt, and regret. They all mix together and marinate in my mind, and the result is misery. When it happens, I sleep a lot, retreat from everyone, stop talking, and often stop working.

Anxiety, for me, is a state of tension—tension between my present and future selves. When expectations of the future self encroach on the present self, I experience what I know as anxiety. I think of anxiety as being in a state of misalignment with who I see myself becoming and who I am in the moment. When this happens, I find myself short of breath, have difficulty focusing, and look for things to numb the feelings. I often experience physical manifestations of my anxiety: itchy skin, stomach issues, an uncomfortable internal vibration, and an overall sense of being unsettled.

My journey has required an untangling of each of these three selves. Knowing each of them has allowed me to recognize them when they appear. For example:

MY YOUNGER SELF

When I think of my younger self, I see a boy around seven to ten years old. I was seven when my little brother was born. That was also the year that my family moved from the single-wide trailer into a house up the road that my dad had built. This was also around the time that I first started experiencing anxiety and depression. That age range was one of challenge and change.

My younger self is a tortured and terrified little boy. He's in a constant state of fear. He thinks and behaves from an instinct to survive. He goes through his young life in a heightened state of awareness. He is unsure as to why, but he's certain that he isn't like the other kids. At home, he never knows what kind of torture his dad will deliver on any given day. Even at his young age, he knows that making his very presence known could be dangerous. He stays quiet. He stays out of the way. He keeps to himself. He plots and functions to survive.

Dominant Emotions: Fear and Sadness[1]

MY FUTURE SELF

I can sense the future version of myself impatiently beckoning to me through time and space. I can see the image of who I want to become, the career I'll have built, the businesses I'll own, the love and support of the people around me, the experiences that I'll have, the adventures that I'll go on. That guy has aged well; he's taken care of his mind, body, and spirit. He's figured out how to develop deeper relationships with others. He's a great husband. He's helped millions of people from around the world get more of what they want out of their life. He lives his personal freedom.

This version of me is full of expectations and anticipation. While he has good intentions, he has unrealistic timelines combined with impatience and perfectionism. He wants to exist in the now and is willing to force the present self out of the way. He's aggressive and doesn't appreciate allowing for a process of personal and professional development. His mantra is: *Hurry up* and *be the best.*

Dominant Emotions: Fear and Anger

MY PRESENT SELF

This is me—right here, right now. My presence allows for gratitude, joy, meaning, satisfaction, and all the things that make our lives worth living. He has confidence in his resilience. He is optimistic and ambitious but unattached to any expectation. He senses oneness with the universe and peace in knowing that he's okay. He is my "best" self, who exists in the here and now.

Dominant Emotion: Happy

WHO IS SHOWING UP?

Over the years, I've learned to mitigate the experience of depression and anxiety by bringing awareness to the alignment of these three selves. If I'm depressed, I search for what's going on in my current circumstance that's triggering a difficult memory or past experience. Typically, I'll find unresolved anger that I've directed inward, toward myself, because I haven't found a healthy way to direct or express my feelings toward the subject of my anger. If I'm feeling anxious, I examine the gap between the way things are and the way I want them to be. Typically, I'll find that I'm bringing uncertainty of the future or unhelpful expectations of an unrealized future into my present self. Bringing awareness to the misalignment of my three selves has been an effective means of understanding my depression and anxiety.

The threes selves are always present—and a mindfulness practice regulates the friction between the versions of the self. But the past and future rarely align with present circumstances. So the question then becomes: Which version of myself am I allowing to be in the driver's seat of my life at any given moment? Through a practice in mindful awareness, we can call on the present self to emerge more readily.

Mindful awareness offers an opportunity to introduce a regulating force in our lives, a perspective that can observe us through an external lens, absent participation in our current state. I call that moderating force my Conscious Observer.

How does the Conscious Observer identify which version is present? When I'm feeling out of alignment (experienced as anxiety or depression), I stop myself and ask, *Where am I? Am I showing up as my past, present, or future self?* Simply asking the question will bring an awareness necessary to navigate the moment, whatever it may be. Asking the question calls on the powers of the Conscious Observer to recognize who I am in the moment and judiciously make decisions that honor all three selves while allowing my present self to emerge. There are times that I stop myself and acknowledge that I'm behaving as the scared kid living in my head. Sometimes I'll recognize that I'm thinking about something in the future, some task or project that I want to get done, only to realize that the mental energy I'm spending solves a problem that doesn't yet exist. When that happens, I chuckle at myself, take a deep breath, and bring myself back to the present moment.

For example, as I was writing this book, a fear emerged that I wouldn't be able to reply to all the questions readers will have about it. There are lots of reasons that a fear-filled thought like that may be silly, but one is that I hadn't even finished the manuscript. I created unhealthy anxiety around a problem that didn't exist in the present and may not even exist in the future. It's prudent to think about the future, to plan, to be thinking ahead. But it's not helpful to think about problems that aren't even a possibility yet. Before I could worry about readers, I had to finish the manuscript. How often do we create and worry about problems that don't yet exist by allowing an unhelpful version of ourselves to emerge? This only sabotages us.

A healthy, mindful mindset requires that we recognize the three versions of our self and engage the powers of our Conscious Observer.

PERSPECTIVE IS EVERYTHING

Imagine for a second that you have an itch on your leg. Your brain senses the discomfort, and then what happens? You instinctively reach down to scratch. Instinctively, without thinking. Our habits and programming cause the same kind of instinctual response throughout our lives—when someone says something to us, looks at us the wrong way, cuts us off in traffic, or even when we sit down to eat. We instinctively react to the stimuli. We get angry. We honk our horn. We eat everything on our plate. Living mindfully is bringing awareness to what you're seeing, hearing, and experiencing so that you may consciously respond—or not respond.

Try this little exercise to show yourself the difference between a reaction and conscious action: The next time you have an itch, don't scratch it. Take a second to acknowledge that you have an itch, then consciously decide to scratch it. If you can stand to give it another second, ask yourself if the itch is on your skin or in your mind. This little exercise will help wake you up and bring your awareness to the present moment.

Mindfulness is being aware of being aware, living with your eyes open, developing the ability to think about your thinking. It's being aware of each part of yourself, as well as all the parts of our lives.

There are so many things I've experienced in my own life that are the result of not being in a practice of mindfulness. Depression, anxiety, and fear are the result of the bad management of my mind. But so is taking unnecessary risk, such as getting overexcited about an idea, overeating, or drinking too much.[2] We can either let our minds run wild and our lives become the consequence of that chaos, or we can learn to better manage our mind. Better management of the mind is a practice in mindfulness. And the first step to better management is to better understand what's going on in our mind. Let's start with a familiar mind activity: thinking.

We think in order to rehearse the future. To rehearse an upcoming conversation, performance, game, or trip to the grocery store. The power of our mind allows us to mentally experience that future event before it happens. The thoughts we have about the future are framed by our beliefs—where past, present, and future collide. Some of our beliefs are inherited from our environment: culture, family, school, religion. Some beliefs are created through life experience and our ability to assign reason to things that have happened to us. Based on what we believe, we imagine how the future will go, how we see it playing out.

Once that future arrives at the present, our minds work to confirm what we've already experienced in our imagination. Thus, our mental rehearsal of the future is based on our current understanding of the past. Those thoughts in the present are based on beliefs that were created in the past and will determine the future. Beliefs are everything—the holy grail of mindset work—and it is through a practice in mindfulness that we become aware of and are able to scrutinize our beliefs.

When examining your beliefs, you'll find that they are tied up in the stories of your past. Because of our linear perspective of life, we tend to see our current and future circumstances through the lens that we created in our past. That past lens created the stories and memories that have made you who you are, defined you, and created your beliefs. If you want to better manage your mind, you'll have to work to examine and, if necessary, create new beliefs. Part of this untangling work will include seeing those past experiences and stories reframed and retold in ways that will empower you in the present. We actually have the power to change our past by changing how we think about it.

Now, let me be very clear right here. What I'm suggesting does not mean that I'm excusing the behavior of the people that did you harm. I don't mean that at all. I am not excusing any abuse; there is no excuse for it. Some of my stories growing up were horrible. So horrible, in fact, that parts of my childhood are blocked out of my mind; there are periods that I just can't remember. But in order to move from surviving (then) to thriving (now), we need a self-narrative of support and empowerment rather than one that will sabotage the present and future we deserve. Even though we were powerless at the time of our abuse, we can reframe the entire experience as one of strength and resilience, not suffering or victimhood.

Reframing our past experiences is important, because what you believe about them will become manifest in your future. Not because you are casting some magical spell, but because our minds only see the things that we believe. This is called confirmation bias:[3] seeking or interpreting what's happening in our lives (giving reason) in ways that support our existing beliefs or ways of thinking.[4] Through confirmation bias, we are actively creating the life we have already decided exists. No one ever wants to think that they are wrong; our brains are wired to confirm what we already believe, not question it.[5] In fact, our beliefs can last longer than any evidence that contradicts them. Evidence will come and go, but our beliefs will remain unless we bring mindful awareness to them and how they are impacting our lives. We have to make the conscious and mindful decision to reframe our experiences and create new beliefs.[6]

Our minds are wired to move forward through life, actively searching to confirm our beliefs. I'll remind you here that our minds are heat-seeking missiles. But it's our job to tell the mind which heat to seek. What you believe, you will create. You won't be able to help it; your mind will actively seek out the heat, which will confirm that belief. If you grew up being told "times are tough," you'll grow up and see the times as tough. If you grew up hearing that "no one but family can be trusted," you'll go through life skeptical of those outside your family. That's because our brains crave certainty, not doubt. Think of how you feel when something is concrete, established, and sure versus when things are up in the air, unclear, or fuzzy. We're wired to confirm the beliefs that already exist. Not only do we seek out experiences that confirm existing beliefs, but we also have a tendency to double down on the evidence that confirms those beliefs.[7]

In a mindfulness practice, every thought receives scrutiny. Questioning yourself means becoming okay with being wrong, even embracing that you've been wrong. A new way of life requires a new set of mindsets. To create the life you want, to experience and live your personal freedom, you must be open to an examination of your beliefs. You can't be limited to one specific dimension of yourself. My journey included the twelve mindsets that I've outlined in this book. As soon as I would bring awareness to one mindset, it influenced others. This may be your experience as well. The untangling process isn't a precise dissection—it's much messier than that. Allow yourself the grace to experience a messy process.

Research has shown that perhaps the only way to overcome the tendency to confirm existing biases is to force oneself to think about exactly the opposite belief. You must be open to flipping your worldview upside down. Along your journey, you've picked up ideas and beliefs from other people, who likely picked up those ideas and beliefs from someone else—someone who likely never scrutinized the belief that they held or passed down. That was certainly the case for me, growing up in an environment where the hard thinking was left to someone else, and the search for answers was cut off by ideas that said, "That's just the way it is." Or, "That's the way it's always been." Or even, "That's just God's plan."

Know that, by doing the work of untangling and inviting a mindful mindset, you'll recover parts of yourself that have been suppressed and discover the strength and resilience of your present self. Know that, by doing this work, you are again breaking a cycle of inherited mindsets.

NOTHING HAPPENS FOR A REASON

Mindfulness is bringing awareness to your life, in the here and now. It's a practice of becoming awake to everything that is—all of it. Once you welcome awareness of the present moment into your life, you can begin to make true and lasting change. This is more than taking responsibility for the way things are; it's accepting the truth of the way things are too. It's seeing things as they are, without attachment to failure or idealism. It's accepting that things are what they are, period.

This can be a difficult concept to grasp; it was for me. The idea of being in the present felt in contrast to the religious teachings I grew up with. I was taught that everything happens for a reason. Reason was assigned and outside of my control; it was predestined or predetermined for me. Life was something that happened *to* me. I was a victim of destiny.

I no longer subscribe to that school of thought. With perspective and reflection, it's not difficult to look at our past and draw a line from the events of our past to the circumstances of our present. That's not destiny; it's an exercise in cause and effect. Nothing happens for a reason; *you* give reason to the things that have happened. Our consciousness gives us the ability to mindfully assign reason to the events and circumstances of our past in a way that supports our journey toward personal freedom.

When you tell yourself that things happen for a reason, from a place of abdicating that responsibility, you're giving away the power of your past, present, and future. If things happen to you for reasons that satisfy someone else's agenda, even when that someone else is God, you don't have to accept responsibility for the way things are in your life, and you forfeit the power to change them. When you assign blame and relinquish control of your life's narrative, you invite chaos, anxiety, and discontentment into your life.

Through the power of your personal narrative, you create your own life. You write your own story. What you do today, what you decide today, and what you say today will show up in your future—because today is the past to which you will one day assign reason. All of our decisions result in outcomes to which we will one day assign reason. Behave with an awareness of yourself today so that tomorrow you may reflect and assign reasons that reinforce your resilience, character, and grit. Create a life arc that shows your resolution to fully experience each moment that brings you closer to the greatest version of who you are.

NOT SMALL ANYMORE

Do you ever wonder why you don't face things in your life more directly? Do you avoid having hard conversations? Shy away from asking for what you really want? Ignore your email, mailbox, or voicemail? That isn't the present version of yourself handling those situations; it's a younger version of you being allowed, through avoidance, to manage your very adult life. This tendency to avoid is a defense mechanism, a way of acting out. There are other ways that the younger self acts out: whining, yelling, refusing to talk, playing dumb, throwing temper tantrums. The adult version of us, who allows the misbehaving younger self to emerge, will find themselves exhibiting behaviors not too dissimilar to those of a child.

In psychology, this emergence of the younger self is referred to as regression.[8] I'm sure you've heard arguing adults say, "You're acting like a child!" Which is exactly right! Regression becomes acute particularly during times of heightened stress, insecurity, or fear. It's a defense mechanism by which we are trying to get back to a time when we had no responsibility, a time when someone would come to our rescue. This younger version of you is likely holding you back from achieving your goals, stopping you from facing your life more directly, and keeping you small. It's stopping you from both confronting challenges and seizing opportunities.

Our younger self is a smart little kid. For me, the most familiar type of regression is the one that tells me to stay small. My younger self had to figure out how to survive—and he did that really well. When he shows up now, he tells me a familiar message. It's the same message he's been telling me all of my life: hold back, stay hidden, be quiet. When I'm small, when I'm feeling worthless and full of doubt, when I physically hurt with loneliness, when I retreat from the world and hide my light, when I shut everyone out,

I'm being compliant with what my father wanted from me. He wanted me small. He wanted me quiet. And for all of my youth, that's what he got.

My misbehaving younger self carries a message rooted in fear, a powerful emotion, and his only motivation is survival, a very powerful motivator. His message of survival has protected me in the past, but now his concerns are inflated. When allowed to go unchecked, he has the potential to overcome my present self.

Your regressions may be staying small, throwing temper tantrums, or somewhere in between. But here's the thing: that little kid in each of us isn't going away. He'll always be there. He is you, after all. He, too, will have a seat at the table alongside your present and future selves. All three versions of you will move through life with you.

If you are going to experience the personal freedom that exists for you in the present, you have to learn how to take care of your younger self. Trying to ignore this self is like ignoring an attention-seeking toddler; their behavior only gets worse. When you notice your younger self showing up, pay attention to the feelings he has, and engage him in conversation. Remind him that he can trust the person you've become, and remind your present self that you're not small anymore.

Your present self has the ability to take care of your younger self so that he doesn't unintentionally sabotage you. Look at that little kid as your responsibility now, as if he's your own child. Listen to and satisfy his needs and desires so they don't overwhelm you. When challenges come your way, you want your adult self to show up, not that little kid. You want that little kid to recognize that challenges don't have to scare him, and he doesn't have to emerge and act out of fear. You want him to understand and take comfort in the fact that you've handled a lot, you've overcome so much, you've survived, and you have the tools now to protect him.

You have to take care of him in a way that is supportive, loving, and safe—something he didn't get enough of while growing up.

Regression and emergence of the younger self isn't all about misbehaving and acting out. Jung, for example, argued that the younger self plays a role in enhancing our well-being by helping us find security, love, and trust.[9] I'm of the mind that it's as important to help the younger self experience and express his joy as much as it is to protect him. We can do that by allowing him to emerge when it's time to have fun and play. The inner child in us has needs that we can and should satisfy.

Learn how to live at peace with your younger self. Doing so means continuing your journey of personal development—the work you're doing right now. That will allow you to find more peace and harmony between your competing selves and go confidently into any situation. Even though his young voice may seem impossible to ignore, remember that just because you hear him doesn't mean you have to listen to him. As you face the challenges and opportunities in your life, don't come to them as your former or future self, but rather as the very best version of who you are today. You are enough, right now in this very moment; you are not small anymore.

So how does someone put mindfulness into practice? Through research and my own experience, I've developed a few ideas: First, you have to bring awareness to historical narratives you are carrying into your present and do the work that reframes those experiences in a way that will support your growth. Second, you have to become grounded in gratitude and intentional about your life. And finally, it's necessary to adopt a mindfulness practice that will become the vehicle for delivering you to the present moment.

BE AWARE OF WHAT YOU ARE BRINGING INTO THE PRESENT

The exercises in this section consist of four parts. But first, you may find it helpful to read some thoughts that I have kept in mind as I have done this work.

Years and years of therapy have forced me to recall the experiences of my past. There are some folks out there that will tell you this is a counterproductive exercise, that your past doesn't matter, only the here and now does. There's a kernel of truth in that; you can achieve short-term gains by gaming your mind in the present. However, it's simply another survival mechanism, no different from the one that we engage in during traumatic times. Until you take the time to seriously consider your past, your experiences, and the programming that has defined who you've become, you will not experience the long-term resolution that will lead to a thriving life. For you to adopt a mindset that is grounded in the present, the present has to be an inviting place for you to want to be. If you can't find peace in your present, you won't want to be there.

It's painful to recount the past. If you still have relationships with the people who were around you when you experienced your trauma, there's potential for this process to be painful for you and them. For me, there was a tendency to want others to come along on this journey with me, and at times I would try to force it. Not everyone is ready for this kind of work. That's okay. But the work is worth it, even if it's lonely at times.

When going through the process of understanding your past and how it frames how you see yourself today, you'll remember things that you've forgotten. Things that happened to you will come back to you in trickles and floods. Sometimes there will be so much information coming back that it will be overwhelming, and sometimes it will feel dry. Remind yourself constantly through the process to be kind to yourself. Schedule breaks and self-care. Sometimes you'll need to be alone, and other times you'll need to be around people who support you.

Be kind to yourself. Make that sentence a mantra. Don't succumb to the inevitable negative feelings that will accompany the memories that come up through this process. When I began to seriously think about being more kind to myself, something strange happened. It wasn't just a mental shift; it was also a physical one. I could breathe easier. Literally, it's like a weight was lifted from my shoulders and my chest. I began to realize the pressure I had put on myself for so many years: pressure to overachieve, to overcome, to look a certain way, to be perfect. There's something to learn about yourself in the exploration of that pressure. I discovered that the pressure to be perfect came primarily from my mother. There was a similar but somewhat conflicting message from my father, who expected me to be perfectly straight and butch and like him. That kind of pressure on a young person is heavy beyond weight.

As you begin these exercises, stay open to the exploration of the beliefs, ideas, emotions, and narratives you have tangled up in your mind, no matter how bizarre, surprising, confusing, and sometimes conflicting the fragments may be. That's the point; breaking the cycle begins with awareness.

I found it helpful to intentionally dissociate myself from my younger self. This can be helpful when reframing your stories. It's a process of stepping outside of yourself, calling on your Conscious Observer, viewing yourself as an outsider looking in. It has allowed me to observe without reliving so that I could put my emotional state of mind into perspective.

Dissociation has also helped me when considering the other people in my stories. With my mother, for example, it's extremely difficult for me to reconcile her actions, or lack of action, when I consider her as my mother. What I've learned to do over the years, though, is to see her not as my mother, but as a human being—with her own emotional trauma, her own experiences, her own life, which is separate from me, her son. I know how odd this sounds. How can I not see her as both mother and human? When I think of her as mother, I center myself—she's mother to *me*. When you think of the whole person as they exist in their relationship to you, you can't objectively see them for who they are: human. Place them in time and space absent your relationship, seeing the person as they are, not just who they are to you. When I do this, I experience a range of emotions. The feelings change depending on my circumstances, but typically, I feel sorry for her. I feel sad for her. Sure, I feel angry too. But overall, I see her negligence to act as more weakness and less malice toward me, and in recognizing the humanity in that, I'm able to untangle from her.

These exercises may also reinforce negative emotions and even amplify them. For example, when I think of my father as human and not as "father," I experience the opposite range of emotions toward him. I can't reconcile his behavior as that of a good human. My dad experienced his own abuse and lived with his own tormentor. But in the end, I can't find a way to see the humanity in his actions. His actions toward me were not kind. His actions were not based from a misunderstanding of love—they were mean-spirited and cruel.

Through these exercises and by constantly examining my beliefs, I was able to determine the relationships I wanted to salvage—the people I wanted to keep in my life—and the relationships I had to eliminate for my own healing. Through these exercises, and others you'll find in this book, I found a way to reconnect with myself in the present and work on relationships with people who were important to me.

EXERCISE

I'd like to invite you to settle into a quiet place, free from distraction, and complete the following steps:

PART 1:
GETTING TO KNOW YOUR THREE SELVES

1. Who shows up more frequently? Is it your past self? Your present self? Your future self? Why do you think this is?

2. How do you recognize and describe your younger self?

3. What are the dominant emotions of your younger self? Happy, mad, sad, scared? (*You can see how I did this exercise and notated the dominant emotions by referring back to pages 175-176*)

4. How do you recognize and describe your future self? Keep in mind that the future self holds the expectations—describe them.

5. What are the dominant emotions of your future self? Happy, mad, sad, scared?

6. How do you recognize and describe your present self? Remember that your present self is the "best self," minus the encroachment of the past and future selves.

7. What are the dominant emotions of your present self? Happy, mad, sad, scared?

PART 2:
DOMINANT SELF-IDENTIFICATION

1.   Choose a topic, idea, situation, or person (see a list of ideas below).

2.   Write down the first three words that come to mind.

3.   Take a minute or two to close your eyes and reflect on the topic and the ideas, beliefs, and memories that come up for you around it. As you journal, let your mind wander, and write down those things that came to you as you sat in contemplation. *I recommend spending at least ten minutes just letting thoughts come to you as you journal.*

4.   Which self (past, present, or future) dominates how you perceive this topic, idea, situation, or person?

Here's an incomplete list of areas worthy of examination:

- ► Ambition
- ► Career
- ► Childhood
- ► Commitment
- ► Community
- ► Connection
- ► Education
- ► Family
- ► Fatherhood
- ► Friends
- ► Future

- ▸ God
- ▸ Health/wellness
- ▸ Meaning
- ▸ Money
- ▸ Motherhood
- ▸ Legacy
- ▸ Love
- ▸ Past
- ▸ Politics
- ▸ Present
- ▸ Purpose
- ▸ Relationships
- ▸ Sex
- ▸ Sexuality
- ▸ Social status

PART 3:
ANOTHER PERSPECTIVE

1. Using the same topic, idea, situation, or person from Part 2, introduce the opposite belief around those first three words that came to your mind. *For example, if the topic is "family," and your immediate reaction is "rejection, challenging, confusing," the opposite idea might be "acceptance, easy, clear."*

2. Which version of self (past, present, or future) would see the topic, idea, situation, or person through this opposite lens?

3. Journal about what that topic would look like for you through the lens of the opposite beliefs that you've introduced. *I recommend spending at least ten minutes letting thoughts come to you as you journal about this reframed experience.*

PART 4:
ENCOUNTERS OF SELVES

1. Imagine that the version of you who gave the answers in Part 1 were to meet the version of you that provided the opposite answers in Part 2. If those two versions of yourself had a conversation, what would they say to each other?

There's no limit to the time you'll spend going through this process. In fact, it's a process that you'll adopt into your everyday life. You may consider making it a part of your morning routine. As you're introduced to new thoughts and ideas, scrutinize each one, and only let them take up room in your head if they support how you want to see yourself and your life.

Thoughts, ideas, beliefs—they don't get to live in your head rent-free. At some point, the rent is due. That rent may come in the form of your own mental well-being but can also come at the expense of those around you and your relationship with them.

When I began this process, I realized that there were areas in my life that felt incongruent. The beliefs I was holding were not in alignment with my experience or what I wanted for my future. This exercise will allow you to reframe and realign those experiences in a way that will support you instead of sabotage you.

HAVING TROUBLE?

I had trouble finding ways to take that information and change the programming. Over the years, I learned that it's not as much *de*programming as it is *re*programming. It's about seeking out new information, new ways of thinking, and new ideas that serve me instead of sabotaging me. We don't know what we don't know.

In order to help myself, I read a lot. I go to therapy every week. I meet with coaches. Outside perspective is an extremely powerful and helpful tool on your journey to better understand yourself.

It's okay (and encouraged) to get help! Surround yourself with books, mentors, and authentic friends. If you're able, get a good therapist and a coach, and join a mastermind group of like-minded people. You can certainly begin the process of questioning your own beliefs, but you may be blind to many alternative beliefs. We are so drawn to confirming our own beliefs and expectations, but doing this only prevents us from seeing anything that would conflict with them.[10] Other people can help, and they will fast-track your progress.

GET GROUNDED IN GRATITUDE

There's one thing my dad did get right. He was a stickler for making sure that we expressed our gratitude. "Did you say thank you?" he would ask. Saying thank you, even for the simple things, instilled an awareness of gratitude in us. My mom and dad prayed with my brother and me at night. Those prayers were largely expressions of gratitude for basic things. Each night, we brought our attention to the blessings in our lives. My folks messed up a lot, but the gratitude thing they got right.

I want to invite you to adopt a practice that I call being

grounded in gratitude. This is a state of being, one that helps you immediately seek and gain perspective throughout every part of your day and your life.

Before I share my ideas for what I think gratitude is and how it will improve your life, let's explore what gratitude is not.

Gratitude is not an antidote to ambition, nor is it settling for what you have. There's a saying that what we resist persists. This is also true with gratitude. If you can't find the blessing of your circumstance, it will persist until you do.

Through my own journey and helping others along theirs, I've found that desire can create conflict or a misalignment with gratitude. Gratitude for what has flowed into your life—whether perceived as good or bad— doesn't mean that it will stay in your life forever. It's a conduit for flow. When we resist, through resentment, overindulgence, guilt, or greed, we interrupt the flow and therefore our growth. Gratitude makes way for more in your life because it brings awareness to what is flowing into your life. Just like we explored in money mindset, the same ideas apply in our mindful mindset. It's a form of awareness that widens the banks of the river of abundance flowing through your life.

Being grounded in gratitude means being grateful for all of it—not just the stuff you're happy with, but all the facets of your life, even the stuff you don't like. Gratitude for the roof over your head, the food you eat, the people in your life, the breath you take. Also, gratitude for the challenges you've faced and your ability to learn and grow from them.

The more gratitude you express for your life, the better your life will become. For example, when you say, "I'm so grateful for . . ." the universe responds by saying, "Well, if you think that's good, let me show you how much better it can be!" Gratitude is like fertilizer. Could your plants grow without it? Sure. Will they grow so much better with it? You're dang right they will.

Being grounded in gratitude . . .

- ▸ is a recognition of self-worth;
- ▸ acknowledges your progress;
- ▸ checks your privilege;
- ▸ means knowing that today's obstacle is tomorrow's victory;
- ▸ halts complaining;
- ▸ ends judgment;
- ▸ ceases criticism;
- ▸ allows you to feel more deeply;
- ▸ draws you closer to others; and
- ▸ honors your journey.

How do you begin the practice of being grounded in gratitude? My goal for you is for you to go through your day living in gratitude. To begin, set aside times in your day to bring awareness to what you are grateful for. Begin your day grateful that you woke up and that you are drawing breath. Bring awareness and gratitude to the fact that you are waking up in a bed, with a roof over your head. Take that gratitude into your meditation practice, which we'll cover in the next section. And then, end your day by journaling your gratitude for the day. Keep a gratitude journal next to your bed and, before you lay your head down, write down three things that you are grateful for and why.

By adopting these practices, eventually you'll catch yourself feeling awkward when you complain. This is a good thing. Recognize that your work is paying off, embrace the feeling, and lean into your gratitude. By journaling at the end of the day, you're training your mind to look for things that are contributing to your journey. You'll start to notice yourself looking for the good throughout your day. All of these practices will help you get grounded in gratitude.

MINDSET PROMPTS:

▸ Today I am grateful for . . .

▸ I am grateful to have come so far. Ten years ago, I couldn't have even imagined that . . .

▸ I am grateful for this struggle because it is teaching me that . . .

▸ I am grateful for this person because they help me see . . . in myself.

PRACTICE IN MEDITATION

Mindfulness is a practice. Just like anything that you have to practice, it requires thought, focus, attention, and energy. Meditation is my primary exercise for practicing the mindful mindset.

Meditation offers me a practice, which I have craved in other parts of my personal development too. Perhaps it's my religious upbringing, but I need some sort of ritual every day that grounds me. I've found that I need that type of routine practice in my life, and meditation offers that. With therapy, for example, while I find it very helpful, the intentional practice is missing for me. Therapy helps me connect the dots between what I went through as a kid and how that has impacted my life as an adult. Meditation, though, is the daily practice of getting my mind in check. Slowing my thoughts down. Stopping the spiraling effect where one small problem causes out-of-control thoughts of permanent demise. Helping me let useless thoughts go and find the present moment without letting my past and future selves overwhelm the present.

There are more books out there on meditating than you could ever read in a lifetime. Because there are so many opinions about meditation, it can seem a little intimidating. The excitement over the practice can be overwhelming for the uninitiated. Most of the books have a cover design that makes the idea look foreign and unapproachable if you don't subscribe to the more woo-woo parts of personal development (there are a few really good exceptions that I'll share in the resources for further reading). Furthermore, there are many guided meditation apps to help you; I recommend Calm or 10% Happier (also a great book).

I can't recommend a meditation practice enough; if you've resisted, let me try to convince you to at least give it a try. The benefits of meditation will penetrate your entire life. The way you show up will be different. The way you interact will be different. The way you see yourself, the people in your life, and the world will be different. In your meditation practice, you'll begin to notice that the ideas you bring intentional thought and energy toward start to show up throughout your day. You'll start to catch yourself being more compassionate, more observant of what's happening in each moment, more curious, and less judgmental.

Let's break down what meditation is and what it's not. Meditation is lowering the volume in your head, silencing the ongoing voice in your head, and becoming still. It's not about creating a new experience or bringing something else into being. It's not transporting yourself to some mystic space. It's about being in observation mode and aware of what is here, right now.

Since I grew up in the Missionary Baptist Church tradition, my first thoughts about meditation were to liken it to prayer. Maybe it's the way I was taught to pray—a lot of talking, either to yourself or out loud. The men in the church used to pray aloud. Each man had a different style of prayer. In that way, I think meditation is similar; everyone seems to have their own style. There are some common traits across meditation practices, and there's a lot of variation. I've meditated with folks who do fast and intense breathing, some who chant, some who move, some who sit silently. But as I reconcile the difference between meditation and prayer, I think of it this way: if prayer is about talking to a higher power, meditation is about listening without hearing anything.

I'm not a monk; I've never even been to a monastery. I'm just a simple guy from Alma, Arkansas, who had to figure a lot of life out on my own, sharing with you what I've learned. When it comes to meditating, I'll outline what I do, and you're more than welcome to try it out. Ultimately, though, you should experiment and do what works for you. Your unique mediation style will bring you the most change. I'm a baby yogi. My practice is so extraordinarily simple. But it's where I started many years ago, in a form that I continue to practice at least once per day. I continue to evolve as I learn more. Even though it's simple, it is extraordinarily effective for me.

When I meditate, my goal is to slow my mind down, to find and be in the present moment. What does that mean? Slowing down my mind means that I no longer hear the critical voice always jabbering in my mind. It means to silence the self-talk going on. Being in the present moment means that when I'm meditating, I'm meditating. I'm not thinking about what's for breakfast, what I need to do today—none of that. If I'm meditating, that's where I stay.

Each morning, I wake up early enough to spend a few minutes meditating before I start the day. I begin by sitting comfortably with my back straight, legs crossed, and hands resting on my knees or in my lap. I close my eyes and begin to breathe deeply. I bring my awareness to my breath, in and out. Sometimes I can hold my awareness on just the breath for a full in-and-out sequence. Sometimes I can't. When I become aware of my mind drifting into thoughts about anything other than the in-and-out of my breath, I gently nudge the thought along. I don't beat myself up about it. I don't punish myself for it in any way. I simply let the thought go and return my awareness to my breath. I return my breathing to a normal pattern.

Close to the beginning of my meditation practices, after I've taken around ten full breaths, I will do a body scan in my mind. I check in with each part of my body, working from the top of my head down to the bottom of my feet, checking in with every limb and section of my body along the way. I bring awareness to any discomfort or tension, and then I release it. I don't make any judgments. I simply become aware of any sensations that I might feel in my body. I do my best to relax each part of myself as I think through this body scan. I drop my shoulders, then relax my tongue, my jaw, and my forehead. I honestly don't know how long my body scan lasts. I've never looked at the clock to see. But once I'm through it, I return to my breath, focusing on the inhale and exhale. I've been surprised over the years at the degree to which the mind responds to the body and vice versa.

The length of my session depends on how practiced I am in my meditation at the time. Don't try to start out being a hero; just sit quietly, in a dignified way, for about three minutes, simply reflecting on your breath. Three minutes may seem like an eternity, but keep at it; it will get easier. Once you begin to feel like three minutes is going by really fast, extend it to four minutes, and so on. It's not a contest—not even with yourself. It really is about the quality and not the quantity of the experience. The frequency with which you meditate will improve the quality.

After you've meditated, spend a few minutes with your calendar or journal and think about what you want to come from this day. We'll explore being intentional in the Productivity Mindset chapter of this book.

As I mentioned, I am a baby yogi. I'm no expert on meditation, but I am an advocate for the practice. In doing your own research, you may find that meditation is where some of the more woo-woo elements of mindfulness exist. If that isn't your scene (it isn't mine), don't let your resistance discount the entire practice.

Stay open to the possibilities, and learn what you can from the aspects that you find most helpful. You'll be glad you did!

You can find resources for more moderate meditative leanings in the online companion to this book at ChadPeevy.com/book.

YOU HAVE ALL YOU NEED

Methods in mindfulness aren't about a new experience or manifesting something else into being. It's about observing and being aware of what is here, right now. It's the awareness that you're still carrying around a younger version of yourself, and you're being drawn toward a future version of you. It's realizing that you are not small anymore; you are enough just as you are. It's about perspective, understanding that nothing happens for a reason. Rather, we give meaning to everything that has happened, and our actions today will have karmic consequences. It's about becoming grounded in gratitude and recognition for everything that has flowed into our lives to help us learn more about ourselves. It's also about putting these ideas into a practice of mindfulness where you can create an opportunity for reflection, evaluation, and, ultimately, grace.

Mindfulness isn't easy. It requires a level of self-awareness that many simply cannot tolerate. Some will prefer the fantasy of the life they've created in their head, rather than the reality that's staring them in the face. Resenting the past, worrying about the future, stressing, falling into depression, or succumbing to anxiety—those things are easy. They can even be addictive. Being mindful, bringing a level awareness to yourself, requires an extraordinary amount of effort. Breaking the cycle of self-sabotage is courageous. It's hard work, but it's worth it.

Mindfulness is about forgiveness, of yourself and others. I know that it can be overwhelming, even repulsive, to think about forgiving those who have wronged you. There's no excusing the cruelty that some people have inflicted, but there is forgiveness. You simply cannot bring your resentment and hatred for another person into your present moment and experience true joy, fulfillment, peace, or happiness. You can forgive without excusing. You can forgive without reconnecting or going back to the way things used to be. You can forgive without allowing that person to have a place in your life. You can even forgive when that person is no longer on this earth. Remember: forgiveness isn't for them; it's for you.

Mindfulness is about detaching from everything we've created to protect us so that the fullest version of our present selves can be revealed to us. Be mindful so that you may recover the forgotten parts of you and realize your potential.

PRODUCTIVITY
CHAPTER 8

Most men pursue pleasure with such
breathless haste that they hurry past it.

~ Søren Kierkegaard

If you took a minute to look up from the busyness of your day, what would you be left with minus the to-do list, calendar, or back-to-back meetings? In this chapter, we'll explore the mindset of productivity. Most specifically, we'll discover how you can start to think about productivity in a way that leads to having the time to experience your personal freedom.

The reason people stay so attached to the busyness of their lives is because without it, they're left with something they're really uncomfortable with: themselves. It's really no different than the awkwardness of sitting alone in a room with a stranger. If you fill your days and, effectively, your mind with mindless and unnecessary obligations, you leave no time or room for you to be with yourself. It's essentially the tactical mechanism by which you deny yourself the opportunity for experiencing your personal freedom. This type of avoidance of self in deference to "productivity" can be hard to see or accept because it seems so noble to be busy, sacrificing yourself, accommodating the needs of those who put demands on you—from work, friends, and family. Have you taken time to consider whether in this deference, you are giving up your precious and limited time in exchange for manifesting your own meaning and purpose? Or are the trappings of these exchanges robbing you of that opportunity?

I used to think that my blacked-out calendar was a badge of honor. Until I noticed that what was on my blacked-out calendar was only blacking me out. There was no room on there for me. I had completely filled my time to satisfy other people's agendas so that I could avoid myself. I'd found a way to numb what I was feeling, what I wanted, and who I was by allowing myself to become a cog in someone else's machine. I had surrendered to this societal pressure to always be "productive" without ever having defined for myself what it meant to be productive. I knew I had to find a way to give myself the room and the time to experience more of my life—for me. This meant I had to find a way to think about being productive that was about more than filling my calendar from dawn to dusk.

A perversion of productivity can lead to a rigidity that numbs your life experience. You may have found in your life that certain identity-reinforcing activities can serve as a medium to escape. For most of us, these activities take the form of our work. You may even justify it by convincing yourself that it's better to be a workaholic than an alcoholic, drug addict, or shopaholic. But I can also imagine that you're already hearing that whispering question that drew you to this book in the first place: *Is this all there is?* If you're hearing that whisper, you're really fortunate. You're being pulled onto a path that can lead you to feel more, love more, and experience life more deeply. Listen to that whispering question and continue the process of answering it before that whisper turns into an unbearable scream.

Productivity has gained a lot of attention in popular culture. While it's critically important as the driving force of the economy, in my view, the discussion around productivity skews dramatically toward work output in a way that has become hazardous to our well-being.

When Henry Ford introduced the forty-hour workweek in his factories, he was replacing the existing forty-eight-hour work-week. If the purpose was to increase productivity, why decrease the work hours? Because Ford understood that more hours of production were actually hurting individual productivity. The long hours didn't allow for workers to have balance; their day was structured in a way that denied them that opportunity (this also denied them the opportunity to buy his cars). To increase the output, Ford wise-ly decreased the time on task, opting for a day that accounted for eight hours of work, eight hours of rest, and eight hours of leisure. When his competitors saw his explosive revenue, they began to follow his lead and, through pressure from labor unions and ad-vocates, this eventually resulted in the Fair Labor Standards Act signed by FDR in 1938.

I'm not saying that there's a perfect work-life balance that can neatly fit into three square time blocks a day—especially these days, when many of us are working from home and redefining what it means to be "at work." Even if there were once some spa-tial boundaries that kept work at the office and personal time at home, these boundaries are disappearing, which is why this topic is more important than ever. The idea of showing up for work eight hours a day is becoming more and more distant for many of us. Our work is less physical and more intellectually taxing, and those kinds of demands alone require another way to think about our productivity.

What I'm advocating for is bringing awareness and consideration to how you are spending your time. I'm advocating for productivity toward your purpose, not time on the task that neglects time on purpose. I'm suggesting that you bring awareness to what you're being productive toward, for whom, and to what end. I'm asking you to examine how you look at productivity, not by measuring activities and checklists, but as a mindfulness exercise that empowers you. Throughout this book, I've asked you to make more room in your life for you to be you. Now I'm asking you to make sure that there is time.

REDEFINE PRODUCTIVITY

I can hear it now: *If I take away time from my work, I'll lose my competitive edge. I'm a workhorse, that's how I get ahead!* Or, *If I'm not being productive with work, I won't be able to have as much or save as much money to do the things that give me freedom.*

Relying on your drive to satisfy basic needs has provided for you, kept you safe, and allowed you to create everything you see around you right now. There's real fear when, even briefly, you entertain the idea of taking your nose off the grindstone. For many of us, though, these are unrealistic fears that we've allowed to go unchecked. The fear you have of losing your edge or not having enough is rooted in the psychology of your most basic needs. Simply asking, "Is this it? Is this all there is?" is an indicator that you are beyond basic. If your basic needs weren't met, your instincts to meet those needs and survive would override those more complex and developed psychological needs.

Maslow's hierarchy of needs states that once your base physiological and safety needs are satisfied, you, as a human being, then need to satisfy your needs for love, self-esteem, and (eventually) self-actualization. In some ways, an addiction to traditional ideas of productivity limits your ability to satisfy these higher needs. By constantly overfilling or oversatisfying the base needs, you leave no time for the higher needs to be satisfied. Until you redefine how you look at productivity, you'll stay caught in this loop of satisfying your base needs. The draw to satisfy those needs is intense, even primal, but you deserve to ask yourself if it's time for more and bring awareness to the state of those base needs. If you deny yourself the opportunity to explore and express your full self, you deny yourself the full picture of who you are—and, ultimately, your answer to that existential question. Yes, there's more love, connection, freedom, experience, and creativity for you to express if you want to. So now it's time to redefine what productivity means to you in order to reach it.

Instead of being afraid of losing your competitive edge or not being able to make ends meet, be afraid of denying yourself the potential to become a fully expressed and fully realized version of who you are. Of leaving parts of yourself undiscovered. Of never allowing anyone to be close to you. Be afraid of not feeling life experiences more deeply. You can't possibly know what else there is out there for you if you don't look up from your spreadsheets to see. Now is the time for you to discover who you are beyond basic survival. What is important to you at this moment of your life? How will you live fully with the time you have left? What do you really want from this short experience?

Give yourself permission to explore whether you have reached a season in your life when it's time for a more compassionate definition of productivity—one that is inclusive of all of you, not just your professional output. It's time to adopt a new mindset that simply says: "I will bring to each moment of every day only that which is necessary for my personal freedom."

During the day, I will often turn that definition into what I call The Productivity Question and ask myself: "Am I bringing to this moment that which is necessary?" This perspective toward productivity is compassionate and realistic. I may, in fact, be taking some time to sit in bed and watch Netflix, but that activity may be necessary for me to rest my mind, to zone out for a bit, to let my mind and body relax for a while. And that activity *is* necessary for that moment. I may be sitting with friends or business associates in a social setting and catch myself getting frustrated and anxious because I could be "working" and being so much more "productive." It's in those moments that I ask The Productivity Question and get the perspective that, by building relationships, I am in fact doing what's necessary. That brief check-in brings me back to the present moment and reduces my anxiety and guilt. But it may also mean that I find myself watching TV, asking that question, and having to answer no . . . I am not brining that which is necessary to this moment.

This adjusted mindset allows for a compassionate approach to productivity that reminds me that I am a whole person who is capable and has permission to satisfy base needs and those needs of deeper meaning. I need to spend time talking to my husband, petting my dog, going for a walk, and also being really focused and intentional with my work. All of these things are important in order for me to satisfy my wider range of psychological needs. This means that, if I am working, then I am working. If I am resting, I am resting. If I am with loved ones, then I am with loved ones. It's about awareness; it's not an automatic response to a clock that says I must work from nine am to five p.m., nor is it an automatic response to satisfying a basic need that is already met.

If you start by thinking of your own productivity through the lens of The Productivity Question, the rest is just figuring out the techniques and exercising discipline.

LIFE AS SEASONS

Summer, fall, winter, and spring all bring with them their own purpose. Each comes and goes, bringing about the next. So, too, do the seasons of our lives. In this moment, what is necessary for you?

Many conversations about productivity center around the idea of output within the constraints of the near-term calendar. But let's expand our thinking to consider beyond the day, week, month, quarter, and year and begin to consider productivity within the context of your life's seasons. An expanded view of time helps bring clarity to that which is necessary in each moment.

When you were growing up, life seasons were prescribed for you: toddler years, elementary school years, teenage years, and so forth. The same is true for adults, but in much broader terms: entry level, young parents, middle age, retirees. Our job as thinking adults is to self-prescribe and bring awareness to the season we're in at any given moment. Maybe you're in a season to raise your kids, to build wealth, to explore who you are, to transition to something new, or to give.

Any self-prescribed definition of productivity that is detached from our purpose is just busy work. So much of what we do every day is just avoidance and distraction disguised as productivity in order to pass the time. So, how do we create meaningful forward motion, output, and contribution in a way that aligns with our purpose and highest self? When you understand what season of your life you're in, it becomes easier to understand that which is necessary. Once you understand what's necessary, you can more easily consider what to bring to this moment.

Some seasons of our lives last many years, and some last just a short time; it depends on what purpose that season is satisfying in your life. You may be in a twenty-year season of raising great kids. You may also be in a three-year season to make a career transition.

Once you know the season, live it out fully. No matter how long or short the season, we can find happiness, fulfillment, and the meaning we crave when we apply our maximum effort toward everything that matters to us in this season.

It would be unproductive to spend time in regret about a season that has passed or in anxiety about a season yet to come. When you have clarity around your season, it's time to be in action toward the purpose of that season. So, be in action! Stop negotiating with yourself about what could or should be. Act toward satisfying this season, and don't waste time.

When thinking about productivity through the lens of seasons, you may resist what you perceive as "slowing down." Remember that there's something to be learned during each season of your life. Don't regret taking in and fully experiencing each season—live them fully. Shortchanging a season leaves the cycle incomplete and leaves you ill-prepared to enter the next. Incomplete seasons are fertile ground for regret, guilt, and ignorance from lessons unlearned. When the lessons we are meant to learn about ourselves in one season are left incomplete, these same lessons will find a way to show up for us in the next. We can experience deeper meaning in the next season of our life when we have a deeper understanding of the one we are in.

When it comes to speeding through the hour, day, week, month, or season, keep in mind the consequences. Daniel Kahneman wrote about these consequences in his book *Thinking, Fast and Slow*.[1] He explains the consequences of speed in terms of the quality of our decision-making. Speed forces automatic thinking. When we go too fast, we don't spend the time necessary to weigh options, think creatively about a problem, or consider novel alternatives. Instead, we default to what we know and go in the direction of familiarity, potentially allowing yet another cycle of that which should be broken to continue. The entire idea to break and untangle is to stop the automatic thinking that is holding us back.

Clearly, there are times when quick decision-making is necessary. I'm thinking of the soldier, the pilot, the police officer. We want people in these roles to have extensive training so that when they need to make quick decisions, they are defaulting to quality training that leads to the best outcomes. Speed is good for when the decision is clearly thought out and in alignment with the overall strategy, especially when the outcome is reversible. Decisions that lead to irreversible outcomes are best deliberated and made thoughtfully. Most of us are not in positions that require flash decision-making, whether personally or professionally. We have the liberty to take a minute to consider our decisions, but too often we move too quickly and rely too heavily on our emotions instead of our logic.

Our entire lives are the consequence of our decisions; so give yourself time to create the best possible life by making the best possible decisions. This is critical to mindful productivity. Show yourself the grace and have the courage to take a breath, to think, to insist on the time and space you need for each season of your life.

MINDFUL PRODUCTIVITY

Through our productivity, we achieve future goals, but productivity isn't in the future; it's in the present. And yet, often we are so distracted by the future goal that we aren't present enough to be attuned to the productivity required to get there.

Setting goals sets the direction for your life's journey. Mindful productivity requires that we set goals that give us an opportunity to reveal more of ourselves and live our personal freedom. The productivity necessary to realize a goal does not exist in the future; it exists in the present moment. Once that goal and direction is set, we must detach from the goal itself in deference to the direction of its realization. Rather than fixating on the destination, bring mindfulness to the journey itself and the steps you need to take today to move your life in the direction you've chosen.

Mindful productivity gives us an opportunity to practice visualizing the future you wish to create without obsessing over an uncertain future. Attachment to the outcome of a goal brings the future self into the present and, with it, anxiety and uncertainty. But those feelings aren't helpful and only limit your ability to focus on what is necessary in the here and now. Mindful productivity leaves room for a mindset of receiving all the purpose, satisfaction, and meaning possible on the journey itself.

Attachment to the goals ignores that the journey, and what is required to achieve that goal, is what allows us to realize our purpose and derive meaning in life. It's a mindset of taking. This attachment to an outcome limits the reward of the journey ahead of you. It's productivity blind to a meaningful life experience. It's a form of productivity that has allowed you to become a cog in the machine of your own making.

Your goals set the direction for your life, but no outcome is guaranteed. You can't control the outcome, but what you can control are the emotions, strategy, work ethic, grace, and generosity you bring to the present moment in pursuit of your goals. That's the magic of mindful productivity—the realization that the process, the journey, is what you truly seek. It isn't really the destination at all. It's not an outward quest; it's an inward adventure. It isn't the one-million-dollar goal for the year. It's who you reveal yourself to be on the journey toward that goal. The bigger the goal, the more challenging the path, and the deeper you will be required to go to reveal who you are. Small goals, small breakthroughs. Big goals, big breakthroughs. Honor that journey and recognize that, no matter the season, you are doing the work of expressing more of who you are. That's the reward, the meaning, the fulfillment you truly seek.

KNOW WHAT'S IMPORTANT

To be mindfully productive, you only have to be productive toward the things that actually matter—those things necessary for the current season of your life. We've allowed the idea of productivity to morph into a notion that we are what we do. And by that logic, if we aren't doing it, then we are nothing. But that just isn't true. What if we expanded our view of productivity to include more aspects of our lives. What if we took a more holistic approach to being productive and adopted the definition of productivity that I've offered you?

By that standard, do you have a productive marriage? Are you a productive parent? Are you a productive friend? Are you a productive citizen?

EXERCISE

Let's get clarity around what mindfully productive would look like for you. Here are some prompts to help you begin the process of changing your mindset:

1. If I were to describe this season of my life, I would describe it as . . .

2. What are the top three priorities for this season of my life?

3. What is necessary for this season of my life?

4. Does my calendar currently reflect the most important things to me during this season of my life?

5. How will I know when this season has passed?

SETTING YOUR INTENTION

If the idea of bringing that which is necessary into this moment seems familiar, perhaps it's because that is the essence of prayer. Prayer is a practical exercise by which we bring awareness to that which we see as necessary. While rooted in the realm of religion, there's power in the simple practicality that such an exercise can offer us—even without the connotations and associations of religion or even the idea of intercession by any higher power outside of ourselves.

I've come to see prayer as a calling to my present self to come into alignment with the highest ideals of who I am in order to face the circumstances confronting me. Put simply: remembering who I am. You can use the act of prayer to invite that sense of your own sufficiency into the present, a means to remind yourself that you are good enough, smart enough, successful enough, lovable enough, and worthy enough to meet any of life's challenges just as you are.

People have a tendency to run to prayer when things aren't going their way. A "Hail Mary" cry for help when they've exhausted all the options available to their conscious mind. A form of surrendering to something outside themselves. While some may see a prayer as a last-ditch effort, I think it should be your first. While some would consider prayer an act of desperation, I prefer to see it as a means of calling on the most powerful force within you to meet the circumstances you face. A reminder that our most powerful resource is within us. It's not an external force on which we are dependent for intercession. We can use prayer as a way to remind our present self of who we are and the intentions we have for our lives.

We can use prayer as a tool to live our lives offensively, rather than reacting defensively. We can turn The Productivity Question into a productive intention:

I will <u>bring</u> to each moment of every day,
that which is necessary for my personal freedom.

Bring is an action verb; it requires some sort of effort on my part. That effort may be time on task, doing physical labor, making the call, or writing the email. But above all else, you must first bring awareness to your intent. It is the intention that directs the effort.

When you woke up this morning, did you set an intention for

the way this day was going to go? What you were going to accomplish? How you were going to feel? How you were going to treat people? How you expected to be treated? Or did you go through your day in reaction to everyone and everything else? Intentions are a way to take our life off of autopilot and bring awareness to the things that we seek. We can use the idea of prayer to organize those intentions in a way that serves us.

Prayer is a simple and powerful tool. And, yes, I believe it's available to people of any faith or of no faith. Don't let the spiritual terrorist rob you of prayerful communion with yourself. A practice in prayer is simply a moment of reflection and intention. If it's easier for you to give this practice another name because of the stigma it may carry with you, that's fine too. I grew up with prayer, so the idea of carrying on that routine worked for me as long as how I thought about prayer reflected my values.

Before I sat down to write this book each day, I said a simple prayer that it might be used as an instrument to bring you love, healing, abundance, and joy. I declared my intention to be a voice that would bring you words to unlock something inside of you—your potential. To help you know yourself beyond your hesitation and resistance. To be a pathway for you to discover more joy, love, and understanding of yourself and others. I prayed that I would sit and give words to your experience so that you could see yourself more clearly.

What are you intentional about each day? What do you get up and pray about? What do you pray your day will look like? What do you pray that you will use this life for?

Be intentional about what you will do with your life each day you are blessed with it. No one wants to spend their day working on something that will have no lasting meaning, relevance, or significance. And yet, day in and day out, we sit at jobs that we hate doing and engage in work that is meaningless. We are all guilty of this. When we leave the day to chance, it's only by luck that our effort will carry much meaning or purpose. Prayer brings our intention to the present. What do you really want? What is really important? What is your intention for this day, this week, this month, this year, this season? Pray on these things. Being intentional and praying about your life is not a wish list; it's an active assessment of everything that's meaningful. Active awareness brings the life you want into being.

EXERCISE

Now, I'd like you to find yourself in a quiet place, free from distraction, and consider the following questions:

1.   What is your daily prayer?

2.   What will you say to invite your intentions for your life into the present?

CHAD'S DAILY PRAYER

Each day, immediately following my meditation, I say this prayer. I say it five times, bringing each of these to mind:

- *myself,*
- *someone I love,*
- *someone I only know in passing,*
- *someone who I'm struggling to love,*
- *and love for all of mankind.*

May your life be filled with joy, peace, and happiness
Good health and well-being
A life of ease and prosperity
The courage to get what you want from this life
The clarity to know what it is
The imagination to not sell yourself short
And the discipline to see it through

ROUTINE

I love to watch a great dancer—someone who can settle into the groove of the music and show you the sounds by the way they move their body. It's beautiful to see how dancers effortlessly control the flow of vibrations through their body.

Routine gives your life a rhythm. It gives your day form and shape. A routine lets you pick the music to which you dance through your day and, in fact, your life. But too many of us are dancing to someone else's tune. It's awkward, hard to watch, and wears us out instead of lifting our spirits.

Having a routine is about knowing what works for you—what makes you feel the day—and then having the discipline to act on it. Routine helps you find your way back when you've drifted off course. Routine allows you to focus on that which is necessary. It shines a light on the things that affect you and allows you to emphasize those things, adjust them, or eliminate them completely, if needed.

Routine is the key to consistency. It eliminates decision fatigue. Once something is part of what you've already decided is your routine, there's no longer a reason to debate with yourself whether it's going to happen. You'll act on it simply because that's just what you do. I shave Monday through Thursday. I hate to shave. But because I decided to make it part of my routine, there's no question about it. When I shower, if it's one of those days, I shave. I spend no time thinking or arguing with myself about it.

Routine has power because it brings with it a cascading effect in your life. If your workday starts at eight a.m., there's a cascade of events that has to happen before then. You might need to meditate, shower, eat breakfast, work out, or walk the dog. This cascade of events becomes your morning routine. It's the intentional sequence of automatic responses.

With your morning routine, you're exercising a practice in personal discipline and collecting good habits. Over time, these good habits add up to benefits to your physical[2] and mental well-being. Routine is a tool to keep you accountable to yourself; it holds you to a minimum self-standard. The reason it's critically important for me to shave on the days I've decided to shave is because I know that once I give up on the little things, how much easier it becomes to give up on the big things. Like everyone, I have occasional bad days. But even on the bad days, I can at least say that I moved through a series of good habits, because that's just what I do. The fewer arguments and negotiations you have with yourself, the better your mental well-being and the more mental resources you have at your disposal throughout the day.

That kind of minimum standard routine establishes control over the day. It introduces certainty into your life before other people get the chance to pull you into their agendas and before other unforeseen variables pop up.

A well-established routine summons your highest self consistently throughout your day, and not just in the morning. If you've made it this far in life, you know that there are things that work for you and things that throw you off course. Pay attention to those things, and become intentional about them. If you know you suffer from an afternoon crash every day, preempt that crash by doing what you need to do thirty minutes to an hour before you know it's going to happen. If you know that you get a better night's sleep when you journal or turn off the screens at least an hour before you sleep, make that part of your routine—not something that you just do when you feel like you need it, but every day. Don't leave your well-being up to chance. Make it part of your routine whether it happens in the morning, midday, or night.

Go to ChadPeevy.com/book and download an outline of my daily routine.

EXERCISE

Let's craft your routine. Take your journal and consider each of these questions:

1. What would you like to do before your workday begins? Meditate? Exercise? Eat breakfast? Walk the dog? Read?

2. How much time will you spend on each of these activities?

3. What time would you like for your workday to begin?

4. Based on your answers to the first three questions, what time will you need to wake up each day?

5. What are the things that you would like to be part of your life every day? What are the things that always happen because their happening is just part of who you are? Continue to journal and write down what you would like those things to be. Use these prompts to help guide your thinking:

   ▶ What do you do every weekday?
   ▶ What do you do every Saturday?
   ▶ Who do you do every Sunday?

6. What do you believe the benefits of this routine will be?

7. After one year of this routine, what will your life look and feel like?

THIS IS AND IS NOT ALL THERE IS

The answer to that existential question, *Is this all there is?* contains both a yes and a no. Your life, your human existence, is and will be what you make of it. You get to decide. If you can't muster up the conviction for what you're being productive toward, you will have a hard time finding the meaning, purpose, and personal freedom you're craving. You have to make the experience of living in your personal freedom more enticing to you than watching Netflix all day, hiding behind your work, or making yourself so busy that you are a stranger to the people in your life and to yourself. If you have the capacity to ask if there's more in this life for you, you have the capacity to get more if you are intentional about making time for it.

Explore a mindset of productivity that empowers you to move intentionally toward something in your life that is worthwhile to you—something you believe will make a difference, that will satisfy your craving for more. Bring awareness and recognition to who you are and the season you are living in, then give yourself permission to be productive toward everything that makes this life precious.

SOCIAL

*how I connect and
relate to other people*

BELONGING

HELP

AMBITION

LEGACY

BELONGING
CHAPTER 9

*This is your life's journey, but that doesn't
mean it has to be traveled alone.*

~ *Chad Peevy*

So much of my existence in Arkansas was defined by my struggle to fit in. Whether it was at school or at home, I wanted to belong, and I was willing to try just about anything to feel that sense of belonging. I tried to be straight; to be athletic; to fit in at church; to be a son my dad could be proud of, despite our differences and his abuse; to be the friend my mother wanted me to be, despite my need for her to protect me. In an attempt to belong, I was willing to sacrifice my needs in deference to the needs of those around me.

During my second year of graduate school, I went back to Arkansas for Christmas. This was before my parents had divorced, and when I got home, they apologized for the way they treated me as a kid. This had become a recurring conversation among us.

I'm not sure if it was guilt that drove these conversations or simply that I had become more vocal about my feelings. This particular conversation was a teary one; there were tears of shame, guilt, anger, and sadness.

The only thing I can remember saying through all the tears was that I needed time and space to process. I didn't have the skills that would have allowed me to hold onto myself during these conversations. All I knew was that I needed to remove myself from the painful reminders of that upbringing. Saying they were sorry wasn't enough for me at that time in my life. I wish their apologies could have been enough. I wish I could have accepted their apologies and moved on. But what I had endured wasn't easy to forgive—and I didn't have the capacity to forgive them. As we'll explore later in this chapter, forgiveness only exists when there's a demand for love. At that time in my life, having only recently come out as gay to them, I was in desperate need of their love—unconditional love. But my dad had made it clear to me that that kind of love and acceptance would not be happening. Withholding his love made my forgiveness impossible. I wanted him to love me, but if he couldn't love me, I couldn't forgive him.

The only refuge I could find was to remove myself from that environment and liberate myself from those relationships. I would liken it to ripping myself up from my roots so that I could replant myself in healthier soil. The pain of having love withheld was so great that I was willing to exile myself from the tribe. I'd worked really hard throughout my life to make myself into someone I thought they would find acceptable. These contortions of self had become too much for me. Everything I needed to do to belong, and the painful reminders of that environment, was no longer worth being a part of that tribe.

CONNECTION IN RELATIONSHIP

Looking back on it now, I realize how brave it was for me to stand up for myself and express what I needed, even if all I knew was that I needed time and space. Recognizing what I wanted is significant in itself. Saying those words out loud to someone, to the person who had tormented me all of my life, was monumental.

What became clear to me after I made the decision to break from my parents was just how conditional love had been for me all of my life. I had to be a certain person, believe a certain way, worship in a particular style, and satisfy the expectations of others over what I wanted for my own life. When I moved away for college, and then went on to graduate school, I got my first big dose of perspective that there are people out there who would accept me for me. Who would let me be my authentic self—even expect that I be my authentic self. This expanded perspective made it clear to me that I needed and wanted people in my life—they just needed to be the right people. People who saw me for who I am, not who they wanted me to be for them. This perspective proved most consequential and important when I met Pasha.

Growing up, I never learned how to hold onto myself when in conversation or disagreement. When my mom and dad got in a fight, my mom would pack us kids up and we would leave—that's the modeling I got for handling disagreements with a partner. My own way of surviving confrontation as a kid was to avoid and hide from it. I had learned that the smaller I could make myself, the safer I was. Pasha was having none of it.

Pasha didn't let me default to my old ways of doing things. Nor did he let me get away with the things I had always gotten away with in other relationships. In the past, if I got into a fight, I wouldn't confront my partner or have a conversation about it, I would just leave—literally, I would leave the relationship all together. It was a behavioral response that was only reinforcing the bad training and modeling that I got as a kid.

Pasha showed me something new—something I had never experienced before. He gave me the space and the safety to express myself, even if expressing myself meant expressing my dissatisfaction with him. I tried to break up with Pasha at least three times. I can't even remember why—that's how insignificant the incidents were. But each time he would insist that we talk out the issue. He was quick to apologize if he was wrong, and he was just as quick to tell me if he believed I owed him an apology. Each time, he made it clear to me that if you care about someone, you don't just leave. You work it out. He made it clear that it was okay for me to stand up for myself. It was okay for me to demand how I wanted to be treated. And it was okay to say if I had a problem with how I was being treated. These were all foreign ideas to me, and it took an outside force for me to become aware of them. Ultimately, learning to stay and work it out caused me to mature in my marriage, and in other relationships too.

I've also had to learn that Pasha can't be everything to me. It isn't fair of me to ask him to be everything to me, and vice-versa. You can't get everything you need from one person. Pasha offers me a safe space—a place where I can share my feelings, my dreams, my fears, and my love. He gets the most intimate place in my life. But there's so more to each of our lives than what one person can fulfill. There's the social, spiritual, intellectual, and business sides of my life. Pasha can partially fill these other parts, but not all of them. Likewise, there are parts of his life that I fill, and some that I can't. Because of that, we have to find our communities outside of our romantic relationships.

Pasha has taught me a lot about connection, specifically how fulfilling it can be to have an emotional connection with someone. As instructional as my relationship with Pasha has been for me, it made clear that there was more work for me to do if I wanted more meaningful connections in my life. My sense of otherness, coupled with the belief that I had to conform in order to be accepted, had a stickiness to it that followed me into adulthood. If I wanted to experience connection and belonging, I was going to have to work at it. I had to work at understanding this status of "other."

Being "other" is a lonely feeling. It's feeling separate from and different than all the rest. And while it may seem as though what makes us different is something to overcome, our otherness is actually our gift. Our life's work is to know ourselves, not the person someone else wants us to be. Otherness helps us identify other people like us in the world—our tribe, where we will find the love and belonging we deserve. Everything that makes us "other" points the way to our tribe. A thriving life is not one lived in isolation, separate from, or other than. Joy, peace, purpose, and meaning are more accessible to us when we are surrounded by people who inspire, motivate, support, identify with, and love us as we are. Life is simply freer when our lives are spent surrounded by people who see us for who we are, and in whom we see ourselves.

LONELINESS

Every man that knocks on the door of a brothel is looking for God.

~Unknown

We live in a world where the potential for connection is greater than at any time in history, so the current epidemic of loneliness and the consequences that loneliness presents seem inconceivable. Technology has made the physical world smaller and the digital one extraordinarily accessible, and yet we live in a time known as the "The Age of Loneliness."[1] Why are so many of us experiencing loneliness? And what can we do to minimize these feelings?

The research on human connection is very clear: We are social beings, and a sense of belonging is critical to our well-being and survival. Loneliness appears in the absence of a bond or connection with other people, and the negative effects are considerable. Being part of a group of people and experiencing a strong bond with others isn't just a nice feeling to have. Belonging isn't a want; it's a need. When that need goes unmet, there are consequences, such as depression, anxiety, and overall poor health.[2] Research has shown that a lack of social connection is as damaging to our health as smoking fifteen cigarettes a day.[3] Social psychologist Timothy Wilson from the University of Virginia conducted a series of studies that showed people would rather give themselves electric shocks than be alone for as little as fifteen minutes.[4] Loneliness has been linked to higher recreational drug use,[5] eating disorders,[6] obesity.[7] It also diminishes our cognitive abilities and immune systems,[8] and can even bring on an early death.[9] Unsurprisingly, research suggests that people who are lonely experience a less satisfied life.[10]

A lot of what holds us back from the life we want is an undiagnosed state of loneliness. The emotions we experience as a result of loneliness can be evasive, because we don't have a good enough understanding of what loneliness is. Loneliness is similar to anxiety in that it serves as a warning that our needs aren't being met—in this case, our social needs.[11] When the feelings of loneliness arise, we can become aware of them and take action to alleviate them. In the research, loneliness is defined as the aversive state experienced when a discrepancy exists between the interpersonal relationships one wishes to have and those that one perceives that they currently have.[12] Others have more simply described loneliness as the feeling we get when our need to belong isn't sufficiently met.[13]

Loneliness research offers us six needs to be satisfied in our social relationships to mitigate the feelings of loneliness:

- ▸ *Attachment:* satisfies needs of security and commitment.
- ▸ *Social integration:* satisfies our needs for companionship, shared concerns, and activities.
- ▸ *Opportunity for nurturance:* satisfies our need to be needed and to experience a sense of responsibility for others.
- ▸ *Reassurance of worth:* satisfies our need to be seen as competent and valued.
- ▸ *Reliable alliance:* satisfies our need for those relationships that create a sense of continuing assistance.
- ▸ *Guidance:* satisfies our need for relationships that offer us trustworthy advice.[14]

These dimensions of loneliness suggest that we can experience both loneliness and belonging in a variety of ways, and the research backs this up. In fact, people who describe themselves as lonely, as well as those who don't, spend similar amounts of time with other people.[15] I don't know about you, but I can certainly relate to the idea of being lonely in a room full of people. Our social needs aren't created or satisfied equally. And so, to feel less lonely, all of our social needs have to be met. We can't substitute one for another.[16]

In fact, research on loneliness[17] has simplified these dimensions by making a distinction between social[18] and emotional loneliness.[19] Even if we have a romantic partner who satisfies our emotional needs, we still have social needs that need to be met. Plus, it's unfair to expect one person to meet all of our needs. That kind of strain is not a recipe for a healthy, long-term partnership. The six needs of social relationships offer an organizing structure that is helpful to us because it creates a means by which we can identify the type of loneliness we're experiencing and take action toward alleviating the resulting feelings.

To overcome the feelings of loneliness and isolation, first you have to bring awareness to the fact that those feelings exist. Is our boredom, aimlessness, anxiety, depression, or emptiness the result of our loneliness? When we say we're bored, are we actually lonely? As with all of the untangling processes, we have to become willing and skilled at observing our feelings and behavior. Then we must be honest with ourselves about what we discover. We crave a deeper level of connection with others, but we often just don't know how to go about getting it. I don't think we consider all the dimensions of social relationships that are necessary to satisfy that craving. Therefore, our loneliness becomes disguised to us as something else: productivity, boredom, success, tiredness, aloofness, hunger. When you finally crave the connection of others but don't have the tools to get it, you'll fill the void with something else: food, alcohol, drugs, gambling, money, work, or anything else that creates a sense of safe connection or numbs you to the feelings of loneliness. Put practically, you may eat when you think you're bored, not because you're hungry but because you're blindly trying to fill the void of loneliness. Sometimes our bad habits are just our way of filling the void of connection.

I filled that void by working all the time. Through my un-tangling work, I realized that so much of what I was working on was so insignificant; it was busy work that I was using to keep my mind occupied and shielded from feelings of loneliness. I want to challenge you to explore what you may be using as a crutch to avoid a connection with others. If you're anything like me, then it's prob-ably a familiar go-to excuse for why you can't connect with others when you have the opportunity. ("I have to work." "I need to go to the gym." "I need/have to . . .") Once you've identified that crutch for what it is, question its usefulness to you. Is it really necessary? Or do you use it to avoid getting close to other people? Is it a way of keeping yourself isolated? Are you trying to protect yourself from other people, only to hurt yourself in other ways? Knowing how you're filling the void of connection is one important way you can get to know yourself. Armed with that information, you're better equipped to catch some of the default programming that is keeping you disconnected.

Through connection we can more clearly recognize our own meaning, feel joy, and experience greater life satisfaction. Loneliness is a barrier to that satisfaction. Understanding what loneliness is and how it shows up in our lives can help us overcome it. When coping with loneliness, we have to acknowledge the role we play in keeping ourselves lonely.

It's true that when we don't feel connection and belonging, we'll go anywhere to find it. To me, the search for God (as stated in the quote at the beginning of this section) isn't saying that the door will open to God himself, but rather that connection is a desire to transcend the pain of loneliness. We all need and are searching for connection—and we will go anywhere to get it.

Understanding your life's journey and discovering your meaning and purpose is an endeavor in understanding the self. Individuation specifically implies singularity, but realizing your individuation doesn't mean that you have to go through life alone. Self-actualization begins with self-transcendence. When you come to know yourself, you have the ability to see yourself in others and connect with them in a deeper, more meaningful way. This deeper connection is fulfilling; it allows you to understand yourself better and be in service of others. A journey that includes other people puts your journey in greater context.

HOW OUR PARENTS SHOW UP IN OUR WORLD

Much of how we connect with others is a reflection of how we attached to our parents.[20] The nature of that attachment, its strength, and its reliability all play a role in how we create connections with others as we grow up. The model of connection created for us as children allows us to adequately predict the nature of our connections as adults. We predict if relationships will be safe, strong, and reliable based on those past experiences. If left unexamined, these models dictate the limitations of our ability to connect with others and experience a sense of belonging. The good news is that, no matter what may have been, we have the ability to learn, adapt, and find new models that will better serve us.

Life sure would be easier if we could see the source of our scars confined to a singular source without the possibility of contaminating other parts of our lives and other relationships. If you remove the tumor, you remove the disease. That's not the case when it comes to the complexities of connection. We carry the impact of these relationships with us: good and bad. This isn't a matter of physical presence but rather the enduring influence of who those people were to you and how their impact follows you throughout your life. This can be a hard circle to square because, like us, our parents also evolve as human beings. Who they are today likely does not reflect who they were to us when we were growing up. But it's that version that we experienced as a child that haunts us and informs the nature of the connections we create as adults.

The parents who raised you will continue to show up as ghosts in your life. Even if you develop a healthier relationship with them as adults, who they were to you as a child will haunt you because of the imprint they made on you as a child. Because those parental figures were important during your most formative years, you will subconsciously seek out people to be in your life who can play the role your parents once played for you as a child. This is what it means to experience transference of mother and father throughout your life.

You'll hear people talk about women marrying their father,

or men marrying their mother. It's as if they unconsciously are attracted to the parental figure and seek their replacement in adulthood. This is common. What is also common, but less talked about, is that we do this in all parts of our lives. This can happen not just with romantic partners, but also with business partners, bosses, friends, and even institutions or companies. As adults, we project the familiarity of the relationships we had with our parents onto the figures in our lives as adults.

How we echo, rebel, or respond to the parent will often be reflected in how we echo, rebel, or respond to the shadows that we've created of them in adulthood. For example, when my husband complains about me not picking up my clothes in the bathroom, I don't hear him asking his partner to contribute to the cleanliness of our home. I hear my mom nagging me. Then, from a place of rebellion, my instinctual reaction to him isn't one based in love, partnership, and common goals—it's a rolling of eyes or picking a fight.

I've even found that my parents have shown up for me in my business. I've found myself allowing clients who remind me of my mom to lure me into offering free services or "helping them" with their business, because I interpret their need as an expectation for me to save them—like I believed my mom needed me to save her from my dad. My dad has also appeared in my business when someone is aggressive with me. When that happens, I notice that my reaction to them is similar to my reaction to my dad as a child. I retreat, become as quiet and small as possible, and am careful to not disrupt or disturb the order of things.

Ask yourself how your parents are showing up for you in the world. How has your experience with them made an impression on your worldview? Where do they appear in your life? Can you recognize them in your environment and your relationships? Can you recognize the shadow of your parents for what it is—a shadow—before you react to the reminders reflected from your spouse, friend, or coworker?

There are opportunities for growth in bringing awareness to the ways in which you make yourself small in deference to the shadow of your parents. Becoming small could mean literally making yourself small, unseen, or unheard. But it could also mean becoming less than your best self; it may show up as acting in a way that doesn't reflect who you really are.

Growth also exists in the awareness that we are shutting people out because we fail to see them for who they are, insisting instead on seeing them through the lens of our propensity for transference. When a person shows a characteristic familiar to your parent, they become that parent in our mind as we regress to our younger self. But your reaction to them is just a trick your mind is playing on you. Your parents are your parents, and everyone else deserves a chance to be themselves.

There's also an opportunity for growth, not just through awareness and understanding, but also through forgiveness. Forgiveness has been a significant part of my process, and I suspect it will need to be for you as well.

FORGIVENESS

I can remember, as an angry young man, how much rage I felt when people would tell me to forgive my parents, knowing full well the circumstances that I grew up in. They would make excuses for them, give them credit for their recent progress, and remind me that I turned out okay despite their failings. But the very suggestion of forgiveness made my blood boil. If you experience those same feelings, I understand. I had to come to grips with the idea of forgiveness in my own way. I'd been physically and emotionally abused for my entire life, so I rejected anyone who told me to for-give and forget. So I'm not going to do that to you. I'm not going to tell you to forgive anyone who has done you wrong—that's your business. But if you'll hang with me through this section, I do want to offer some ideas around forgiveness that have helped me and, as a result, allowed me to develop closer relationships with other people.

Let me start by saying that the way I've managed my relation-ship with my family was my way; it was what I deemed necessary for my own well-being. I'm not encouraging you to mirror what I've done. But I want to encourage you to give yourself some grace and, ultimately, permission to do what is best for you, to find your own way—a way that is 100 percent in your best interest. A way forward that's not about what you think society might expect of you, what might be best for your parents, what your friends or ex-tended family might think. You have to do what's right for you on your journey to heal and discover your path to personal freedom.

My own experience with forgiveness had to begin with the understanding that my younger, present, and future selves had to acknowledge that my parents also had different versions of self. My younger self experienced my mother differently than my present self experiences her today. We are both different people now. Likewise, with my dad, forgiveness required that I confront the tormentor living in my head—a version of him I experienced as my younger self. People often say to me, "Chad, your dad has really changed." But, even though it may be true, it's not the present version of him that I have to contend with. The reality of who he is to me is the version that tormented me as a child. That's the version who lives with me, who haunts me, that I have to deal with day in and day out. It's the one that gets reflected into my world and tries to keep me small. The work I had to do on my journey was to confront this version of him. I needed the strong, capable, and loving person that

I've become to take care of my younger self. I've actually visualized my present self standing between my dad and seven-year-old me. I put my thriving and capable self between them to protect that little kid. That's what that little kid needed then. And I have the ability to give that protection to him now.

The untangling process requires confrontation of the versions of those who wronged you who still live in your head. The person they are today, in the present, isn't the person they were when you were wronged. All that's left of that version of them is what you are carrying around with you. Achieving personal freedom requires that you acknowledge that neither the version of them nor you exists in the present—both are memories. Our untangling requires that you encounter these versions in your head, under the supervision of who you are today. Conversations between current versions of selves may be helpful, but the resolution that's required isn't between the people you've become; it's between who you were. Forgiveness requires that the rage you feel be exercised and directed appropriately toward the object of your anger. Since the person who wronged you lives in the past, this part of the untangling process doesn't require any interaction with the version of that person in the present. You can heal by taking on this work on your own, with a therapist, a coach, or a trusted confidant—absent the person who wronged you. Only when I realized that, and understood what forgiveness is and isn't, did I come to a place in my life where forgiveness became a palatable part of my journey.

Forgiveness is a gift to yourself. But the power of forgiveness is in what comes after it. The next step is taken by a version of you that isn't small anymore. You get to define the terms by which you proceed with the person you've forgiven. That may mean a regulated place in your life with clear boundaries (as I have done with my mom), or it may mean that there's no longer a place for that person in your life at all (as I have done with my dad). Forgiveness doesn't require an obligation to continue a cycle, repeat their mistakes, or allow their shortcomings to be detrimental to our life's experience.

Forgiveness is allowing your younger self to move from a state of fear and rage to a state of youthful joy,. You can accomplish this by acknowledging the power of the present self to give voice to the rage, disappointment, frustration, sadness, and hatred that you've harbored. It gives your younger self permission to trust your present self because it requires that the feelings of the younger self be acknowledged and heard. Only then can you consciously let it go—not for their benefit, but for your own. Forgiveness is recognition of your own growth and capacity to love yourself.

Forgiveness doesn't mean that everything has to go back to an idealized form of the way things used to be. It's not an excuse of past behavior. It doesn't mean giving someone a free pass. It isn't sweeping things under the rug. It isn't surrendering to the other person. It's surrendering to the strength of who you have become in this moment, because forgiveness exists in the present.

To withhold our forgiveness is to hold onto our fear that a transgression will be repeated. Forgiveness withheld, or a grudge, reminds us that this person did us harm and can do it again. Meanwhile, it undermines us because it discounts our ability to protect ourselves in the present and to cope with the transgression against us. I have forgiven my parents, not because what they did was okay, but because I've come to realize that I'm okay. Until we can forgive and find our strength in that forgiveness, we will continue the transference of the past version of the person who hurt us into our current world. We will continue to see them everywhere as a means of self-defense and protection. Holding onto them leaves no room for healthier relationships to take their place. When we forgive, we open ourselves up to the love and belonging that exists in the world for us.

Forgiveness only arises with people we love or want to love us.

When we get cut off in traffic, there isn't usually a conversation in our head about forgiving that nasty driver. We may get angry and, in our best moments, think to ourselves, *Just let it go*, but rarely is that slight ever framed in terms of forgiveness. Forgiveness is reserved for those relationships in which there is a desire for love.

I couldn't forgive my parents, especially my dad, for so long, because what I was really craving was his love. My younger self held onto the hope that my father would unconditionally love me. Who I am today doesn't need my father's love in order to experience my personal freedom. Forgiving him allowed me to free myself from him and my need for him to love me. Who I am today has the capacity to care for and love my younger self. That's the power of forgiveness. I'm okay, despite the fact that I don't have his love, but only by forgiving him was I able to break free from my attachment to his love and open up to the love of others.

We're all human, and we all make mistakes. But the mistakes that our parents make are the ones that haunt and impact us the most. Their mistakes show up in the ways we echo, rebel, or otherwise respond to the influence of our upbringing. I hear the constant drumbeat of self-help experts that say things like, "Stop blaming your parents," or "Stop playing the victim of your childhood." To them I say, "You are intellectually and emotionally lazy." Is there a place for focusing on the present? Focusing on peak performance? Yes, of course. But you can't truly be your best self if you are not in touch with who you really are, and who you are was shaped by your upbringing. There is no magic pill or "hustle" routine that will serve as substitute for that arduous work. Short-term gains and outward success can be achieved. We may temporarily substitute true meaning and satisfaction with material possessions, but if we ignore the work of seeking the self, we deny ourselves the opportunity for the deeper joy, love, connection, and meaning that we crave—and need. It's as if you're driving a Ferrari with a cracked engine. It may look good on the outside, but it's just a matter of time before it breaks down. To experience personal freedom, you have to confront everything that haunts you, putting in the long, hard work of understanding what makes you, you.

Connection and belonging elude us because we confuse the people we see out in the world with people from our past—when a younger past version of ourselves was powerless in their presence. When we sort that out and recognize the strength of who we've become, it's then that we are able to open our hearts and minds to the loving relationships that await us.

MAKE A LIST

If I'm being honest, I've worn my fierce streak of independence as a badge of honor. I thought that being "on my own" and "standing on my own two feet" was something to celebrate. I embraced those ideas because they allowed me to avoid the vulnerability of connection. I had embraced an identity of independence because going about life apart from others is what has allowed me to survive, or at least I used to think so. This was immature and naive of me, as I later realized just how much my so-called independence was causing me to miss out on in life.

This is a consequence of spending so much of my life in survival mode, since surviving meant depending on myself. It was too dangerous for me to trust anyone else. Perhaps because I was afraid people would discover I was gay, I kept everyone at bay so as not to reveal any sign of vulnerability. It felt, to me, like everyone had an agenda for me that contradicted what I knew as my truth. But I did need people; I just needed the right people.

Once seen as a badge of honor, the self-described, "fiercely independent" person may feel uncomfortable with that characterization after adopting a mindset of belonging. That discomfort is a doorway to growth, so I would like to offer you a couple of ways to move through that discomfort. One is to make a list of friends, and the other is to identify your family of choice.

When I'm feeling anxious or depressed, I know, logically, that I need to reach out to other people, but too often I'll do everything but that. Reaching out to be in community with other people is far down on my list of remedies. To help me remember how important it is to reach out, I keep a note in my phone that says: *These people are your friends. Be their friend and let them be your friend.* And then I have a list of names of people who are my friends. For some of you, this may sound crazy. But for someone with a history of not trusting people, this was necessary for me. When I'm feeling down or could use support, my first instincts are to go inward, to count on myself to fix whatever I might be facing. I've learned, though, that the thriving mindset doesn't ask, *How do I fix this?* Instead, it asks, *Who can help me through this?* On the days that I'm feeling isolated and alone, I have a handy list of people that I can reach out to. People who reflect a part of me back to me, who allow me to see myself from an empowering perspective. Having this list of people who know you, who accept you, and with whom you belong is a powerful remedy to the symptoms of loneliness. I have found that the symptoms of anxiety and depression are overinflated when the only audience for our internal dialogue is ourselves. Friends allow us to get all that stuff in our head out. They also help us establish proportionality to our thinking.

As an adult, I've created what I call my family of choice. You could also call these people your innermost circle. My innermost circle has eight people. It includes my husband, my in-laws, cousins, and old friends. These are people that I have *decided* to treat like family. They get a special place in my life because I've made the decision to give it to them. No one gained automatic entry because of their familial relation. These are the people who see me for who I am, not for who they want me to be. I have rules for myself when it comes to these people: When they call, I answer. When they text, I reply. Even if that's to say, "I can't talk right now. Can I call you back?" I don't do this because I'm obligated. I do it because it creates a sense of belonging for me, a belonging to my family of choice. I have one hour on my calendar each week to reach out to at least one of the people in this group. I may call, text, or send them something in the mail. I put in the effort to belong in their lives because I've decided that I'm better when they belong in mine.

Friends and families of choice make our lives bigger and more fulfilling and help us to see our life's meaning more clearly. Having these tribes helps us see different parts of ourselves more profoundly. Creating this structure makes it easier to access a means of connection on the days that are more challenging. It's in these relationships that you will find comfort in sharing your life's journey with people you trust and even love, with people who will support and encourage you as you travel.

EXERCISE

Now, I'd like to invite you to take your journal and:

1. Make a list of your friends. If you don't have friends, make a list of people that you have an interest in becoming friends with.

2. Make a list of your "family of choice." Put their faces or names in a place where you can easily see them. Mine are on the lock screen of my phone.

3. What are the rules or obligations that you want to hold yourself to with these people?

SCHEDULE SOCIAL DATES

Research tells us that those experiencing loneliness are more passive in their approach to satisfy the needs of connection.[21] Instead of seeking to remedy the loneliness, they withdraw. Knowing that this is the case, it's important to take steps that will mitigate your tendency to perpetuate your default programming. I suggest you do this by scheduling at least one face-to-face social experience per week. You may choose to find four different friends with whom you schedule a monthly get-together. That gives you a face-to-face interaction once per week for most months.

When you ask your friends to commit to this scheduling idea, be open and transparent about why. I think you'll find that if you're feeling like you need to create more connection and social interaction in your life, your friends do too.

Don't feel weird about scheduling social appointments. Your parents likely scheduled playdates for you as a kid, and recess was scheduled into your day. If you were in any type of organization in college, there were scheduled social activities, and this is no different. People are busy; you're busy. Taking the time to invest in these connections will only help you; it will make you feel better, less isolated, understood, and happier. Putting that activity on your calendar is simply insurance that it happens. In fact, I think you'll find that people appreciate that you made the effort to connect with them. I also think they'll appreciate that you're asking to schedule that time. It indicates that you think spending time with them is so important that you want it on your calendar. They'll be flattered.

The key to this exercise working is to limit your invitations to quality people only. Only make time for the people who build you up, make you feel good about yourself and your life, help you breathe a little easier, and make you smile and laugh. People who don't do that for you will only make this exercise feel like work, and you'll end up stopping it. Be aware of who you are attracting and inviting into your life.

Connection is important enough to make time for it. Reach out to schedule some time to hang out with at least one person per week.

FIND A TRIBE

It's in our biology to be part of a tribe. A tribe keeps us safe. It looks out for us. It gives us something to which we can contribute. But the nature of the tribe has dramatically changed with technology. You're no longer limited to a tribe of like-minded people who are geographically close to you. Your tribe can be anywhere, connected through the technology that our time in history affords us.

Finding a tribe means finding those people with whom you feel understood. They are people who have a shared interest, goal, or bond. Your tribe makes you realize that you're not alone. It gives you resources for how to navigate what you're experiencing. It helps you make sense of your life experience, holding up a mirror so that you can see yourself more clearly. Your tribe makes life's journey less lonely.

You can be a part of as many tribes as you would like. You could be part of a fitness tribe, a reading tribe, a personal development tribe, a professional tribe—the options are limitless.

What part of you needs more exploration? What are you trying to figure out right now? Where could you use more clarity? Find a tribe that is actively seeking an answer to that question. You don't have to figure your life out on your own. Find a tribe that can offer you some perspective. Their perspective will fast-track your insight.

When you a join a tribe, remember that self-actualization happens through self-transcendence. The tribe is where you can put that advice into practice—to heal or learn more about yourself by helping others.

To help you get into action toward feeling a deeper sense of connection, here's an easy three-step process you can follow:

1.   Identify three tribes that will make you feel more connected and less alone.

2.   Join those tribes!

3.   Participate in the tribes. Keep in mind that you will get from the tribes what you give. Lead with generous giving and contribution to others.

If you experience loneliness, here's a quick word of caution for you as you take these actions. Be prepared for a lot of internal resistance. People who experience loneliness have a tendency to misinterpret or exaggerate the hostile or affectionate intent of others.[21] There are a number of studies that show that people who experience loneliness not only have negative views of themselves, but they also look at other people through a negative lens. They look at others with more skepticism, are less accepting, and are more likely to expect to be seen negatively by others.[22] So, as you do this work, remember that it's your default programming showing up that is making you feel and think this way. It's allowing the past into the present—a way of looking for those negative experiences of our past to resurface in the here and now. The way I see it, we can approach people in one of two ways: 1) We can resent them for not being more like us and not being how we want them to be, or 2) We can see them for who they are, respect and appreciate what makes them different from us. The first will keep us isolated and lonely; the second will create potential for connection.

INDIVIDUALITY VS. LOYALTY

That Christmas trip home to Arkansas led to my taking a break from speaking to my parents. My dad and I are still on that break—a break of more than ten years now, as of this writing. My mom and I have been slowly and deliberately working on our relationship. Breaking the relationship was what I needed to heal. You may need something different. But if you are waiting for permission to take that break, here is that permission. Culturally, we are programmed to think that family ties are never to be broken. Growing up in the South, I was taught to value loyalty over individualism. I absolutely call nonsense on that notion. That being said, let me be clear: I am not advocating that you remove people from your life who challenge you, frustrate you, push you, or disagree with you. Tension is a necessary part of any meaningful relationship and will contribute to your growth. This does not mean that just because the other person is different, they must be bad and therefore removed. I'm not saying that at all. I'm talking about those people who belittle you, abuse you, and intentionally keep you small to make themselves feel bigger or derive pleasure from your misery. Anyone who would deliberately cause you harm, physically or emotionally, has no "familial right" to be in your life.

Belonging and connection aren't as elusive as we like to pretend that they are. I hear folks all the time say that it's so hard to make friends as an adult, that college was so much easier. Well, of course it was easier—your whole life was certainly more convenient in college, if not easier. You had structure, accountability, and planned social events. You can have the same as an adult, but you have to create them for yourself. We tend to figure that secret out when it comes to things like our productivity (or a boss helps us figure it out). But, for some reason, when it comes to belonging and connection, the secret remains elusive. Like most things, though, this can be figured out.

Opportunities for connection exist if you look for them and work at them. Simple steps, like making a list to bring awareness to those who are already in your life, to scheduling times to be social with them, to expanding who you know by finding a tribe. All of these are practical ways to develop more connection.

The connections you develop over the course of your life will give your life flavor. Resolve to savor that flavor! Resist the default programming to go inward all the time and give yourself the gift of belonging.

HELP
CHAPTER 10

Shoot for the moon. Even if you miss,
you'll land among the stars.

~ Norman Vincent Peale

I hate asking for help. It makes me feel weak, dependent, and out of control of my own life and destiny. My anxiety kicks into overdrive when I think about being dependent on other people to help me achieve my goals, live a better life, live fully. My internal dialogue, my chatterbox, says things like:

I can go faster if I go it alone.
Other people are just going to let me down and disappoint me.
Other people just don't understand me.
If I want something done right, I have to do it myself.
If I need someone else, I must not be good enough.
I want to maintain complete control of my life.
I'm fine. I've got this all under control.

This has been my internal, and often external, dialogue for much of my life. And even though I may feel this way about asking for help, I have come to understand that my life is better when I ask for, receive, and gracefully accept help from others. I eventually realized that not asking for help was a way that I had learned to keep myself small, hidden, and repressed. That chatterbox was just a string of excuses I could replay in my head to reinforce keeping myself down. By not asking for help, I was complying with my survivor's mindset that told me to stay quiet and trust no one.

Survivors are people who have overcome their past; they've come out on the other side of adversity, heartache, and trauma. But on the other side of all that, survivors can adopt an unhealthy mindset of self-reliance, believing that they are completely self-sufficient and that they don't need anyone or anything to help them. They've survived and therefore they've "got this." What's underlying their internal dialogue is a resistance that says something like: *Don't mess with my approach. It's what saved my life.*

This way of thinking makes sense. Your life has been defined by buckling down, making things work, and successfully coming out on the other end. Your history wasn't defined by a reliance on anyone else; you had to rely on yourself. And when you did, it worked. You learned a lesson: if you want to do something, if you want to survive, do it yourself.

You may have good reason to not trust anyone. You may have been let down by the most important people in your life. When you needed help the most, and asked someone you loved for help, they may have disappointed you. Or worse yet, you never even felt safe enough to ask for help. As we'll explore later in this chapter, these ideas may have formed while you were a baby; Mom or Dad may not have been attentive or responded to you in a way that you needed. If the most important people in your life wouldn't help you, why would anyone else? I get it.

It may be true for a while that you don't need anyone else—at least that might be how you'll see it. For me, that was true until it wasn't. It was true in my survivor's mindset; it was not true for a mindset of thriving. My life got to the point where growth required help and support. Imagine your personal growth like building blocks, one stacked on top of the other. You can stack a bunch of building blocks on top of one another for a while, you can rise to a certain level of thriving, but at some point you need structural reinforcement to prevent a collapse. At some point you will need help.

I really started to notice how stubborn and resistant I had become to asking for help when I saw how Pasha would handle situations where he needed to go beyond his own skills and abilities. When I face a challenge or feel stuck, my first instinct is to think, *How am I going to do this?* Pasha's first instinct is always, *Who am I going to ask to help me do this?* Recognizing Pasha's approach and how foreign it seemed to me made me realize that I had an opportunity to discover a new way. I had to learn to think about the need for other people's help as a means for getting more of what I want out of life, instead of seeing it as a deficiency. I had to come to see that being able to recognize my own needs and asking for help is a sign of strength, growth, and maturity, not a weakness.

Getting help doesn't require that you completely cede control of your life to someone else; you'll never hear that from me. We are all ultimately responsible for our own decisions and our own lives. But don't you think you would benefit from the help of someone or many someones who have your best interests at heart, who want to see you succeed, and who can offer you some perspective? Wouldn't it be to your benefit to allow people into your life who can help you discover those parts of you that you're blind to? Isn't your life worth asking for the help that will allow you to grow beyond what you can do on your own?

THE WORLD IS A MIRROR

In the movie *Shutter Island*, Leonardo DiCaprio is shipped off to a mental institution on an island. He's a detective who believes he is being sent there to investigate the disappearance of one of the patients. Much to his surprise, and to the surprise of the movie watcher, he isn't there to investigate at all—he's there as a patient.

This jolting realization DiCaprio's character experiences mirrored my own when I joined a therapy group. I resisted my therapist's recommendation to join group therapy for years before finally giving in. This particular group meets weekly, with the supervision of a therapist, to explore how to improve our interpersonal skills.

I'm a fixer; I always have been. In my very first session, a member of the group began to describe something they were going through, and it was like looking in a mirror. I recognized that problem. I could relate to how they felt, and I knew I could give them my shortcuts to help them through this experience. So, I started doing what I do: asking questions and trying to help them see the breakthrough that was right in front of us.

When our interaction ended, another member of the group turned to me and said, "You really scared me." I didn't understand what they meant. I had just helped this person through a tough situation, so how could they be scared? In my second session, I learned from others, including the person that I thought I was helping, that that person was also scared of me. They asked me if I was angry at them or angry at the situation. I was so sad, because I wasn't angry at anyone. I thought I was being helpful!

All of a sudden, it hit me hard that I wasn't meant to be the fixer in this group. We were all there to help one another. That meant that I, too, was there to be helped. This group was helping me recognize a form of cognitive dissonance, a gap between how I saw myself and how other people saw me. What I thought I was doing to help wasn't being received that way—and I was blind to it.

I was embarrassed but also relieved at the opportunity for growth. All of a sudden, I began to see that what this group was telling me was a more impactful and more direct version of what family, friends, employees, and clients had been telling me for many years: that I'm too serious, too intense. This group showed me how I had been making other people feel: scared. I saw myself as helpful, a results-oriented doer. Others perceived me as arrogant and intimidating. I learned that my poker face can confuse people and that I have a tendency to go too fast when trying to be helpful. This group has helped me see that it's hard to connect with me when I lead with an analytic mind instead of a feeling mind. All of these were important lessons that I couldn't have learned on my own; I needed help. This wasn't a wide gap that I had just ignored. I had never realized there was a gap at all.

Asking for and accepting help will bring you perspective. We experience the world looking through a mirror, not a window. When we recognize that, we also recognize that we have blind spots that make it impossible to see parts of ourselves. That view can't be expanded unless infringed upon by an outside force—and that outside force is what we call perspective.

Opening yourself up to allow others to help you see things in another way, or more clearly, is truly a gift. By accepting others' help, you will be able to access different parts of your self that may go untapped without prodding from the outside.

This experience in group therapy made me realize another way that I could be helped, which would allow me to get more of what I wanted in my life. Allowing others to hold up a mirror for us helps us see different dimensions of ourselves. Bringing awareness to how I was showing up in the world showed me how I was sabotaging my own efforts to be close to others and develop relationships. I understood, through help from others, a better way to show on the outside what I was feeling on the inside.

Remember that asking for help isn't surrendering or admitting defeat. It is, in fact, the opposite; asking for and accepting help is actually a form of taking control. It will bring you to a new level of depth, meaning, and untapped potential. Asking for help can show you different sides of yourself, help you move from one point to another, and allow you to share the burdens of life. Receiving help gives you the room to experience more of your life's journey.

Asking for and receiving help will allow you to live a more fully expressed life. When you don't ask for help, you are resigning yourself to a limited version of your personal freedom. You are keeping yourself small and in the grips of survival. You are building a cage around yourself. A cage in which you starve yourself of what you really need. For me, resisting help is one of the ways that my dad keeps me in his grips. When I don't ask for help, I'm allowing him to maintain his hold on me. I am allowing him to keep me small. When I ask for and accept help, I break that grip. Asking for help is saying, *I am here. This is my space. I have needs, and they deserve to be met because I am worthy.*

WHY WE RESIST HELP

When you don't ask for or accept help, this is the ultimate action to keep yourself small. Here are some of the reasons we don't ask for or accept help:

- ► Fear of looking weak
- ► Embarrassment[1]
- ► A loss of independence
- ► Being perceived as imposing
- ► The illusion that you are the only one who does it right

Numerous studies have explored the cost of asking for help. When we ask for help, we are paying a psychological price. First, we have to admit a personal limitation to ourselves in order to recognize that help is needed. This can be hard for many people. Some studies suggest that people with higher self-esteem are *less* likely to ask for help than those with low self-esteem. This actually makes a lot of sense when you begin to break it down. It may seem counterintuitive at first, but consider why it rings true for so many people.

What is self-esteem anyway? It's having confidence in our abilities. A survivor mindset requires self-confidence. If you didn't have confidence that you could and would survive, you might not have. When we ask for help, we threaten that part of us that says, *I've got this. I can handle this. I'll survive this.* When we ask for help, we are volunteering that we might not have it all figured out. That there's a need for someone else. It's an admission that there is a chink in our armor.

Studies have shown that people are even less likely to ask for help in areas where they perceive themselves as having more control.[2] For example, we are less likely to ask for help from a life coach or therapist because the problems that they help us solve are central to our own sense of self. But we might be more willing to seeking advice from an electrician, since they solve problems that are further separated from our selves. It's less likely that we understand the intricacies of electricity; therefore there's less embarrassment or shame associated with asking for the kind of help that they might offer. Where did we get this idea in our head that we should have this kind of unassisted understanding of self?

Resistance to asking for help can also be a manifestation of old programming or scripting—very old programming that you may have absolutely no recollection of in your conscious memory.[3] This is a type of narcissistic defense mechanism developed when we're young, wherein we pick up the idea, from either of our parents or both, that our needs are a burden to them. At some point, we begin to believe that what we want or need is too much for them to handle. Our perception may be that they have too much to deal with and can't handle any more, especially in relation to us. Therefore we hold onto those needs, we learn to not ask for help, and we begin suppressing our own desires in deference to theirs. This can happen at a really young age, from the days of crying in the crib. The result is unhelpful programming that likely got reinforced through many circumstances over the years.

It's not hard to see how the impact of that kind of experience would show up for you as an adult. If you picked up on an idea when you were young that your needs were an imposition that went unmet, why reach out to people for help, even if you know you should? Why would you trust anyone to do anything for you? It would be easier to just make excuses for other people when they let you down, saying they are incompetent, unable, or unwilling to be of help. But that's not healthy. This approach can cause a lot of pain and undue emotional suffering. When we have needs, our very aliveness lies in our reaction to those needs. When we respond by asking for what we need, instead of suffering in silence, not only do we get what we need and the satisfaction we feel when our needs are met, but we also grow as human beings.

We are tribal, social creatures, who were made to rely on one another. We've survived as a species because we've relied on one another. We stayed alive by reacting and responding to our environment and those around us. Lean into that primitive instinct to react and reject the programming to deprive yourself of what you need.

HOW TO ASK FOR HELP

How does someone who has a hard time asking for and accepting help even ask? There are so many circumstances that would influence the answer to that question, and every circumstance will require your personal finesse. Nonetheless, there are a few things that transcend circumstance and can help you adopt a mindset that allows you to ask for what you need:

First, direct your ask wisely. I would ask Tiger Woods for golf advice, but I would not ask him for marriage advice. I would ask Warren Buffet for investing advice, but I would not ask him for dance lessons. You wouldn't ask your mechanic about your digestive issues, and you wouldn't ask your doctor about your transmission problems. Be specific and purposeful about where you direct your ask. While I respect my husband's opinion on many things, there are topics on which I wouldn't rely on his advice. I might rely on his perspective about the style of my delivery, but not on the substance of my expertise. He might ask me for advice about his teaching business, but he would never ask me about a violin fingering or bowing, since it's not my expertise.

Being purposeful about where you direct your ask will get you the best help you can get and reinforce a mindset of asking for and accepting help. Just make sure your ask aligns with the ability of the person you're asking.

Second, when asking for help, be direct. Don't make the person you're asking work to try to figure out what you're asking of them. Keep your head up, stand firmly and squarely on your feet, and ask. Being direct will bring clarity in deciphering what you really need and will allow the person you're asking to see how they can best help. Don't try to position your request as a bargain, or explain why they should help you, or bring up that one time that you helped them and therefore they owe you. Also, don't make promises that you'll return the favor one day. Just ask. If they want something in return, trust that they'll ask.

Finally, be respectful when making your ask: respectful of the other person's time, attention, and boundaries. And be respectful when they deny your request. Always express your gratitude to them whether or not they agree to help you.

As previously discussed, there is a psychological cost to asking for help. Asking for help reveals our vulnerability. Following an expert-focused approach can help you bridge the gap between completely resisting asking for help and beginning to get more of what you need. Research tells us that we underestimate how willing people are to help us.[4] Help is just an ask away.

ACCEPT HELP WITH GRACE AND GRATITUDE

To live a bigger, more fully expressed life, we have to invite other people to contribute to the richness of our experience. But, in addition to extending that invitation, we have to learn how to accept it.

Receiving help can sometimes be more painful than asking for it. Ideas of being indebted to someone, or being weaker than our helper, or feeling a sense of inadequacy can be overwhelming. I hope that, by now, I've convinced you that this way of thinking is just nonsense. You were not meant to go through this life alone. Helping and being helped is an important part of who we are.

No one got to where they are on their own. Contrary to popular belief, no one is "self-made." Everyone who ever did anything has had help of some kind. There's absolutely no shame in that. Because no one is self-made, there are people out there with unbalanced karmic accounts who want to be in service to others, to help someone in the way that others have helped them. These people may show up in the form of good parents, mentors, coaches, and teachers, to name a few. Who are you to deny their efforts to live their purpose of helping? Asking for and accepting help allows others to fulfill their purpose. Don't deny them the opportunity.

When you are the object of their grace, accept it with grace and gratitude, with the knowledge that you have been given a gift that you are welcome to pay forward through your own purpose.

I understand the resistance to accept the grace and kindness of others. But being in connection with others means being part of the full cycle of giving and receiving help. Allowing others to be part of our lives requires us to listen to and then check our survivor's ego when that resistance inevitably shows up. Someone with a survivor's mindset might think:

I've survived. I did it without anyone, and I'm fine without anyone now. People annoy me. They disappoint me. They just want something from me. They don't understand me. They have nothing to offer me. I don't want to owe this person anything. What's their real motivation for helping me?

But this mindset limits our lives. Instead, we should work toward developing a mindset to thrive. Someone with a mindset to thrive might think something like:

I've survived, and I'm stronger because of my life experience. I know that there's still another level of life for me. There's a more joyful life for me that feels more meaningful, more connected. I know that I'm a strong, smart, confident, and capable person. I know that there are other people in this world that can contribute to my life experience in a way that makes life more satisfying. I understand that other people are not perfect; they are flawed and will make mistakes. Even so, I will engage without judgment or offense, with grace, and with gratitude. As I adopt this new mindset, I know that I, too, am flawed and will make mistakes. I will show myself the grace, humility, and forgiveness that I so easily show others. The benefit of my growth outweighs any discomfort of the journey. I accept the gift of love and connection from others. I will allow them to see me, connect with me, and help me.

Open your heart and your mind to a new way; you might be surprised at the goodness you allow in.

CONNECT SOME DOTS

Take the opportunity to connect some dots between where you were and where you are. Asking for and accepting help are actions (less hidden internal thought patterns) that make it easier for us to recognize. The following exercise will help you start connecting some dots and allow you to explore what's stopping you from asking for and receiving help from others:

EXERCISE

To help you untangle your resistance to asking for help, take your journal and write your reflections on the following questions:

1. Was there ever a time in your life when you needed help from someone, and you asked but didn't get it?

2. Was there a time in your life when you expected to be helped by someone without having to ask them and didn't get it?

3. If either of the previous questions yielded a yes answer, what do you imagine the motivations were of the person who denied you?

4. Do you believe those motivations were real or imagined?

5. If they were to deny you that help today, as the person you are today, what do you imagine your response would be?

6. How have these experiences shaped your mindset for asking for and receiving help?

Let's switch things up a bit:

1. Was there ever a time in your life when you needed help from someone, asked for it, and got it?

2. Was there ever a time in your life when you didn't expect to be helped by someone, and they helped you?

3. If either of the previous questions yielded a yes answer, what do you imagine the motivations were of the person who helped you?

4. Do you believe those motivations were real or imagined?

5. Can you imagine yourself offering that kind of help to someone in need?

6. Are there lessons in your responses that can be used to reprogram your mindset for asking for and receiving help?

Imagine for a moment that you've found yourself in a situation where you need some help. Maybe you're moving, you need a ride to the airport, you're having a really bad day, or you just won the lottery and don't know what to do with all that money. When you've got that situation firmly in your head, and you're holding on to the awareness that you need help, answer these questions:

1. What do you feel in your body right now? Do you feel any physical sensations that came about?

2. What are you feeling emotionally? Is there one dominant emotion (happy, mad, sad, scared)?

3. Is your mind wandering somewhere else in order to avoid or resist the idea of asking for help? If so, where did it go? Does that tell you anything about your avoidance tendencies or resistance?

4. Who can you imagine asking to help you with this situation?

5. How would you go about asking them? How would you reach out? What would you say?

6. What do you imagine their response would be?

7. How do you imagine you would feel about their response?

8. How can your responses inform a better mindset for asking for and receiving help?

Now, let's imagine the roles were reversed. What if that person you asked had instead asked you for the same help?

1. How would it feel to be asked?

2. How can you imagine responding to their request?

3. Would you expect something from them in return for your help?

4. What do your responses tell you about the way in which you ask for and accept help from others?

START WITH A SMALL ASK

Begin to adopt a mindset of asking for and accepting help by taking small steps in that direction. If you're already easily asking for and accepting help from others in a healthy and safe way, feel free to move on to the next chapter. But if you struggle with allowing others to help you meet your needs or if you're aware that your resistance to accepting help is holding you back, give the next couple of exercises a try.

EXERCISE

For the next week, use this question at least once per day:

"Could you _____ , please?"

Memorize that sentence. Start small. Seriously, small. Your one ask a day might be something like:

To a friend: *"Could we talk about this at another time, please?"*

To your child: *"Could you help me unpack the groceries, please?"*

To a coworker: *"Could you let me talk something out with you, please?"*

To a stranger: *"Could you grab the door for me, please?"*

Think of a small ask and activate it each day. You can ask the same person or someone new each day. The purpose of this exercise is simply to get you to bring an awareness to and put into practice asking for and accepting help from other people. By inviting others to participate in your life, you're inviting the opportunity to form a new bond or deepen an existing one.

Slow yourself down and pay attention to your body as you make the ask. Be aware of how you feel when they respond to you, and show them grace and gratitude in return. Remember, this isn't about negotiating their compliance; it's about beginning to make space for yourself in this world. No matter their response, you are getting the benefit of the practice.

PRACTICE ACCEPTANCE

One of the easiest ways to practice acceptance is to accept compliments without responding by qualifying them. You may not think of a compliment as help, but it certainly is. A compliment is an unsolicited boost of self-esteem, confidence, and validation. By complimenting someone, you acknowledge that person by recognizing and seeing them. Compliments are a great and simple way for you to bring awareness to accepting help with grace and gratitude.

How many times has someone complimented you and your response downplayed the compliment? Maybe someone complimented your shirt, and your response was something like, "Oh, I've had this forever." Or, "Oh, thanks. I got it on sale." The next time someone compliments you, let them. Don't diminish the compliment or dismiss it. Just say thank you. Allow the other person to give you that compliment; it's a gift.

When someone compliments you, it's a way for them get closer to you, to connect with you. When you diminish or dismiss their compliment, you are resisting their attempt at connection. For the next week, practice accepting help by accepting compliments with grace and gratitude.

PURPOSE EXERCISED

*When I was a boy and I would see scary things
in the news, my mother would say to me,
'Look for the helpers. You will always
find people who are helping.'*

~ Fred Rogers

There are people who cannot live their purpose until you embrace and live yours. There are people who cannot live their purpose until you let them know that your life is an opportunity for them to express theirs. This is the cycle of our connection with one another.

There are so many reasons to love that Mr. Rogers quote, but one, for me, is that it puts into perspective the timing of the helped and their helpers. We are helped in our times of need. And we help others when they are in a time of need. I think there's a tendency when we resist help, either consciously or unconsciously, to think that we aren't enough, and that, by accepting help, we are permanently inadequate and in need of assistance. That just isn't true. We all have moments of needing help, and we all have moments of being able to help. There's nobility in both roles and in how we express and accept being the one in need and the one who fulfills the need. One doesn't exist without the other. When we refuse to ask for or accept help, we deny the helpers and those in need of fulfilling their purpose. We deny ourselves the opportunity to be closer and more deeply connected to others. Don't deny others their opportunity to be of service. Ask for help and accept it with grace and gratitude.

AMBITION
CHAPTER 11

Ambition is the drive we allow others to see.

~ Chad Peevy

In ancient Rome, when candidates were running for public office, they had to go around asking people for their votes. The Latin word for this effort was *ambitio*, which came from *ambire*, a verb that means "to go around."[1] Ambition isn't something that sits within us; it's the evidence of what's inside of us. It's how we show, through our efforts, what's important to us. The word *ambition* and its meaning (to go around, advocating for yourself) carried a special significance to me as a gay man. In the root of that word, there was a familiarity with what I recognized and had experienced in "coming out."

Whether or not you identify as gay, when you break the cycle of your past, or break out of what someone else expects of you and embrace who you really are, you're experiencing a form of coming out. You are coming out as someone who is willing to see yourself for who you really are. When you start a business, get married, get a divorce, quit your job, declare your political affiliation, decide to embrace the religion you grew up with or reject it, these are all forms of coming out. You are declaring who you are to others and to yourself.

Any type of coming out is your ambition in practice that, regardless of the shape it takes, is an audacious act of courage. Coming out is a process, consisting first of deep internal deliberation in search of your truth, which is ultimately a revelation of who you really are. It is a process that brings you a deeper understanding of yourself, and a declaration that allows others to know how to become closer to you.

THE DECLARATION

At first, I saw my coming out as a sexual declaration; but I've since come to see it as a spiritual one. A declaration that chipped away at my ego and the attachments of what others thought I should be. It was an act of becoming closer to the truest version of myself, a step forward toward personal freedom, and an invitation for the most important people in my life to see me as I really am.

Coming out is a form of rejecting an inherited mindset. A rejection of the status quo in our lives, whether that's coming out of the closet, ending a relationship, transitioning careers, or changing college majors. Coming out is that awakening to an intolerance to the things that are blocking our way to our personal freedom.

A coming out is a statement about what's important to us, and how we choose to show up in the world. It reveals our deepest values. The more you come out in more areas of your life, the clearer you will see yourself. The more you come out, the more you allow others to see you. The more you come out, the more comfortable you become in your own skin. The more you come out, the more you'll feel free to reach for what you want out of life.

COMING OUT

My mom was a smoker, but she didn't smoke in the house. She would go outside on the porch to sit on her bench and smoke her cigarette, no matter the weather. Sitting on that bench and talking became our routine over the years. I couldn't stand the cigarette smoke, but sitting out there was my chance to get some time with my mom. One particular day on the bench was different than any of the days before it. I had just told her and my dad that I was gay.

I was twenty-two years old, a senior in college, when I came out to my parents. I had hit a wall with the denials. I had grown tired of lying about dating girls and pretending to be interested when they would suggest potential girls for me to date. I had come out at school, but there wasn't any sort of announcement—it was just known that I dated guys. I knew that the news of my sexuality would be received quite a bit differently at home.

I want to remind you that, when I was growing up, gay people were equivalent to the boogey man at church. My dad wouldn't let us watch television shows or movies with Black people in them, much less gay people. This was rural Arkansas in 2002. Telling my parents that I was gay was paramount to aliens landing a spaceship in our backyard.

"Mom, Dad, I'm gay."

I really don't know why they acted so shocked. There had certainly been more than a few clues over the years, and I had heard my dad say some things about me to my mom when they thought

I was sleeping and unable to hear them. I think the shock was less about my being gay and more about the real-time disintegration of their fantasies for my life. With those few words, I destroyed their hopes and dreams for me, and what those hopes and dreams meant for their lives. I changed how they saw themselves, and I instilled a fear in them of how they thought other people would see them now that they had a gay son. Even if they had suspected it, they hadn't prepared themselves for the reality of it.

So, there we sat. No one, including me, knew how to process that information or what to do next. This sort of thing happened to other people, not us. But after the initial shock wore off, the tears and words began to flow. Some of those words stuck out more than others.

My mom asked, *"Who is going to take care of you when you get AIDS?"*

My dad said, *"Don't you ever bring some faggot home."*

And in an effort to reassure them that I could still have a "normal" life, I said, *"I'm going to have babies with lesbians!"* I guess I was thinking that I might be able to split the difference with them by getting a woman to donate her eggs. That way I could be me and still give them a piece of what they wanted for me.

There were a lot of things said that day that I have no doubt we all wish we could take back. While it was the *present* version of myself who sat there that day with courage and came out to my parents, it was the *younger* version of me who waited for, heard, and reacted to their response.

My coming out was so messy. Sometimes our journey gets that way. Who we are, what we want for our lives, and what life path is revealed to us doesn't always align with the expectations of the people in our lives. They aren't always ready to know more of us in the same way that we seek to know more about ourselves.

Regardless of how messy and how painful it was, I have never regretted coming out. My life has been full of love and joy because I made the decision to know myself and to be true to that awakening. But there are two things that I wish I could have done differently that day.

First, I wish I hadn't given them false hope that being gay might be a phase. I didn't tell them that it could be a phase, but when they suggested it, I didn't dispute the idea. All I wanted was to be loved. So when things got uncertain for me in that moment, that younger, scared version of me was willing to retreat to a position that was more accommodating to their expectations and less accepting of my own truth. To them, that little bit of hope meant that I was willing to be "fixed." But I realized the cruelty of that false hope when one day, not long after the day I came out to them, my mother handed me brochures for conversion therapy. Only then did I summarily reject the idea of this being a phase.

I allowed them to hang on to hope for what they wanted for me. But I should have given them hope for what I wanted for myself. I knew that I would never be straight. I knew without question that I was gay and that it was no phase. I had known, hid, and denied my sexuality since I was a kid. I did all of us a disservice and caused us more pain by not fully and unapologetically holding onto myself and my truth. Looking back, I realize that my ambition for what I wanted for my own life wasn't greater than my desire to satisfy what I thought they wanted for my life. Even in a moment of extraordinary courage, part of me was willing to compromise myself for their fantasy. That kind of ambiguity denied us all the clarity that situation deserved.

By allowing that ambiguity, I denied them the clarity they would need to begin their own journey. I don't think she always knew how, but I never questioned that my mom loved me. I believe she brought me those conversion therapy pamphlets not only because it would have satisfied what she wanted for me, but also because my ambiguity left open that I was open to the idea too. With time, and with more clarity, my mom found the courage to embark on her own journey of understanding me. She found other ways to express her love that were in alignment with what was my truth, and ultimately hers too—that her love was unconditional. In fact, she was one of my biggest supporters when I founded the Austin Pride Foundation. She was right there alongside me at the parade and festival. And to top it off, she loves my husband.

Second, I thought that my experience was unique to me, and so I went about my coming out all alone. Granted, there weren't as many resources available to me in those days, but I made no effort to seek out the resources and support that were available. I wish that I had surrounded myself with like-minded, compassionate people who understood what I was going through so that I wouldn't have felt so lonely and isolated.

YOU NEVER STOP COMING OUT

Human beings imitate one another in order to connect. In an effort to be liked, accepted, and loved, we conform to what others have signaled that they expect from us. But our ambition rebukes conformity. Ambition is an act of breaking the cycle of what is expected of you and freely expressing who you are. Whether it's taking a stand for what you believe in or who you love, coming out isn't a one-time declaration; it's a lifetime commitment to taking a stand for yourself.

You will never stop coming out. The pressures and expectations to conform, the assumptions that you are like the status quo, the pull to fall in line and to be like everyone else will never stop. As humans, we want to see others as we wish them to be, to make them match our worldview. As such, we all work to make one another fit our own worldview because that makes our experience with one another more comfortable. Our own desire to fit in is a natural defense mechanism: the more we fit into our tribe, the more protection we receive from them, and the more likely we'll survive. That desire to create conformity limits our ability to connect more deeply with others. It makes it harder for us to learn from people who don't experience the world the way we do. Because that push and pull to conform is so strong, the necessity to come out will never stop. True personal freedom means that you won't be satisfied with just one foot out of the closet. You can't be out to one person or group of people, but not others. You can't act a certain way with certain people and another way with other people. This sabotages your identity, self-expression, ability to connect, and personal freedom. You'll remain chained to the expectations of others instead of fully knowing, embracing, or expressing your truest self. How can you be *you* just part-time?

On average, I have to come out to someone about once a day. Why? Why do I feel the need to correct someone when they make an assumption that I have a wife and not a husband or a boyfriend instead of a husband? There are four compelling reasons.

First, to deny who I am, and to effectively hide who I am, keeps me small, where I remain unseen in deference to someone else's worldview. This isn't freedom. This isn't a thriving life. The impact of diminishing yourself will show up in every part of your life. Be proud of who you are.

Second, I feel like I have an obligation to honor the sacrifices that have been made for me by people who came before me. The reason I can legally be married to a man, the reason my entire life looks the way it does today, is because someone like me stood up on my behalf many years ago. They will never meet me, nor I them, but they are my ancestors, my brothers and my sisters, and I owe them the respect of honoring their sacrifice and fulfilling the promise of a better future they fought so hard for. The reason you can fly your freak flag,[2] no matter what that flag represents, is because someone before you sewed that flag with bloody fingers.

Third, I don't know the impression that I'll have on the person I'm coming out to. I may be the first gay person they've ever met, or even a "different kind" of gay person that this person has never met. I don't know the impact that I can have to help them break their cycle of prejudice, stereotyping, or discrimination.

And finally, I have an obligation to continue to pave the way for the people like me, who are coming up behind me—my younger brothers and sisters who are making their way through the world. I want to make it easy for them to have opportunity, to have equal protection under the law, to not be seen as outsiders, to get the same opportunities that the "insiders" have. The ease and prosperity of their journey will be a reflection of how I spend mine. I refuse to minimize myself to make others feel comfortable—not when the stakes are this high. Suicide is the second leading cause of death among young people between the ages of ten and twenty-four, and gay youth are five times as likely as their heterosexual peers to have attempted suicide.

When you stand up for who you are, when you hold on to who you are in this very moment, to the person you've worked so hard to become, you are honoring the work you've put into yourself and the people who have made it possible for you to live that truth. You are living freely and ambitiously as your truest self. It takes courage to participate in this life—from saying what you want to taking the steps necessary to get it. Your courage must be ever-present.

The only thing standing between you and the life you really want for yourself is fear. To move past that fear, you'll need the courage to take the next step to get closer to your truest and highest self. Take those steps with people like you, who support you. The more steps you take, the more you stand up for yourself and for others like you, the less it will feel like courage, and the more it will feel like freedom.

When you allow people to make assumptions about who or what you are, you are allowing them to unintentionally rob you of a little bit of your freedom. Yes, there will be times when you don't want to stand in your truth. You may tell yourself that you don't feel the need or that it's not necessary this time. I would suggest that you to just go ahead and assume that you won't ever "feel" like it. But you don't have to feel like it—you just have to do it. Do it because you owe it to yourself to be *you* every single day.

In a speech in 1978, Harvey Milk, famous gay rights icon and the first openly gay elected official in California, said;

> "Every gay person must come out. As diffi-
> cult as it is, you must tell your immediate
> family. You must tell your relatives. You
> must tell your friends, if indeed they are
> your friends. You must tell your neighbors.
> You must tell the people you work with.
> You must tell the people in the stores
> you shop in. And, once they realize that
> we are indeed their children, that we are
> indeed everywhere, every myth, every lie,
> every innuendo will be destroyed once and
> for all. And once you do, you will feel so
> much better."

I believe those words are as necessary today as they were when they were said in 1978. No matter how different or "other" you may feel, let each time you come out be a reminder of your strength and your gift. Honor your journey. Honor those who came before you. Recognize that your difference is your strength. And realize the purpose that exists in making this path easier for those traveling behind you.

What could it mean for you, people you care about, people in the world who are like you, and people like you who haven't been born yet if you made the decision right now to raise your ambition? How different might the world be if you dreamed a little bigger, reached a little higher, and loved a little harder? What kind of difference and impact might that slight variance make? What if you leaned into your purpose, helped one more person, who then turns around and helps one more person. What kind of exponential difference could that make?

Ambition isn't a dirty word. It gets a bad rap, especially for women and other marginalized groups who some believe should tamper their ambition as it threatens their perception of stability and predictability. Ambition isn't bad. It's what kept me alive as a kid: dreaming about a life out of Arkansas, a life where I could feel safe, where I could just be me. That ambition was a belief that there was something better, a fiery desire that said there's more out there, and it can be yours.

We wouldn't have the world we have today without the ambition of those who came before us. What's your vision for what the world will be like for the people who will come after you? There's no thriving without a higher sense of ambition. Your ambition will change the world. It's time to raise your ambition.

RAISE YOUR AMBITION

There I was, going through life not doing anything that I was particularly proud of. But I was making it, and I was comfortable. All my basic needs were met. I wasn't worried about money. The business was doing well. My marriage was going well. I exercised regularly, and I ate well. My life was steady. Then one day I found myself sitting at a Brendon Burchard event. Brendon is a charismatic nerd who used language that resonated with me unlike anyone I had ever experienced. His message was positive, but it was grounded in the reality that life is full of struggle. I completely got what he was saying; it was as if he was talking just to me.

Brendon went to his big whiteboard and drew a graph that went from zero to ten. Then he said, "You've been living your life at a five. You're going through life living a five because it's better than you were a year or two ago. The five feels better, but it's not all you're capable of; you have more in you to give and to offer the world. It's time for you to raise your ambition." I was all in.

Having gone from unable to get out of bed with depression to a comfortable state, I didn't just hear his words—I felt them. The thoughts of not being able to get out of bed, of scouting out bridges to live under, and the memories of my Progresso soup diet came back to me.

I knew I was living at a five. A five is comfortable. It's the goldilocks number—not too good, not too bad. It just is what it is. A five can feel really good because it's not a one anymore. The one was misery. Two was painful; it hurt, almost to the point of being unbearable. When I hit five, it was like I was able to breathe again. I was able to move again. I was able to get out of bed, function in society, work, and contribute at home. I didn't need Brendon to tell me I was living a five—I knew it. But the wake-up call he offered me was priceless. A five isn't a life of thriving, and while it's better than a one, it's still just surviving.

The words kept ruminating in my mind: "You have to raise your ambition."

I knew right then that, while I was grateful for having pulled through the worst depressive episode of my life, I had been playing it safe. I knew I was letting fear get in my way. I knew that it was my time to make a mark. It was my time to make a contribution, to give back. It was my time to live fully as the person I had worked so hard to become. I knew it was time to raise my ambition.

That was the moment I gave myself permission. It was as simple as making the decision. I promised myself that I would not exit this world leaving anything on the field. I wasn't going to sit in the bleachers and watch the game of life; I was going to get on the field and play full out. This is my time!

This is your time too! Step fully into who you are.

You have my permission to live fully as the person you have worked so hard to become. My greatest hope for you is that you will give yourself that same permission.

Raise your ambition.

CONSEQUENCES OF COURAGE

In the book *The Psychology of Courage*,[3] the authors present two different types of prosocial behavior on display. Here is how they describe them:

The first:

"...took place in Munich, Germany, January 13, 2001: About 20 Nazi skinheads harassed a young Greek and started to beat him up in a most brutal way. Five young Turks witnessed the situation and decided to intervene. Risking their own lives, they were able to save the disabled and blood-stained victim from being beaten to death."

The second:

"...occurred in Asia: After the big tsunami wave in Southeast Asia in December 2004, more than 165,000 people lost their lives and more than one million people were made homeless by the floods. Shocked by this horrible natural disaster, people all over the world wanted to ease the victims' suffering. Thousands of volunteers went to Southeast Asia to help on the ground and in Germany, for example, more than 250 million Euros were collected in private donations to help the tsunami victims."

While both groups reached out to help the people in need, the consequences of courage for these groups stand in stark contrast to one another. One group put their personal safety in danger in order to help someone. The Nazis could have turned their violence toward the helpers and attacked them.

The people who came to the aid of the people in Southeast Asia, while courageous in their efforts to help, were faced with fewer perceived risks and even gained social recognition for helping (particularly by making donations). Both are admirable, but one carried a significant risk and the other less so.

When you come out, you are declaring how you are different. This will both repel and attract people to you. By coming out, you are essentially saying, "I am this and not that."

Come out and identify as gay, marry someone of a different race, make your political ideology public, stand up for someone who is different from you in the face of a powerful majority or vocal minority, and there will be consequences for your courage.

When I came out as gay, and also came out as someone who was hell-bent to break the cycle that I was born into, I lost my relationship with my dad, and my relationship with my mom was dramatically altered. It's made a relationship with my brother nearly impossible, and I agonize over the distance it has created between the two of us, and between me and my niece and nephew. All the while, I gained a loving life partner, in-laws who love me like their own son, and a community of people like me.

It's up to you to understand and weigh the consequences of your courage—they are real, and some of them will hurt. You may lose people, status, power, a job, clients, children, faith, community, and even your safety. But, odds are, you'll also gain many of those things from a more authentic and meaningful place.

I don't say this to discourage you. I say it to make sure that you're awake to your reality and the risks. Most women in the United States wouldn't think twice about running to the grocery store without their heads and arms covered; it's unlikely that a woman in a Muslim country would do the same without consequences.

The consequences of your courage could depend on a number of factors: your country, gender, financial independence, network, mental well-being, age, education, and so on. I decided to call them Mindset *Methods* for a reason; these are ways to think about how you live and not be cavalier about it. The ambition to come out as anything takes courage, and it carries risks. Those risks should be weighed and thought about methodically.

When we take risks, we are doing something different, contradicting conformity and predictability. Taking a risk is changing our future—for good or bad. Most people would rather live a life half-lived than take a risk on themselves out of fear for what might come. That fear is usually based on only half of the possibilities— the bad ones. Consider the full range of possibilities for what taking a risk might mean for your life. Don't over- or underestimate the potential danger the consequences of your courage may carry.

If there's someone in your life with whom you feel safe, try this exercise with them. Let them offer you their perspective on the parts of your situation that you may be too close to in order to see clearly. Sometimes the consequences of courage are overplayed fear that's built up in your head; sometimes those risks could represent overwhelming consequences. A trusted confidant can help you navigate the two.

Ultimately, though, this is your journey. Weigh the consequences of your courage.

EXERCISE

To help you bring awareness to the possible consequences of your courage, take your journal and write your reflections on the following questions:

1. What is your personal coming out, your personal ambition? What's worth perpetually coming out for? What is worthy of your courage? I'm coming out as _____.

2. My courage to come out will make me an insider with people like . . .

3. My courage to come out will make me an outsider with people like . . .

4. If I come out as _____, the worst thing that could happen is _____.

5. The best thing that could happen is _____ .

THE COURAGE MULTIPLIER

> *Community is a courage multiplier.*
>
> ~ *Chad Peevy*

Groupthink is a psychological phenomenon that happens when a group of people who are seeking harmony or conformity make irrational or dysfunctional decisions in their effort to achieve that state.[4] My impression from the research is that, while the idea of groupthink has been widely examined, it is largely viewed through a negative lens (particularly in Western cultures where individualism reigns supreme). You'll find a lot of articles out there on how to avoid groupthink. And honestly, my independent streak tends to align with the idea of avoiding going along with the "sheeple." After all, there are some potentially negative consequences to groupthink; the Challenger Disaster and the Jonestown Massacre immediately come to mind. I'm reminded of the impact that blind following has when someone uses the phrase, "drinking the Kool-Aid" (even though it was technically Flavor Aid that was used in Jonestown). Your teachers probably encouraged independent thinking when they asked; "If all of your friends jumped off a bridge, would you jump too?" And the truth is, you probably would. Why? Because we imitate other people in order to fit in with them. We assume that, to be liked and accepted, we have to go along to get along.

The definition of groupthink casts it into a negative light, suggesting that members of a group always make irrational decisions in order to conform. But here's the thing: making better decisions or engaging in healthier behavior that will lead to a thriving life may seem irrational compared to what your default programming, popular convention, or the people around you are telling you. It might seem irrational to call your sponsor instead of drinking. It may seem dysfunctional to have a hard conversation with your spouse instead of stewing in your anger. It may seem irrational to schedule your meals instead of just eating when you're hungry. Holding yourself to a higher standard might seem irrational to the people around you.

Most of the research paints the idea of groupthink in a negative light, since we live in the age of the individual. But when we need desperate change, we turn to it. Parents send their kids to reform schools when they want a dramatic behavior to change. People go to rehab to receive intensive help for addictions of all kinds. And believers find congregations that align with their belief systems. We volunteer ourselves for groupthink all the time when we subject ourselves to an environment that subscribes to a particular system of goals, beliefs, and behaviors. Putting ourselves in an environment that supports a desired behavioral outcome that is common to the group can be very effective.

Peer pressure is a similar idea that can also be seen as negative until it crosses over into peer support. To me, peer pressure implies stasis; the pressure comes from the people already around you. It's important to find a group that supports your identity, a group that reflects who you are and where you want to go. That kind of association can serve as a source of morale and solidarity, and it strengthens your motivation to persist[5] in troubling times.

There are also positive examples of groupthink. You can even leverage it to your advantage. Here's what I mean: Once you've weighed the consequences of expressing your courage and made the decision to come out or raise your ambition, you can use the power of groupthink to find connection, to put yourself in a community that enhances your journey. Your courage will multiply exponentially when you're with a group of like-minded people. It's as if you get to borrow one another's bravery.

Programs like AA offer a community of people who think a certain way about addiction, and the pressure of the group members plays a role in maintaining an individual's sobriety. Sports teams have reminders in their locker rooms to prompt the members that their team thinks, behaves, or plays in a certain way. Group therapy or support groups, where you maintain your individuality but are committed to working toward a common goal, improve how you relate to other people. Group members commit themselves to an ideal that pushes them toward a common cause.

Groupthink is a courage multiplier when leveraged wisely and with awareness. The easy thing is to go along with what the group, the family, or the tribe has always done. What I'm asking you to do—to break the cycle and approach life in a different way than you were originally taught—isn't easy. But it can be easier when you find a group to help you express your true self—whether that's a support group, mastermind, group coaching program, or other network. That kind of immersion helps you practice your new programming so that your default becomes, "People like us do things like this." Where "things like this" are those things that reflect who you really are.

Courage multiplies exponentially when it's expressed with the support of like-minded people.

EXERCISE

To help you bring awareness to your community, take your journal and write your reflections on the following questions:

1. Think about the groups you're a member of now; do those groups support the vision you have for your life?

2. When you think about the direction you want for your life, what groups align with that vision?

3. What steps can you take today to get involved with those groups?

THE OTHER SIDE OF COMFORT

We choose to go to the moon in this decade and do the other things,
not because they are easy, but because they are hard.

~ John F. Kennedy

People who strive for more personal freedom often aren't comfortable being comfortable. Comfort is the sly enemy of a thriving life, but we are conditioned to believe that comfort is the goal. Comfort is death's waiting room. It's a state where we allow ourselves to become numb to life, and it deprives us of the joy we can realize through the hard work of reaching for our higher selves. Those who thrive know that it is in the struggle where we find meaning and purpose.

Comfort is letting the tension out of the rope that stretches between where you are and where you want to be. Without that tension, the rope sags. But with the right amount of tension, that rope becomes a bridge to your greatness.

If you are reading this during a time in your life when things are good—your needs are met, you're doing well for yourself, your family is well-fed—and yet you find yourself in the quiet moments asking if this is it, if this is all there is to life, then it's time to raise your ambition.

Borrowing from Maslow, once our physiological and safety needs (air, food, water, shelter, clothing, personal safety, good health) are met, there are opportunities to experience another dimension of life's needs: those of self-actualization.

EXERCISE

Write the number that corresponds to your answer in the space provided.

> *1 = I'm extraordinary | THE VISION*
> *2 = I want more / better | THE TENSION*
> *3 = I'm comfortable | THE DANGER*

LOVE & BELONGING

☐ I'm part of a community of like-minded people

☐ I have a deeply intimate relationship with someone

☐ I feel free to show my love for the people I care about

ESTEEM

☐ Others would say that I show them respect

☐ I move confidently through my life

☐ I feel respected by others

SELF-ACTUALIZATION

☐ I accept myself for who I am

☐ I'm curious about other people

☐ I am living my best life

To help you bring awareness to your life's ambition, take your journal and write your reflections on the following questions:

1.   On a scale of 1 to 10, how would you rate your overall level of ambition throughout your life?

2.   What do you imagine your life would look like should you adopt a higher sense of ambition?

3.   Describe the impact you could you make with a higher level of ambition?

4.   For any of the statements from the previous page for which you indicated that you're living in the danger or tension zone, what might you do to raise your ambition in those areas?

5.   What part of you would need to be discovered, or come out, for you to make the vision for your life a reality?

WHAT'S WORTH IT?

Some men die at twenty-five and aren't buried until seventy-five.

- Benjamin Franklin

Ambition is ultimately about realizing, expressing, and becoming more of your true self.

Whatever your personal coming out might be, whatever part of you that requires ambition and courage to bring you closer to your personal freedom, my hope is that you find the community that can help you make the inevitable suffering on that journey most meaningful. Constantly coming out, sharing your life experience, revealing your truth can feel like a burden. Along the way, don't expect to be understood or accepted by everyone, but do expect to become a better communicator and advocate for yourself and those like you. Don't expect others to take up your cause on your behalf, but if they do, let them know how much you appreciate and value them. Don't expect to find comfort in a world that isn't as brave as you are, but do expect to find meaning, purpose, joy, and peace in your progress.

It's Pollyannaish to think that the world will change around you and learn to love you all on its own. Real change comes from within and expands outward. We teach people how to treat and talk to us. Educating others about our life experience is part of the coming-out process and our own self-discovery process. Coming out as anything is inherently messy; it's an interruption of what people are used to and what may be expected of you. So, expect some mess. Through it all, remember to exercise grace, patience, courage, and humility. You'll need it.

The questions you now should contemplate are: What is worthy of your ambition? What about your life is worth standing up for? What do you believe in enough to endure the inevitable discomfort of growth? I believe we answer these questions best when we understand our legacy.

LEGACY
CHAPTER 12

It takes the whole of life to learn how to live, and
—what will perhaps make you wonder more—
it takes the whole of life to learn how to die.

~ Seneca

One day in tenth grade, my history teacher, Ms. Shirley Donahue, called me a racist in front of the entire class. I have no idea what we were discussing that day, but Ms. Donahue made it clear that she didn't approve of my contribution. If I remember correctly, her exact words were, "Chad Peevy, you're a racist." Ouch.

Her comment shut me up real quick as I sat and stewed in bewilderment, shame, and anger. Even in small town Arkansas, I knew racist was a label I didn't want assigned to me, and I wasn't happy about it.

I carried that anger with me for the rest of the school day and all the way home. I waited patiently for my mother to get home, sure that she would be as outraged as I was. I ranted on and on about it, and finally, after a nudge from my mother, I convinced myself that the right thing to do would be to call Ms. Donahue at home and set the record straight: I was no racist.

Calling a teacher at home was entirely out of character. I had never done it before, but she had really pushed a button with me. So, I called her. I don't remember the specifics of our conversation, but what had an impact on me was that she had the courage to force me to confront something about myself that I had been unaware of. Without fear of what I or the other kids might think, without fear of what her boss or my parents might think, she boldly called out something she saw brewing in me. And by doing so, she did me a great favor.

No one at home ever sat me down and told me that we were racists. We didn't go to Klan meetings or wave the Confederate flag. So how could I possibly be a racist? While I wasn't offered any formal training on how to become a racist, looking back, I realize that I was certainly growing up in an environment where racist ideas would be allowed to flourish.

I guess there might have been some clues, like I wasn't allowed to watch any television show that featured people of color. *The Cosby Show*[1] was a big hit when I was a kid, and I really wanted to watch it. I would turn the volume down and pretend like it wasn't on. My dad would notice and yell at me to "get that off the TV."

Ms. Donahue was also one of the most respected and influential teachers I've ever had. She probably didn't think much of it when she made that comment to me in class. She was a strong-minded, progressive, very opinionated teacher—a real Ann Richards type. Everyone wanted to be in her class. On one random afternoon, she fearlessly challenged the way I was learning to see the world. She forced me to confront some ideas that I had picked up from my environment, and she made me examine a part of myself that may have otherwise gone unchecked. Just by unapologetically being herself and being unwavering in her values, she changed my whole life. She didn't erase every racist thought I may have had as a teenager growing up in rural Arkansas—I'm not that naïve—but she certainly played a role in breaking a cycle, a pattern of thinking that had been a part of my family history. In so doing, she was creating a part of her legacy—interrupting and changing what would become my legacy.

LEGACY OF INFLUENCE

> *I heard you die twice, once when they bury you in the grave and the second time is the last time that somebody mentions your name*
> *So when I leave here on this earth, did I take more than I gave?*
> *Did I look out for other people or did I do it all for fame?*
>
> *~Mackelmore, "Glorious"*

I think in the end, people on a path to personal freedom want to be able to look back on their lives and say that it all mattered, that it all meant something. We want to feel like our potential was realized and our gifts and talents were used for good. We want to leave this world and feel like we will live on in the people whose lives we touched. That's legacy.

Legacies are created by the living. By becoming intentional about the type of legacy you want to create, you can shape the future by the values you uphold. Even if you're unaware of it, you are creating your own legacy while also becoming a part of other people's legacy. Legacy is the act of living consequentially.

W. Dale Warren, my band director from the University of Arkansas, taught me how to work a room and bring the charm. When he walked into a room, everyone knew because the energy in that room instantly changed. He never sat me down and gave me the steps to work a room. His authenticity radiated from him, so there was nothing to teach. I simply observed. *How* he showed up, in his genuineness, is what made an impression on me.

I met Karen Thompson through my work with nonprofits in Austin. She's a pastor at a local church, and she taught me that people of faith don't all look like the spiritual terrorists I grew up with. She never explicitly made that distinction to me. I simply saw the evidence in how she embodies her faith and how she treats people.

I got to know David Woolly when I was in high school; he was our school superintendent. He was very involved in the band program and, when I graduated, he and his wife gave me a scholarship to offset some of my college costs. The dollar amount didn't matter. What mattered to me was that he made me feel seen and like I mattered at a time in my life when I needed that boost of confidence and encouragement.

Brendon Burchard, my business mentor, taught me that it's okay to be a little nerdy and academic in my approach to personal development. He didn't tell me that; it's just who he is.

Les Brown, the motivational speaker, taught me that it's okay to not be perfect, and it's okay to share the messy parts of my life story.

Dan Harris, author of *10% Happier*, made meditation accessible for me and changed how I experience my life day-to-day.

Were it not for Shirley Donahue, and the way that she challenged one of my inherited mindsets, I might never have considered dating, much less marrying, a person of color.

Some of these people were my teachers in school, some were my coaches or mentors, some I've never met and only know through their work. But just by being who they are, their authentic selves, I (like many others) have become a part of their legacy.

Sometimes we think that legacy is something reserved for

rich people who add their names to football stadiums or school buildings. Sure, those are forms of legacy, but they aren't the only ways to make a lasting impact. And just because you may not have the money to name an arena after yourself doesn't mean that you shouldn't be mindful of your legacy. Even actions that seem small can have a huge impact. Everyone can have an impact if they have the courage to embrace the responsibility. Everyone can have a legacy of influence.

What are you choosing to do with your life? How is your legacy being made? Whose legacy will you carry on? How will the legacy you're creating influence other people? How will your life cause a ripple effect of good, peace, joy, happiness, and contribution? Not just after you're dead and gone, but right now, in the here and now? Are you taking deliberate and methodical steps to break whatever cycle in your past needs breaking? Is your life being used to make the world a better place?

The answers to these questions aren't just a matter of external influence; they are deeply meaningful in how we live and experience our lives.

THE PERSONAL IMPACT OF LEGACY

A legacy mindset lives and dies in peace.

-Chad Peevy

For many of us, the idea of a legacy starts to show up somewhere in our mid- to late thirties and early forties. That timeline tracks with Stage 7 of Erik Erickson's Theory of Psychological Development.[2] Erickson was a famous German-American psychologist who postulated that, throughout our life, our personality develops as a result of psychosocial crises,[3] which could result in either a positive or negative outcome. As we face the challenges in our life, we are presented with opportunities to benefit and grow from those experiences. His theory suggests that, at around forty years of age, human beings are confronted with the idea of generativity versus stagnation: leaving your mark on your world or failing to find a way to contribute beyond yourself.

It's around that mid-life point that most of us realize that our time on earth is limited. We begin to wake up to the fact that we are not invincible, and we, too, will one day pass.[4]

As humans, we are wired to keep ourselves alive at all costs. Yet, we carry with us the knowledge that we will one day die. From a distance at first, we see death as something that happens to other people. And then one day, through our psychological development or experience, we awaken to the realization that our lives, too, will one day end. If ever there was an anxiety-inducing gap between the way things are and the way you want them to be, this is it.

When that awareness occurs, our knowledge conflicts with our instinct to survive, resulting in what we often hear referred to as a mid-life crisis.[5] But it need not be a detrimental crisis. In fact, I think that moment of awakening to our mortality can be liberating. In fact, I would love to see our culture celebrate the mid-life awakening instead of making a parody of it. Based on society's stereotype of mid-life, how often are you compelled to bring images to mind of middle-aged men dying their hair, getting plastic surgery, and trading in their spouses and cars for newer models? These reactions to our mortal awareness are futile efforts to hold onto our youth and invincibility.

It makes you wonder: When the inevitability of our death becomes present in our conscious reality, how do we even function? Why has this reality not caused us to be a species that is completely selfish, violent, and chaotic? Why do we do anything other than eat, sleep, and have sex knowing that our time is limited? Why do we not live in a world where those who have come to this realization don't just stop working, give up, and give in? Why, instead, do we see so many people double down on their work, their giving, their contribution? How did the world evolve and develop when our individual lives are so short? It took 182 years to complete the building of Notre Dame Cathedral in Paris. The men who started the construction never saw the finished product. Why work that hard on something when you'll never see or experience the final outcome of your efforts? Why even dream up something like that, knowing that you will never see the end result?

Again, the answer lies in our most basic instinct: our need to survive. But not just our own survival—the survival of our species. Our brain knows that, while we as individuals will not survive, we as human beings must. Eventually, we come to see ourselves as part of something greater than ourselves. We see our lives as one piece of a greater human experience. That kind of connection to something greater than ourselves is powerful and, ultimately, it is what has allowed human beings to survive, evolve, and thrive.

Death is terrifying. It's terrifying because we don't know when or how it's going to come for us, and we don't know what, if anything, happens to us once we're dead. Is there a heaven or hell? Neither you nor I have any evidentiary insight into what exists on the other side of this life. We must, with humility, acknowledge that we don't know what happens after we die. Again, with so much uncertainty, why don't we just devolve into chaos? Because to manage that anxiety, we've constructed two ways to cope: faith and legacy.[6]

FAITH AND LEGACY

By seeking to understand our fear of death, researchers have developed the Terror Management Theory,[7] or TMT. Inspired by the writings of Ernest Becker,[8] TMT proposes that one of the reasons for human anxiety is that we are both aware of our impending death and also actively working to prevent it. We've developed coping mechanisms to help us reconcile this juxtaposition and manage that terror. When facing the reality of impending death, many find comfort in the idea that the spirit leaves this plane and passes over to some other dimension where we go to heaven or reincarnate in some other form. But at the end of the day, we don't actually know what happens. Nevertheless, we need a way to cope with that level of uncertainty. The idea that we keep going in some form once we die is one of these ways. Faith is a way to manage the fear and anxiety we have about death.

Is it any wonder that religion has endured over time and amassed most of the world's population as followers? Religions offer an answer to a question that has been asked by every person to ever live, and it's a question that can't be answered. By offering an answer, faith helps bridge that anxiety gap. Faith introduces a sense of certainty, which mitigates our fear of death.

The concept of legacy is also a coping mechanism. Legacy can serve as an intentional allocation of our life to the people, causes, and organizations that we want to endure. Through our impact and influence, we get to "live" forever. This symbolic immortality gives us something to live for, and it informs the way we live. It gives meaning to the struggle in our lives and a sense of peace to our death.

Researchers refer to this idea as the "legacy motive": the personal motive to make life better for future generations to cope with the anxiety of our own mortality.[9] When faced with your own mortality, it can make you do things you might not have done otherwise.[10] It gives reason to your life's purpose.

Knowing that you did something meaningful in this life, that your life mattered, helps you cope with your mortality and creates motivation for you to live a full life of love and contribution.

While faith is the substance of things hoped for, the evidence of things not seen,[11] legacy is created and made manifest in the here and now. Our legacy can be created through a lack of awareness of our own influence. Or intentionally as a consequence of our life's purpose.

INTENTIONAL LEGACY

Did any of the people who had an impact on my life know that I was becoming a part of their legacy? Was it intentional? Does it matter?

What if you could adopt a mindset of legacy on purpose? What if you were intentional about how others experience you? What if you could direct your life to create a legacy you can be proud of?

Fear of death keeps us alive, and eventually, that fear teaches us how to live. Legacy mindset is a strategy that informs your day-to-day life. When you become intentional about your legacy, you know who you're working in this life to become. You know who you are to others. You know your purpose. This is your one life and the one opportunity that you know you've been given with certainty. Give yourself permission to discover and then live your legacy every day.

With your life, you have temporarily taken the wheel of history. You get to steer the future in one direction or the other. The responsibility of being this navigator, even temporarily, is a heavy burden. But it's one worth the lift for people who want to do what's right by all of us now and for those to come.

It's no accident that I opened this chapter with a story about a history teacher. This is because, as I've written in the next section, we can discover the way forward by understanding our past.

KNOW YOUR HISTORY

Our legacy honors those who came before us and will come after us. Research has shown that when people know how they've benefited from those who came before them, they consider their own legacy and the positive contribution they can make to the world.[12]

Throughout this book, I've referenced the three selves that live within us all the time: the past, present, and future selves. When we adopt a mindset of legacy, we introduce a fourth version—postlife—to see ourselves as a part of history.

Thinking about legacy from the perspective of the dead self helps us gain perspective.

Our legacy is as much about honoring the journey we're on as it is the impact we're making on others. For me, I think about the LGBTQ+ people who came before me. Those who fought and bled for the rights that I enjoy today. Even though I will never meet those people, I am living a life that is a part of the legacy that they handed down to me. I feel like it's my responsibility to honor them in the way I live my life.

When gay marriage was made legal in 2015, Pasha and I had been together for more than five years. We got married in 2015, not only because we loved each other and were committed to spending our lives together, but also to honor the sacrifice made by those who came before us to make our marriage possible. We understood that we were part of a lineage, and we embraced our role in that movement.

Professionally, I bring awareness to what I do and the privilege I have to be able to do it. Representation matters. When Pasha and I see someone who is sharing a similar life experience to ours, it is empowering in its own right. Being true to who you are is like being a temporary torchbearer for your cause in this moment.

If you're a woman, a person of color, gay or lesbian, transgender—an outsider of any stripe—you're part of a lineage of champions who blazed the trail for you. Even professionally, you're part of a lineage. Doctors, lawyers, plumbers, and band directors (among others) are all beneficiaries of those who came before them in those jobs.

What will you do to advance your lineage, and how will you make your temporary custodianship uniquely yours? Do you recognize your role in the history of your lineage, whether that history is related to your family, your identity, or your profession?

It's important to know your history. Learn from whom you are the beneficiary. Know the sacrifices made by the people who fought for the life you're able to live today. Know your role so you can be more than the recipient of a legacy. You can be a force for progress that honors the past and creates a better future. Ultimately, your legacy is your purpose made manifest. It's within your power to make it happen.

BREAK THE CYCLE

Someone once told me the definition of Hell:
The last day you have on earth,
the person you became will meet
the person you could have become.

- Anonymous

Research tells us that being reminded we are going to die doesn't just cause us to consider the impact we have on future generations, but it also causes us to make better long-term decisions overall.[13] Awareness of our death actually makes us better people.

There's a piece to this idea of legacy that can't be ignored, and that's in recognizing the role you're playing and the connection you have to the people who are part of your life. A recognition of the place you occupy in the lives of the people around you. The resulting clarity will reveal the depth and potential of your impact. An impact that can create and contribute in ways that will outlive you—even if that might just mean *not* perpetuating a cycle. Simply making the decision to do something different with your life (to treat your spouse and kids better than you saw modeled as a kid, for example) is a legacy in and of itself.

My hope is that you'll make the decision to improve that lineage, make it better for the generation coming after you. Just remember that it doesn't start with the next generation—it starts with you. Make your life the best it can possibly be, and everyone around you now, and those who come after you, will benefit.

This is what I mean by "break the cycle." At a minimum, breaking the cycle is about not perpetuating a bad legacy.

Breaking the cycle starts with you. Break *your* cycle. Bring awareness to who you are and who you've been trained to be. Then, question all of it. Recognize the cycle, the patterns, the default programming, and then be the one brave enough to break it, if necessary. Renew the world by renewing yourself.

Join me in breaking the cycle. Join me in my movement to break the cycle of trauma, abuse, racism, bigotry, anti-intellectualism, spiritual terrorism, and all other impediments to our personal and collective freedom. Let's create a better world, one that leads with love and compassion for others. You deserve to live that life.

It won't be easy. Breaking the cycle requires courage. It requires that your mindsets of ambition and legacy meet. It may be uncomfortable for you to step into who you are, because the path you traveled was so difficult. You may feel doubt and uncertainty.

I had the privilege of talking to a famous violinist who shared with me his resistance to teaching. Even though he is now a famous concert artist known worldwide, he still carries with him the scars he had accumulated from his music teachers. He was so influenced by what they put him through, that he had decided he couldn't teach because he couldn't do to others what had been done to him. He was breaking the cycle, but he was neglecting a part of his legacy. A couple of bourbons into our conversation, he was able to see that he was actually able to teach his way. He began to realize that, even though the methods of the past were "the way it's always been done," he had the power to stop it—at least with his students—and choose to do things another way.

Your own healing will come through active and intentional creation of your legacy. Self-actualization comes through self-transcendence. If you want to see yourself more clearly, clarity will come when you get into service beyond yourself.

Don't shirk from your responsibility or play small with your life. You don't have to be like those who came before you. This is your time, your opportunity to have an impact in a way that is purely your own.

WHAT DO YOU NEED TO BREAK?

Begin to think about what cycles exist in your history that you need to break. This exercise has the potential to bring up a lot of shame and guilt, so I want to give you permission to acknowledge those feelings, but don't take them seriously. You're doing something amazing just by bringing awareness to the cycles that need to be broken. You are incredibly brave to face the cycles that may have been passed onto you. Honor that courage as you complete this exercise.

I had a lot of cycles to break. From my family alone, I had to consider cycles ranging from racism, to homophobia, to anti-intellectualism, to fundamentalism, to marriage. Give some thought to the cycles that exist in your family, but give yourself permission to also look at your profession, the causes you believe in, parenting, connecting with other people, and more.

EXERCISE

1. Make a list of the areas in your life where cycles need to break.

2. For each of those areas, write specifically what ideas, actions, beliefs, and inequalities you reject.

3. For each of those things that you reject, write down your vision for that thing.

4. Write down at least three ways how you can live that vision day-to-day.

FOR EXAMPLE:

Area: My profession (band director)

Belief I reject: Women don't lead marching bands; the guys do that.

My vision: Women dominate the marching band industry and are recognized as the best directors, drill designers, and arrangers.

Day-to-day:

▶ I will feature women band directors in my classes—both past and present.

▶ I will hire women to clinic (guest teach) with my band.

▶ I will encourage young women in my organization who want to be band directors and actively create opportunities for them.

HEADLINE YOUR LIFE

Alfred Nobel got to peek into the future when a French newspaper printed his obituary by accident. It was, in fact, his brother who had died. The headline read:

"The Merchant of Death Is Dead!"

I'm sure you're aware of a part of Alfred Nobel's legacy, the Nobel Prize. But did you also know that he invented dynamite? And the use of this invention led to countless deaths. When he realized that he was destined to be remembered as an agent of destruction and death, he made strides to change how he would be remembered. He did so by directing his energy into recognizing those who were working toward improving the human condition, valuing peace above all else.[14]

You may not have the experience of previewing your obituary in the newspaper the way that Nobel did. But I bet if you just took a minute to reflect on your life up to this point, you could come up with a couple of headlines to sum it up.

EXERCISE

Here's your exercise:

1. Ask five friends to write a headline for your life. Here's what you say: "If something happened to me and I passed away, and you were asked to write an essay about my life, what would the first line be?"

2. (Optional) If you're feeling brave, take to social media and ask the same question.

If these headlines are in alignment with what you want for your life, that's great. But if not, there's still an opportunity for you to put the work into writing something different about your life. Creating your Life Map can help you chart such a course.

LIFE MAP

Too many people only look into the future about as far as their next meal. Some can look out at their lives about a year from now. But how many are looking at their lives as a whole, congruent existence that will define their time here?

You don't have to plan every second of every day or become so regimented with your life that there's no room for spontaneity, but you can create a lifetime of purpose and legacy. When you do mindfulness work, it becomes clear that starting each day with intention has a positive effect on the outcomes of our day. But what about an intention for your lifetime?

EXERCISE

For this exercise, find a quiet place free from any distractions. You'll want to give yourself an hour to do the exercise and to process what comes from the experience.

1. Take a blank sheet of paper and draw a line down the middle of the page (you can also find a worksheet for this exercise in this book's companion course at ChadPeevy.com/book).

2. The left side represents your past. Write the significant experiences that have happened in your life on the left side of the page. They don't have to be in any particular order. Just list the experiences that you would consider having made such an impact on you that they contributed to who you are. (some examples: first-generation college student, cheerleader in high school, valedictorian of my high school, rookie of the year at my job, got married, my grandpa died)

3. Look for both the good and the bad. There's no wrong answer or wrong way to do this exercise. As you write, think of the different parts of your life—your relationships, your career, your health, your mindset, your accomplishments, your happiest moments, and your past. Just write what flows naturally.

There are a couple of ways to look at the left side of the paper: 1) You could look at it as all the things that have happened to you, how the world has wronged you. You could see it as all the excuses for your current circumstances and future prospects.

You could see it as your peak. Or, 2) You could look at it as the lessons that you've learned, the experiences that have prepared you to go forward to help other people and make a difference in this world. You could see it as preparation for your legacy. The choice is yours; how you look at it is up to you.

When you go to the eye doctor, he puts the big contraption up to your eyes and asks you to focus on the letter in front of you. As he switches one lens for another, he says, "Which is better? One or two?" Think about this in the context of your own life. How do you want to see the world: this way or that way? Ignorant to the lessons of circumstance? Or as a student of life? As someone who was hurt or someone who has been prepared?

4. On the right side of the page, write who you want to be. What's the impact you will make? What's the legacy you will be remembered for? There's nothing you could write that is too small or too grandiose. Nothing is out of reach for you. Don't apologize, don't qualify—just write it down.

5. Look at just the left side of the page. What if that was your legacy? Would you be pleased? Would you be okay leaving the world with just the left side of the page completed? When I did this exercise, I wasn't. But I, like you, have a choice. I have a decision to make. Will I allow my past to define my legacy? Will I allow my past to dictate who I will be in the future? It's a choice. Which choice will you make?

My dad treated me horribly as a child. I've made some serious mistakes in my past. I've been wronged, and I've wronged others. Will I allow the left side of that sheet of paper to define who I am? Will I let my dad's behavior creep onto the right side of the page? Will I allow the mistakes that I made to cross that line in the middle? Will I allow the old version of myself to define what I write on the right side of the page? It's a decision that is all mine—made daily. And it's yours too.

6. Now, turn that piece of paper over. On the back, write your current age and put a line over the top of it. Then down the page, write out the decades that you have left in your life through your nineties. Put a line over the top of the numbers. For the decades remaining in your life, what would you like to be the theme of your life for each one?

7. Write that theme on the line above your current age and above each decade.

When I did this exercise, I discovered that there were so many things that I wanted to do! After I listed those things out for each decade, I looked for a common theme among the things I had listed. Look for those themes and write them above the decades.

Why do I want you to create this Life Map? Because it helps us live with intention. It's a wake-up call that there's a lot of life left. It brings attention to the fact that, while so much may have already happened to or for you in your past, there's so much more ahead of you. What if you went into your future with intention? What if the theme of your future life was a theme that you chose?

I found myself writing down decade themes like creation, contribution, and mentorship. These are themes and a legacy that I look forward to, that I'm excited about; they're ways that I know can make a difference. These themes don't define my death (which is how we typically think about legacy). They define everything that will become a necessary part of my everyday life.

IT HAD TO BE

We were planting seeds of change, the fruit of which we might never see.

~ Michelle Obama

Guess what? You're going to die. It's a harsh thing to say, but it's the absolute truth. I don't need a near-death experience to know that, and I hope you don't either. We only get one life. There is no re-draw, re-do, start-over, or try again. This is it.

To close this chapter, let's revisit Erikson and see how he describes the eighth stage of psychosocial development: Ego Integrity vs. Despair. This is when we look back on life with "the acceptance of one's one and only life cycle as something that had to be."[15] That just about sums up the whole idea of legacy for me. Did I use this life, the only life that I get, for something that just had to be? Did I truly live my purpose each and every day? Will the world be better because I was here?

I hope that you are able to find a way to go out there and make your life something that just "had to be." I hope you'll discover something worth your effort despite the fear, the difficulty or the emotional struggle. When you're able to think about making the world a better place instead of only thinking about your own survival . . . well, it's liberating. It's showing you are becoming more human and living fully as the person you have worked so hard to become. The world needs you to be you. It's ready for your legacy.

THE OTHER SIDE
CHAPTER 13

The other side of survival left me with two surprising feelings: one was guilt, and the other was a sense of responsibility.

I found myself feeling guilty for my post-survival life: guilty for my emotional well-being, for my improved financial situation, for getting out of my old mindsets, for finding love. I felt guilty for being different, for seeking out a better life, and for being happy about it. For some reason, guilt would cling to me as I rose above my upbringing.

Although I couldn't shake the feeling, I knew that by diminishing myself through these unhelpful notions of guilt, I was perpetuating the psychological stranglehold that my father had on me. The guilt was a reminder of his control, which kept me small, kept me apologetic for who I am, and forced me to put on this porcupine exterior to protect myself.

The more I learned about guilt, the more clarity I gained around what it was. Fritz Perls, the father of Gestalt Therapy, said that on the flip side of guilt is resentment.[1] A shift in mindset to see it that way made sense to me. I had plenty to resent. There was no reason to allow this shadow of my dad living in my head make me feel small anymore. And I had no reason to feel guilty for rising above my upbringing. Therefore, my resentment became my defiance. By defying that feeling of guilt, I was defying him. A defiance that I now recognize as part of my personal freedom.

Along with the guilt came questions of responsibility. Was it my responsibility to save the family I loved but had left behind? Was there an obligation to make sure that my family shared in my success? Was it my job to help other members of my family overcome a shared set of inherited mindsets?

The weight of responsibility that I was feeling was blinding me to the opportunity to help those who wanted that help—and to heal myself in that process. But first I had to learn to respect that while equally important, our journeys are separate paths. I needed to learn that while I can be helpful to someone, it's not my place to assume what is necessary for other people's journey. Ultimately, I am only responsible for my life path.

Your responsibility is to live your best life, to live fully and freely. Not to diminish who you are, not to be small anymore. And even if this is all you do—to bravely and unapologetically live your best life—you are doing something remarkable.

Perls goes on in his work to say that behind every resentment is a demand. My demand became my purpose, my cause: to help those who are ready to do the work, break their cycle of inherited mindsets that are sabotaging and causing them pain, and to untangle those beliefs that are holding them back from living the life they want.

Both my guilt and sense of responsibility were masking the same resentment, the same righteous anger. But righteous or not, I had to learn how to channel my anger in a way that served me.

Because here's the thing about personal freedom: You're free to be *all* of you. You're even free to be mad.

One of the ways I've learned how to channel that anger and all the other emotions is through personal development. My umbrella for that term is broad and includes everything from psychology, to philosophy, to storytelling. I see personal development as all things concerning the development of a person's mind, body, and spirit. It's in that work where I feel at home with myself. Because it seems to me that the study of personal development is filled with a bunch of people who are trying to make right the ways that they were wronged—something to which I can relate. And I can't think of a more noble cause. So I would like to close this personal development book with some ideas about the path of personal development.

PERSONAL DEVELOPMENT

If a person gave away your body to some passerby, you'd be furious.
Yet you hand over your mind to anyone who comes along,
so they may abuse you, leaving it disturbed and troubled
—have you no shame in that?

- Epictetus

I came to personal development during a time in my life when I felt like I had nothing to lose. I was living a comfortable life. I had pulled out of a major depressive episode and was okay, but it just felt like I was going through the motions of life. I was constantly asking myself, *Is this it? Is this all there is?* So when I stumbled onto personal development, it's as if I had found direction. It was a direction that allowed every part of my life to blossom in new and refreshing ways. But it was a direction that required guidance.

If you're someone who has a hard time trusting, who desperately needs guidance in your personal development but doesn't know how to get it, who needs help but is terrified to ask, I want you to know that I was the same way. I had to look for a different way to get what I needed. I found that mentorship satisfied that need.

Mentorship can take many forms. To me, traditional mentorship meant that some old man with gray hair—a substitute father—would take me under his wing and show me all the ways of life. But that old man never showed up for me. And honestly, if he had, I'm not certain that I would have allowed for that kind of a relationship. Nonetheless, I still needed guidance. So, I began to expand my view on what mentorship could be for me.

In many ways, a mentor is both a substitute for what you wished you had growing up and the parental figure you need in your life right now. As we discussed earlier, we seek out replacements for our parents in the world who offer us a familiar feeling. Mentorship gives us an opportunity to choose that parental substitute intentionally. If a parental figure is a bridge too far for you, you can look at your mentors as a big brother or sister, or a favorite aunt or uncle.

Let's all take the liberty of expanding our view of how we define mentorship. An expanded definition that includes any person, living or dead, with a life, cause, or message that you admire. Think of your favorite authors, YouTube personalities, your peers, your spouse, your sibling(s), your boss, your coach, an organization, a cause, a company, a group, an artist, a movement that you believe in as mentors. They all provide a form of guidance.

It can be scary to look to someone to help guide your journey—especially when you've been hurt and let down by people in the past. But you're not meant to go through life all on your own. And you shouldn't have to figure out everything by yourself. There are so many mentorship opportunities for you in this world when you broaden your definition of mentorship. There are so many resources that will help you answer for yourself, *Is this all there is? Actually, no, it's not!* Be open to these relationships; they can enhance your life's experience in ways that you can't even imagine yet.

WHY WE NEED MENTORS

> *If I have seen further than others, it is by standing upon the shoulders of giants.*
>
> - Isaac Newton

Too few people had great role models growing up. But what we were denied in our youth is not an excuse for a lack of mentors now. We can make the effort now to seek out and fill our lives with the mentors we've always deserved. And then we can carry them with us into the world and listen for their voices when we are having a hard time finding our own.

When I have rough days, I hear motivational speaker Les Brown's voice in my head: *"If you fall down, and you will, make sure you land on your back. 'Cause if you can look up, you can get up!"*

If I'm having a hard time with something in my business, I think of author Brendon Burchard: *"Stop being afraid to be seen starting small."* I think about the stories he's told about his own journey of struggle and progress, and I'm filled with the inspiration and confidence to carry on.

If I'm feeling afraid, stuck, or indecisive, I hear life and business strategist Tony Robbins in my head: *"Stop negotiating with yourself."*

If I'm worried about money, I think about financial coach Bari Tessler's books, which taught me so much about my relationship with money: *"You can choose to update your financial identity anytime you like."*

In addition to carrying their message with us, mentors allow for expanded possibilities in our life because of the perspective, speed, familiarity, and community they offer.

Good mentors can help you gain perspective. Not just on the big stuff but on the small stuff too. They can help you visualize the big picture for your life and figure out the very next step to take. Mentors also offer a shift in your thinking and help you see problems through a new lens.

Good mentors can help you go faster. Borrowing from the lessons of their journey, we are shown the shortcuts to get us where we want to be, helping us eliminate or lessen the amount of time we might waste on our own.

Good mentors help you recognize the familiarity of their stories in your own. They don't just show you the end result; they show you the difficult, messy, and confusing journey they took to get there. They illuminate our path by sharing their own stories of struggle and progress. Listen to their stories. Learn from their mistakes. See and recognize their struggles, hopes, and successes in yourself.

Good mentors make the journey less lonely. As a young adult, I found myself stumbling through life. My circumstances had taught me that I had to be self-sufficient to survive. I had to have all the answers, to chart my own destination, and navigate the way—all by myself. From the outside looking in, this may have looked like confidence; in reality, it was more likely arrogance. The way I presented myself was nothing but a mask to cover up and disguise the fear underneath. I was afraid to admit that I needed help. And honestly, I didn't have the vocabulary to even ask for help. I was afraid of messing up, being judged, being wrong, and disappointing other people. Instead of confronting those fears, I masked them with my ego. It's lonely behind that mask. It keeps other people at bay, skews their view of you, and maintains a barrier between you and those who could help you, if only you were brave enough to let them.

With help, our journey of personal development can be more meaningful when we leverage the knowledge and experience of those who have come before us. My hope is that your dreams for your life are so big and so important to you that you don't have time to learn from your own mistakes, and that you'll be vulnerable, smart, and humble enough to learn from someone else's. In fact, many of "someone else's" mistakes.

CREATING A COMMUNITY OF MENTORS

The relevance of your mentor's messages will flow in and out of your life as your circumstances change, so create a community of mentors in a wide range of areas. I'd suggest finding two to three mentors for each of the 12 Mindset Methods outlined in this book. Find specialists for the areas of your life that are important to you. People are people, and just because they are a really good mentor for one thing doesn't mean that they're necessarily good for another area of your life. For example, I may look to someone as a financial mentor but not a marriage mentor. I may have a mentor for my career, but they wouldn't also be a mentor for my health.

There are mentors all around you if you look for them. Some of whom you may see every day, others you may never meet in person. As a result of this expanded view of mentorship, we're left open to accidental mentors. But whether intentional or accidental, these mentors are teaching you something about life and about yourself.

If you fill most of your time with trashy TV, conversations with toxic people, and friends or family who tear you down, they are teaching you something. You're also being taught something when you surround yourself with people who see the best in you, who fill your head with messages that inspire and lift you up. Every minute of every day, you are learning. What you allow into your mind is teaching you something. So, what are you learning?

Mentorship is a filter for what you allow in your life. Building a community of mentors isn't just about who you bring in; it's also about who you filter out. Create a community of mentors who will empower you. I firmly believe that the quality of your community of mentors will determine the quality of your life.

You can see my community of mentors in this book's online companion course at ChadPeevy.com/book

BE A GOOD MENTEE

Once you embrace this way of looking at mentorship, you can be intentional about what kind of mentee you want to be. I see three possible levels of being in a relationship with your mentors: fan, patron, and benefactor.

Being a fan means you follow your mentor on social media, listen to their podcast, watch their videos on YouTube, or subscribe to their e-newsletter. You're a casual observer of their work. You appreciate their message, and it resonates with you. You pay them with your time and attention, but not with money. You enjoy the complimentary resources that your mentor produces.

When you become a patron, you've moved from a casual observer to someone who is willing to invest financially in your relationship with your mentor. This means you're ready to be closer and go deeper. You may buy their book, purchase their online courses, participate in their group programs, engage them for coaching, or pay to attend their live events. You may also be reciprocating the value they are delivering to you with your effort. You leave reviews for their books or their podcast, share their social media posts, and comment on their YouTube videos. You tell your friends about what you're learning.

As benefactor, you've seen firsthand the change that your mentor's message can create in a person's life. You've experienced a transformation as a result of their message. You've reached a place where you want to share their message, and you're willing to invest in the effort to spread that message. You buy their books, not just for you, but to give them to other people. You're willing to purchase their premium offerings, like a mastermind group. You invite them to speak to your organization. You volunteer at their live events. You begin to see their message as your message, and you direct your energy toward advancing this message.

In your appreciation for how your mentors are helping you, maintain your awareness that they, too, are just human.

YOUR MENTORS WILL DISAPPOINT YOU

Your mentors will disappoint you; they will inevitably let you down. They will do something or say something that you don't like or agree with. They may have a gaffe. They may slip up. They may do something stupid. After all, they are human.

When that happens, I want you to first pause and avoid the urge to jump to outrage. If your mentor is a public figure, the media will make them out to be Satan, because that will get them more clicks and views. Don't fall for it.

If they are a good mentor, teacher, and role model, they are going to take whatever has happened and use it as an opportunity to teach. They will find the lesson in their experience, and they will share those lessons with you. That's what mentorship is. They make the mistake so you don't have to. If you dismiss them, you miss out on the lesson and the opportunity for growth.

We all have a right to evolve, to learn a better way. And we all need to experience and exercise more grace toward one another. I say this as a gay man who lives every day working with people who I know, at one time, thought that my very existence was an abomination. They were wrong. They have learned. They are human. And I have the capacity for grace and forgiveness toward people who are willing to grow. While I'm not advocating that you issue your mentors a blank check for bad behavior, I am suggesting that your best mentors will be generous with the lessons of their growth. In turn, be equally generous with your grace.

Your mentors will disappoint you. See all of them, even their mistakes, and you will come to see more of yourself in them and the lessons they have to offer you.

When you show your mentors the grace to be human, extend that same grace to yourself. Because someone out there needs you to be a mentor for them. For the survivor who has risen above their upbringing but is unsure of how to thrive. For the person who is working hard but hardly making progress. For the person who goes through the motions of life but never really feels a sense of satisfaction. You may be the only person who can help them see and move through what's holding them back.

IF NOT YOU, WHO?

Be a rainbow in someone else's cloud.

- Maya Angelou

Mentorship, both being and having a mentor, helps us see our place along life's path. It gives perspective and direction to our journey. Being a mentor to the people coming up behind us helps us see how far we've come. It also allows us to live our purpose and empowers others to live theirs.

A practice in mentorship is an effective way to put the 12 Mindset Methods into practice. By helping others, we heal ourselves in the process.

Eventually, you have to stop limiting your questions to *why* and expand your range of possibilities to *how*. Eventually, you reach a time in your life when it's just not as helpful to keep asking why you're different, or why you were thrown into that circumstance, or why you had to learn that particular set of lessons. There comes a time when these mindsets that always ask why will no longer serve you. Instead, you have to start asking how you are going to use your differences to make a difference.

The most powerful path to your own everyday happiness and personal freedom is to help someone else find theirs. Your particular grooves, indentations, and style are exactly the key that will unlock the door for someone else's transformation. Because of your particular and unique journey, you are needed.

▶ Will you show the courage to break the cycle you were born into?

▶ Will you put in the effort to untangle knots of your inherited mindsets?

▶ Will you step into who you were meant to be?

▶ Will you give yourself permission to live fully as the person you have worked so hard to become?

If you are to discover your personal freedom then you must grant yourself that permission. The only person with the freedom to be you, is you.

DID THIS BOOK HELP YOU?

Honest reviews help readers find the right book for their needs. If this book helped you, I would love to hear about it. You can go right to the Amazon review page for this book by entering the following URL into your web browser:

ChadPeevy.com/ReviewBreakBook

Thank you!

SUMMARY GUIDE

SUMMARY GUIDE

SELF :: PURPOSE

Our Common Purpose

Our common purpose is to serve one another. Purpose is revealed to us as a result of our action toward it. It need not be large in order to be meaningful. Sometimes our purpose is our contribution to better ourselves. How we manifest our purpose need not be a life sentence because our lives are made up of seasons. How we chose to serve others through our purpose will be guided by seasons as well.

Discover the *How* versus *Why* of Purpose

Why is great for self-reflection, but *how* puts us in action toward our purpose. *Why* leaves us in our head, while *how* has the potential to bring us to the here and now. What we're really asking when we question our purpose is: *Who am I, and why am I here?* We gain clarity around that question through our active struggle to answer it.

Purpose Is Not Happiness

To experience a meaningful life, we must embrace life's inevitable struggle. Purpose transcends emotion, so don't chase the emotion—chase the meaning. Through our purpose and through our lives, meaning and satisfaction will be found by experiencing all of our emotions. Emotions are like indicators on a dashboard; they are not the engine itself.

SELF : : INTERNAL DIALOGUE

<u>On Belief Origins</u>

The circumstances of our upbringing heavily influence the ideas and beliefs we come to accept as our own. But they are rarely our own. When our beliefs conflict with the reality of our lives, we experience anxiety. The real work of personal development is to evaluate these inherited beliefs and replace them with those that will serve and not sabotage us.

<u>BEATS</u>

There are several schools of thought that illustrate the notion that our beliefs lead to our emotions and then to our actions. Our life's outcomes can be untangled by examining this model and changed when we have the courage to break these patterns.

<u>Emotional Range</u>

A limited emotional range may be the result of those emotions being stifled as a child. When we limit our emotional range, we limit our full human experience. We have to bring awareness to and express our full range of emotions in order to experience more, and to avoid the danger of holding on to those emotions that can cause us harm when left unexpressed.

SELF : : IDENTITY

<u>What Is Identity?</u>

Our identity is a collection of stories that we have come to accept as our truth. Often times these notions of our identity are formed by the expectations that others have for us. If our thoughts created reality as we know it, then they are also able to create something different. We can't confuse what we've *done* with who we *are*.

Manifest Identity Fixation

This describes a fixation on the manifestation of who we are, rather than the attributes that allow us to experience the manifestation. How we manifest our identity is just an outlet for who we are, but oftentimes we confuse the manifestation with the core of who we are. This kind of thinking blinds us to knowing ourselves more deeply—out from behind the mask of a job, title, position.

Freedom from Identity

Freedom exists when we are free from any attachment to our manifest identity. When we expand our perspective of ourselves, we can see ourselves more clearly for who we are. Releasing yourself from your manifest identity doesn't turn you into a different person; it merely allows you to express who you have been all along.

SELF : : UNITARY FUNCTIONING

Our Mind, Body, and Spirit Are Connected

The connection of mind, body, and spirit brings awareness to the influence that one system has over the others. It also gives us insight for how our negligence of one system creates deficiency in another.

Take Care of Your Body

Exercise and nutrition have an overwhelming impact on our mental health. It's never too late to have the healthiest year of your life. And it's never too late to get educated on how to take better care of yourself. Consider functional medicine as one route for navigating your physical health.

Pick Your Own Journey to God

Don't let a history with religion deny your spiritual journey.

Spirituality allows us to ask deeper questions about our existence: *What is the meaning of life? How did I get here? What is the meaning of love, loss, and death?* Howard Gardner referred to spirituality as "existential intelligence" and described it as a pursuit of understanding and making sense of the world so that we can make decisions about how to live in it.

STRATEGY : : BECOMING

Personal and Professional Development

Personal development is about the journey of getting to know yourself, while professional development is a process of deepening the skills through which you contribute to the world. Both are necessary parts of our becoming. To feel the satisfaction of our purpose, we must be committed to the mastery of our contribution. Deep skills help alleviate uncertainty and anxiety.

Decisions

Our decisions are what have gotten us where we are. To decide is to cut off all other options. Our process of becoming is one of being decisive.

There Is No Destination, Only a Direction

Death is the only real destination. Be open to the journey and all the lessons that the journey itself will offer you. Make decisions about your becoming that will give you a journey in which you acquire a sense of meaning. Set a personal curriculum for your life that will allow you to grow into the person you want to be.

STRATEGY : : MONEY

The Purpose and Power of Money

Money is neither good nor bad. It's simply a tool. But often we give money a special power in our lives that we need to understand. Money allows us to acquire things that meet our basic needs. It also allows us to express our values. Money isn't about self-worth; it's about self-expression.

The Source of Money

Money flows . . . It flows in and out of our lives. Money carries intent and energy with it from whence it flows. It's important for us to examine if the source of our money is in alignment with what we value.

Receiving Money

Our money mindset will influence how we receive money and our reaction to it once received. Our financial health can be measured by our reaction to receiving money. The beliefs we have about money impact those reactions and the opportunity for growth exist in untangling those reactions.

STRATEGY : : MINDFULNESS

Perspective Is Everything

We choose how to see the experiences of our lives. The quality of our lives depend upon the quality of those choices. We have to learn how to better manage our mind, which includes making different choices about how we see our life's experience.

Nothing Happens for a Reason

Nothing happens for a reason. We give reason to the things that have happened. When we assign blame for our lives, we relinquish control of our lives. Less control and responsibility leaves open the possibility for chaos, anxiety, and discontentment.

Not Small Anymore

Avoiding life's circumstances are a way of keeping oneself small. It's a way of facing the present life as the younger self. We have to learn how to take care of the younger self so that he doesn't sabotage the present self. Bring awareness to what you are allowing your younger self to bring into the present.

STRATEGY : : PRODUCTIVITY

Redefining Productivity

The fear associated with staying busy is associated with satisfying base needs of survival. For most reading this book, those base needs are satisfied and are only shadows of a survival mindset. It's time to redefine what it means to be productive—a definition that is more inclusive of your higher psychological needs.

Life Is Seasons

No life sentences. Life is made up of seasons. A redefined definition of productivity requires that we bring more compassion and a deeper sense of what it means to satisfy the demands of productivity. We have to take the time to learn the lessons that life is offering us the opportunity to learn for each season.

Mindful Productivity

Being mindfully productive means that we have to detach from our goals in deference to the direction of that goal's realization. It requires that we bring attention to the struggle in the present moment as we move toward that goal without suffering from the anxiety of the unrealized future. Mindful productivity is about appreciating the journey.

SOCIAL : : BELONGING

Loneliness
We are social beings, and a sense of belonging is necessary for our well-being and survival. Often, the effects of loneliness are what get our attention because we haven't learned to recognize what loneliness is; therefore it remains undiagnosed. There are six needs that must be satisfied in order to mitigate loneliness. One cannot substitute one for the other, and all are necessary for feeling a sense of belonging.

How Our Parents Show Up in the World
Much of how we connect to other people in the world is a reflection of how we connected to our parents. The strength of that connection is often an indicator of the strength of other relationships. The parents living in our heads are not the parents that exist in the present. Our work is to resolve the issues with the parents living in our head.

Forgiveness
Forgiveness is a gift to yourself. Forgiveness is a signal that the younger self has come to trust the present self. Forgiveness only arises with those people for whom we have a demand for love. To withhold our forgiveness is to hold onto our fear that a transgression will repeat itself.

SOCIAL : : HELP

<u>Why We Resist Help</u>
There is a cost to asking for help. It reveals our vulnerability and requires that we acknowledge our own limitations. We are less likely to ask for help when it comes to matter of the "self" because of the misperception that we should be knowledgeable about addressing those issues on our own. Often, our resistance to help stems from how our parents responded to our needs as children.

<u>How to Ask for Help</u>
We should direct our ask for help wisely—asking the appropriate person for assistance. We should be direct with our ask. We should ask respectfully and maintain that respect for the other person and ourself should we be denied.

<u>Accepting Help with Grace and Gratitude</u>
Do not deny other people their opportunity to help you. When help is offered, accept it with grace and gratitude. By accepting help, you are allowing someone else to live and lean into their purpose. There are seasons for helping and being helped. Be open to the full cycle of that season.

SOCIAL : : AMBITION

<u>Coming Out</u>
Ambition means to advocate for yourself. Advocating for yourself is a form of coming out as more of who you are. That coming out is your ambition in practice and an audacious act of courage. It brings you a deeper understanding of self and allows others to know how to be closer to you.

You Never Stop Coming Out

Humans imitate one another in order to be loved and accepted—a coming out rebukes that conformity. Because of that, you'll never stop coming out. To deny who you are is to deny yourself a full human experience. Coming out is a tribute to those who came before you to make your declaration possible. When you live your truth, you have an impact on the people who get to know you.

Raise Your Ambition

Being comfortable leaves one susceptible to stagnation and a life lacking purpose. Live your life full out. Whatever has been your level of ambition (for advocating for yourself and what you want the world to look like), raise that level. Permission granted!

SOCIAL : : LEGACY

Legacy of Influence

Legacy isn't reserved for the rich. We can all have a legacy. Our legacy is left whether or not we realize it—just in how others experience us. How you show up is teaching the people in your life who you are. Being unapologetically you, standing for what you value, is a means of leaving a legacy.

Personal Impact of Legacy

We're all going to die. Some time in middle age this realization hits us. For some, this leads to crisis; for others, it leads to a doubling down on making sure their life counted for something. Death is terrifying, and in order to manage that terror we have formed ways to cope; two of which are faith and legacy.

<u>Break the Cycle</u>

Awareness of our death actually makes us better people. We're all having an impact on the people around us. That impact is either carrying on an inheritance of mindsets that may or may not be healthy, or we are passing on the best of who we are. At minimum, "breaking the cycle" is about not perpetuating a bad legacy. That process begins with you by breaking *your* cycle, rising above your upbringing, and choosing to do something different with your life and legacy.

WHAT TO READ NEXT

Thank you so much for reading my book. I hope that you found something that will help you on your journey. If you would like to read more on the topics that I wrote about in *Break & Untangle*, then I would encourage you to visit my online library at ChadPeevy.com/library. From there you'll be able to see all of the books—from a wide range of topics—that I keep in my library.

I would also like to invite you to be a part of my community by either signing up for my mailing list or getting the online resources that I've created to accompany this book. Both can be found on my website at ChadPeevy.com.

ABOUT THE AUTHOR

Author and teacher Chad Peevy grew up in an emotionally and physically abusive family in rural Arkansas, and spent years learning to overcome the trauma, depression, and anxiety that followed him into adulthood. After earning a Master's degree from the University of Texas at Austin, Chad founded several businesses and nonprofits. Among these are the Austin PRIDE Foundation, as well as the in-house marketing agency for the world's largest real estate office, an online training company, and, with his husband, The PS Foundation for the Arts. Following his passion for personal development, Chad has created a system for supplanting damaging beliefs with healthy mindsets, and now offers guidance and support to all who want to find the same freedom.

Meet him at ChadPeevy.com

ACKNOWLEDGMENTS

I've always thought I was pretty good at taking on big projects. This book, though, this was something of another magnitude. None of which could have been possible without my husband, Pasha. Pasha kept me going and believed in me on the days when I didn't believe in myself. He was always supportive of me seeing this project through, and for that, I am eternally grateful to him. I love you very much, babe! I'm so proud of the life we've built together, and I consider myself so fortunate to get to share this human experience with you.

It wasn't just the writing that made this book hard for me, but the emotional drudgery that made it such a beast. It took me around four years from the time I started writing down the ideas I had for this book until I saw it complete. My therapist, Allen Lambert, helped me immensely through the process. He kept me sane. Helped me further form and develop my thoughts. He helped me hold onto reality. Thank you, Allen. For everything.

Thank you to those people in my life who I brought with me along the writing journey. Mom, I'm glad that we have both decided to put in the effort to have a relationship, despite everything.

Thank you for supporting this project even though you knew it would hurt. I know you want our experience to help someone else have a better one. I will do everything I can to make sure that happens. Thank you, Granny Marie, for trying to protect me when I was a kid. I know it often got you into trouble and caused you a lot of hurt, but I'll never forget that you tried. And even though no longer with us, my Granny and Grandaddy Peevy played a big role in shaping who I am. I miss and love them both.

Farideh and Bob, I couldn't have asked for, or ever even imagined it possible to have, such amazing in-laws. You are both remarkable human beings, and you have taught me so much about family and love.

Denise McIntyre, thank you for being my friend, for listening to me, for making me laugh. Amanda Kaufman, thank you for our weekly conversations. Your friendship.is an inspiration.

There are a few people who were instrumental to making this book a reality by allowing me to experiment on them with some of the ideas that I've presented; especially April Todd, Gina Killough, Sara Driver, Philip Oubre, and Ashley Boyd. Thank you for your curiosity and open-mindedness.

To the people who kept my company going so that I could focus on writing, I thank you. In particular, Andrew Bernas, Anna Dickerson, Collin Findlay, Emily Rhoads, and Erin Ashby.

To everyone who helped by offering that little nudge or push, checking in to see how the writing was going, thank you. Especially Amy Harris, Karen Thompson, Brian Wolfe, Amanda Beatty-Salter, Jasen Edwards, Dathan Goff, Laura Vinson, Ken Granger, and Laura Tilley.

Kent Sorsky was my first editor. My manuscript was such a mess that he fired me. It was the biggest favor he could have done me. Thank you for giving me the kick in the ass that I needed, Kent. For helping me so much with editing and getting this book over the finish line, thank you Vanessa Ta, Olivia Peluso, Jenna Love, Jeni Martens, and Dennis Kouba. Thank you for helping me communicate my message more clearly.

To my fellow mastermind members, thank you all for the inspiration and encouragement to share my story. Especially Patti Moore, Sheila Kloefkorn, Patrick Mosher, Kathy Mauck, Candy Valentino, and Niyc Pidgeon.

To my coaches and mentors: Your guidance changed my life and for that I am grateful. Michael Coffey, thank you for listening to my ramblings week after week and for keeping me accountable regardless of the resistance. Brendon Burchard, thank you for the clarity and perspective.

And finally, to all the giants on whose shoulders I stand, thank you for the vulnerability to be you and to share your story. Thank you for using your life so that mine could be better.

REFERENCES

The following works contributed to the research for this book. In addition to resources below, I have created a place on my website for this and additional references to live as new research emerges on the topics covered in this book. You can find that list at:

ChadPeevy.com/BUreferences

Becker, E. (2007). *The denial of death*. Simon and Schuster.

Berne, E. (1996). *Games People Play: The Basic Handbook of Transactional Analysis*. Ballantine Books.

Brenoff, A. (2016, April 28). *Early Retirement May Be The Kiss Of Death, Study Finds*. HuffPost. https://www.huffpost.com/entry/early-retirement-may-be-the-kiss-of-death-study-finds_n_57221aa3e4b01a5ebde49eff

Bry, A. (1984). *Est: Erhard Seminars Training: 60 Hours That Transform Your Life*. Avon Books.

Burchard, B. (2017). *High Performance Habits: How Extraordinary People Become That Way*. Hay House Inc.

Camus, A. (2013). *The myth of Sisyphus*. Penguin UK.

Chen, A. (2018, June 22). *A social psychologist explains why we should ask for help more often.* The Verge. https://www.theverge.com/2018/6/22/17475134/heidi-grant-reinforcements-help-social-psychology

Clear, J. (2018). *Atomic Habits: An Easy & Proven Way to Build Good Habits & Break Bad Ones.* Avery.

Coch, L., & French Jr., J. R. (1948). Overcoming resistance to change. Human Relations, 1(4), 512-532

Coelho, Paulo. (2014). *The Alchemist.* HarperOne.

Covey, S. R. (1991). *The Seven Habits of Highly Effective People.* Provo, UT: Covey Leadership Center.

Csikszentmihalyi, M. (2008). *Flow.* Harper Perineal Modern Classics.

DePaulo, B. M., & Fisher, J. D. (1980). The costs of asking for help. *Basic and Applied Social Psychology, 1*(1), 23-35.

Dweck, C. S. (2008). *Mindset: The New Psychology of Success.* Random House Digital, Inc..

Eker, H. T. (2005). *Secrets of the Millionaire Mind: Mastering the Inner Game of Wealth.* Harper Business.

Ellis, A. (1999). *How to Make Yourself Happy and Remarkably Less Disturbable.* Impact Publishers.

Ellis, B. J., Bianchi, J., Griskevicius, V., & Frankenhuis, W. E. (2017). Beyond risk and protective factors: An adaptation-based approach to resilience. *Perspectives on Psychological Science, 12*(4), 561-587.

Elrod, H. (2016). *Miracle Morning.* First.

Frankl, V. E. (1985). *Man's Search for Meaning.* Simon and Schuster.

Goldstein, J. (2016). *Mindfulness: A Practical Guide to Awakening* (Reprint ed.). Sounds True.

Goswick, R. A., & Jones, W. H. (1982). Components of loneliness during adolescence. *Journal of Youth and Adolescence, 11*(5), 373-383.

Hansen, M. T., Amabile, T. M., Snook, S. A., & Craig, N. (2018). *Purpose, Meaning, and Passion (HBR Emotional Intelligence Series)*. Harvard Business Press.

Harris, D. (2019). *10% Happier Revised Edition: How I Tamed the Voice in My Head, Reduced Stress Without Losing My Edge, and Found Self-Help That Actually Works--A True Story* (Anniversary, Reprint ed.). Dey Street Books.

Hawkins, D. R. (2014). *Letting Go: The Pathway of Surrender*. Hay House Incorporated.

Heinrich, L. M., & Gullone, E. (2006). The clinical significance of loneliness: A literature review. *Clinical psychology review, 26*(6), 695-718.

Ho, D. Y. (1995). Selfhood and identity in Confucianism, Taoism, Buddhism, and Hinduism: contrasts with the West. *Journal for the Theory of Social Behaviour*, 25(2), 115-139.

Holiday, R., & Hanselman, S. (2016). *The Daily Stoic: 366 Meditations on Wisdom, Perseverance, and the Art of Living*. Penguin.

Jeffers, S. (2012). *Feel the Fear and do it Anyway*. Random House.

Jones, E. E., & Davis, K. E. (1965). From acts to dispositions the attribution process in person perception. In *Advances in Experimental Social Psychology* (Vol. 2, pp. 219-266). Academic Press.

Keller, G., & Papasan, J. (2013). *The One Thing: The Surprisingly Simple Truth Behind Extraordinary Results*. Bard Press.

Kinder, G. (2012). *The Seven Stages of Money Maturity: Understanding the Spirit and Value of Money in Your Life*. Dell.

Kohen, A., Langdon, M., & Riches, B. R. (2019). The making of a hero: cultivating empathy, altruism, and heroic imagination. *Journal of Humanistic Psychology, 59*(4), 617-633.

Kornfield, J. (2009). *A Path with Heart: A Guide Through the Perils and Promises of Spiritual Life*. Bantam.

Kornfield, J. (2019, March 12). *No Self or True Self? — Identity and Selflessness in Buddhism*. Tricycle: The Buddhist Review. https://tricycle.org/magazine/no-self-or-true-self/

Leahy, R. L. (2008). The therapeutic relationship in cognitive-behavioral therapy. *Behavioural and Cognitive Psychotherapy*, 36(6), 769-777.

Leahy, R. L. (2012). *Overcoming Resistance in Cognitive Therapy*. Guilford Press.

Lee, F. (1997). When the going gets tough, do the tough ask for help? Help seeking and power motivation in organizations. *Organizational Behavior and Human Decision Processes*, 72, 336-363.

Maltz, M. (2015). *Psycho-Cybernetics: Updated and Expanded* (Updated, Expanded ed.). TarcherPerigee.

Martela, F., & Steger, M. F. (2016). The three meanings of meaning in life: Distinguishing coherence, purpose, and significance. *The Journal of Positive Psychology*, 11(5), 531-545.

McDonald, B. R. K. A. C. (2012, July 23). *Do those who retire early live longer?* BBC News. https://www.bbc.com/news/magazine-18952037

Michalowicz, M. (2017). *Profit First: Transform Your Business from a Cash-eating Monster to a Money-making Machine*. Penguin.

Nadler, A. (1983). Personal characteristics and help-seeking. In B. De- Paulo, A. Nadler, & J. Fisher (Eds.), *New Directions in Helping: Vol. 2. Help Seeking* (pp. 303-340). New York: Academic Press

Nadler, A., Peri, N., & Chemerinski, A. (1985). Effects of opportunity to reciprocate and self-esteem on help-seeking behavior. *Journal of Personality*, 53(1), 23-35.

Nadler, A., Shapira, R., & Ben-Itzhak, S. (1982). Good looks may help: Effects of helper's physical attractiveness and sex of helper on males' and females' help-seeking behavior. *Journal of Personality and Social Psychology*, 42(1), 90.

Needleman, J. (1994). *Money and the Meaning of Life* (New edition). Doubleday.

Nemeth, M. (1997). *The Energy of Money*. Sounds True.

Newport, C. (2016). *Deep Work: Rules for Focused Success in a Distracted World*. Hachette UK.

Perls, F., Hefferline, R., Goodman, P. (1951). Gestalt Therapy: Excitement and Growth in the Human Personality. *The Gestalt Journal Press*

Perls, F. S. (1969). *Gestalt Therapy Verbatim*. The Gestalt Journal Press.

Perls, F. S. (1969). *In and Out the Garbage Pail* (Revised edition). Gestalt Journal Press.

Pianalto, M. (2012). Moral courage and facing others. *International Journal of Philosophical Studies, 20*(2), 165-184.

Robertson, D. (2019). *The Philosophy of Cognitive-Behavioural Therapy (CBT): Stoic Philosophy as Rational and Cognitive Psychotherapy*. Routledge.

Robin, V., Dominguez, J., & Tilford, M. (2008). *Your Money or Your Life: 9 Steps to Transforming Your Relationship with Money and Achieving Financial Independence*. Penguin.

Roshi, P. K. (1989). *The Three Pillars of Zen: Teaching, Practice, and Enlightenment* (Revised, Updated, Anniversary ed.). Anchor.

Seligman, M. E. (2004). *Authentic Happiness: Using the New Positive Psychology to Realize Your Potential for Lasting Fulfillment*. Simon and Schuster.

Seligman, M. E. (2006). *Learned Optimism: How to Change Your Mind and Your Life*. Vintage.

Seligman, M. E. (2012). *Flourish: A Visionary New Understanding of Happiness and Well-Being*. Simon and Schuster.

Shapiro, E. G. (1983). Embarrassment and help-seeking. In B. DePaulo, A. Nadler, & J. Fisher (Eds.), New Directions in Helping: Vol. 2. Help Seeking (pp. 143-163). New York: Academic Press.

Singer, M. A. (2007). *The Untethered Soul: The Journey Beyond Yourself* (1st ed.). New Harbinger Publications/ Noetic Books.

Singer, M. A. (2015). *The Surrender Experiment: My Journey into Life's Perfection* (Illustrated ed.). Harmony.

Smith, A. (1979). *Powers of the Mind*. Ballantine Books.

Sokol, L., & Fox, M. G. (2019). *The Comprehensive Clinician's Guide to Cognitive Behavioral Therapy*. PESI Publishing & Media.

Stanny, B. (2007). *Overcoming Underearning: A Five-step Plan for a Richer Life*. Collins.

Tracy, B. (2017). *Eat That Frog!: 21 Great Ways to Stop Procrastinating and Get More Done in Less Time*. Berrett-Koehler Publishers.

Twist, L., & Barker, T. (2003). *The Soul of Money: Transforming Your Relationship with Money and Life*. WW Norton & Company.

Wade-Benzoni, K. A. (2002). A golden rule over time: Reciprocity in intergenerational allocation decisions. *Academy of Management Journal, 45*(5), 1011-1028.

Wade-Benzoni, K., Sondak, H., & Galinsky, A. (2010). Leaving a Legacy: Intergenerational Allocations of Benefits and Burdens. *Business Ethics Quarterly, 20*(1), 7-34. doi:10.5840/beq20102013

Whorf, B. L., Carroll, J. B., & Chase, S. (2011). *Language, Thought, and Reality: Selected Writings of Benjamin Lee Whorf*. Martino Fine Books.

You're Likely to Live Longer If You Retire After 65. (2016b, October 31). Harvard Business Review. https://hbr.org/2016/10/youre-likely-to-live-longer-if-you-retire-after-65

ENDNOTES

In this section I have included a list of notes and citations for each chapter in the book. Make no mistake, mistakes have been made. If I have misattributed or not given attribution where it is due, let me know. Please email me at chad@chadpeevy.com so I may correct the error.

INTRODUCTION

1.   Masten, A. S., & Wright, M. O. D. (1998). Cumulative risk and protection models of child maltreatment. *Journal of Aggression, Maltreatment & Trauma, 2*(1), 7-30.

2.   Sternberg, R. J. (2005). The theory of successful intelligence. *Interamerican Journal of Psychology, 39*(2), 189-202.

3.   Masten, A. S. (2014). *Ordinary Magic: Resilience in Development.* New York, NY, US: Guilford Press.

CHAPTER 1

1. Qvortrup, M., & Nielsen, E. (2019). Dwelling Narratively: Exploring Heideggerian Perspectives in the Narrative Paradigm. *Philosophy & Rhetoric, 52*(2), 142-162. doi:10.5325/philrhet.52.2.0142

CHAPTER 2

1. S. Dweck, Carol. (2017). From needs to goals and representations: Foundations for a unified theory of motivation, personality, and development. *Psychological Review.* 124. 10.1037/rev0000082.

2. *Impact of Fear and Anxiety.* (n.d.). Taking Charge of Your Health & Wellbeing. https://www.takingcharge.csh.umn.edu/impact-fear-and-anxiety

3. Ropeik, D. (2004). The consequences of fear: Our modern world is a risky place and evokes many well-founded fears. But these fears themselves create a new risk for our health and well-being that needs to be addressed. *EMBO reports, 5*(S1), S56-S60.

4. Las Vegas Convention and Visitor Authority (LVCVA, 2002)

5. Zaab, A. T. J. A. L. C. (2017, October 27). *What Happens in the Brain When We Feel Fear.* Smithsonian Magazine. https://www.smithsonianmag.com/science-nature/what-happens-brain-feel-fear-180966992/

6. Hendricks, L., Bore, S., Aslinia, D., & Morriss, G. (2013). The effects of anger on the brain and body. In *National Forum Journal of Counseling and Addiction* (Vol. 2, No. 1, pp. 2-5).

7. Segerstrom, S. (2011, March). The structure and consequences of repetitive thought. *Psychological Science Agenda.* http://www.apa.org/science/about/psa/2011/03/repetitive-thought

8. Stewart L. Aledort, (2002). The Omnipotent Child Syndrome: The Role of Passionately Held Bad Fits in the Formation of Identity. *International Journal of Group Psychotherapy*: Vol. 52, No. 1, pp. 67-87.

9. Ibid.

10. Murguia, E., & Díaz, K. (2015). The philosophical foundations of cognitive behavioral therapy: Stoicism, Buddhism, Taoism, and Existentialism. *Journal of Evidence-Based Psychotherapies*, 15(1).

11. Ellis, A. (2007). *How to Make Yourself Happy and Remarkably Less Disturbable*. Atascadero, CA: Impact Publishers.

CHAPTER 4

1. I first heard of the term "dark passenger" from Dexter, a Showtime series about a man who leads a normal life, except for the fact that he's a serial killer—the part of himself that he calls his "dark passenger." While I relate to having this other part of myself, I don't relate to killing people—just to be clear!

2. I use the term "suffer" as Viktor Frankl applied the word in Man's Search for Meaning.

3. There are many, these are a small sampling:

Richardson, C. R., Faulkner, G., McDevitt, J., Skrinar, G. S., Hutchinson, D. S., & Piette, J. D. (2005). Integrating physical activity into mental health services for persons with serious mental illness. *Psychiatric Services*, 56(3), 324-331.

Callaghan, P. (2004). Exercise: a neglected intervention in mental health care?. *Journal of Psychiatric and Mental Health Nursing*, 11(4), 476-483.

Guszkowska, M. (2004). Effects of exercise on anxiety, depression and mood. *Psychiatria Polska*, 38(4), 611-620.

Taylor, C. B., Sallis, J. F., & Needle, R. (1985). The relation of physical activity and exercise to mental health. *Public health reports*, *100*(2), 195.

4. Sharma, A., Madaan, V., & Petty, F. D. (2006). Exercise for mental health. *Primary Care Companion to the Journal of Clinical Psychiatry*, *8*(2), 106. doi:10.4088/pcc.v08n0208a

5. Raglin, J.S. Exercise and mental health. *Sports Med* 9, 323–329 (1990). https://doi.org/10.2165/00007256-199009060-00001

6. Migdal, A., & Macdonald, A. (2013). Clarifying the relation between spirituality and well-being. *The Journal of Nervous and Mental Disease*, 201(4), 274–280. https://doi.org/10.1097/NMD.0b013e318288e26a

7. Akbaraly, T. N., Brunner, E. J., Ferrie, J. E., Marmot, M. G., Kivimaki, M., & Singh-Manoux, A. (2009). Dietary pattern and depressive symptoms in middle age. *The British Journal of Psychiatry*, *195*(5), 408-413.

Sánchez-Villegas, A., Delgado-Rodríguez, M., Alonso, A., Schlatter, J., Lahortiga, F., Majem, L. S., & Martínez-González, M. A. (2009). Association of the Mediterranean dietary pattern with the incidence of depression: the Seguimiento Universidad de Navarra/University of Navarra follow-up (SUN) cohort. *Archives of general psychiatry*, *66*(10), 1090-1098.

8. Zainuddin, M. S. A., & Thuret, S. (2012). Nutrition, adult hippocampal neurogenesis and mental health. *British Medical Bulletin*, *103*(1), 89-114.

9. Dog, T. L. (2010). The role of nutrition in mental health. *Alternative Therapies in Health and Medicine*, *16*(2), 42-46.

10. Nemme, Kori, Nurturing the inner lives of children: an exploration of children's spirituality in three educational settings, PhD thesis, Faculty of Education, University of Wollongong, 2008. http://ro.uow.edu.au/theses/651

Clark, K., Burton, C., Hughto, J., Bränström, R., Keene, D., & Pachankis, J. (2020). Sex, status, competition, and exclusion: Intraminority stress from within the gay community and gay and bisexual men's mental health. *Journal of Personality and Social Psychology.* https://doi. org/10.1037/pspp0000282

Hay, D., & Nye, R. (2006). *The Spirit of the Child.* Jessica Kingsley Publishers.

11.   Gardner, H. (1999). *Intelligence Reframed: Multiple Intelligences for the 21st Century.* New York, NY: Basic Books.

12.   Mayer, F. S., Frantz, C. M., Bruehlman-Senecal, E., & Dolliver, K. (2009). Why is nature beneficial?: The role of connectedness to nature. *Environment and Behavior,* 41(5), 607–643. https://doi. org/10.1177/0013916508319745

Lawton, E. (2017). *The Relationship between the Physical Activity Environment, Nature Relatedness, Anxiety, and the Psychological Well-being Benefits of Regular Exercisers.* Frontiers. https://www.frontiersin. org/articles/10.3389/fpsyg.2017.01058/full

Capaldi, C. A., Passmore, H.-A., Nisbet, E. K., Zelenski, J. M., & Dopko, R. L. (2015). Flourishing in nature: A review of the benefits of connecting with nature and its application as a wellbeing intervention. *International Journal of Wellbeing,* 5(4), 1-16. doi:10.5502/ijw.v5i4.449

CHAPTER 5

1.   Pepler, D., & Ross, H. (1981). The effects of play on convergent and divergent Problem Solving. *Child Development, 52*(4), 1202-1210. doi:10.2307/1129507

Smith, P., & Dutton, S. (1979). Play and training in direct and innovative problem solving. *Child Development, 50*(3), 830-836. doi:10.2307/1128950

Oppezzo, M., & Schwartz, D. L. (2014). Give your ideas some legs: the positive effect of walking on creative thinking. *Journal of Experimental Psychology: Learning, Memory, and Cognition, 40*(4), 1142.

Coker, B. L. (2011). Freedom to surf: the positive effects of workplace Internet leisure browsing. *New Technology, Work and Employment, 26*(3), 238-247.

Jaeggi, S. M., Buschkuehl, M., Jonides, J., & Perrig, W. J. (2008). Improving fluid intelligence with training on working memory. *Proceedings of the National Academy of Sciences, 105*(19), 6829-6833.

Gardner, B., Lally, P., & Wardle, J. (2012). Making health habitual: the psychology of 'habit-formation'and general practice. *British Journal of General Practice, 62*(605), 664-666.

CHAPTER 6

1.   Now I admit that I have no idea how my parents actually managed their money. All I know is what I was told—and that's not necessarily accurate. Whether or not it's accurate isn't important. What's important is how I saw and experienced their saving and spending habits, which caused me to develop my own relationship with money.

CHAPTER 7

1.   I'm noting these dominant emotions here and in the other explanations of self for your reference. They will also be outlined later in this chapter with exercises for you to implement.

2.   This is my own life experience. I'm not asserting that there aren't other causes of depression, anxiety, overeating, or alcoholism.

3.   Stangor, Charles. *Principles of Social Psychology.* University of Maryland. 2013.

4. Koslowski, B., & Maqueda, M. (1993). What is confirmation bias and when do people actually have it? *Merrill-Palmer Quarterly, 39*(1), 104-130. Retrieved April 23, 2020, from www.jstor.org/stable/23087302

Nickerson, Raymond. (1998). Confirmation bias: A ubiquitous phenomenon in many guises. *Review of General Psychology.* 2. 175-220. 10.1037/1089-2680.2.2.175.

5. Klayman, J. (1995). Varieties of confirmation bias. *Psychology of Learning and Motivation, 32*, 385-418.

6. Stanovich, K. E., West, R. F., & Toplak, M. E. (2013). Myside bias, rational thinking, and intelligence. *Current Directions In Psychological Science, 22*(4), 259-264. doi:10.1177/0963721413480174

7. Anderson, C. A., & Sechler, E. S. (1986). Effects of explanation and counterexplanation on the development and use of social theories. *Journal of Personality and Social Psychology, 50*(1), 24–34.

8. Lokko, H. N., & Stern, T. A. (2015). Regression: Diagnosis, evaluation, and management. *The Primary Care Companion for CNS Disorders, 17*(3), 10.4088/PCC.14f01761. https://doi.org/10.4088/PCC.14f01761

Freud, S. (1977). *Introductory Lectures on Psychoanalysis.* WW Norton & Company.

9. Jung, C. G. (1953). *Collected Works: Symbols of Transformation.* Pantheon Books.

Balint, M. (1968). *The Basic Fault. Therapeutic Aspects of Regression.* London (Tavistock) 1968.

10. Fiske, S. T., & Neuberg, S. L. (1990). A continuum of impression formation, from category based to individuating processes: Influences of information and motivation on attention and interpretation. In M. P. Zanna (Ed.), *Advances in experimental social psychology* (Vol. 23, pp. 1–74). New York, NY: Academic.

CHAPTER 8

1. Kahneman, Daniel. *Thinking, Fast and Slow.* New York : Farrar, Straus And Giroux, 2011. Print.

2. Kumar, A., & Jhajharia, B. (2018). Effect of morning exercise on immunity. Chicago

CHAPTER 9

1. Monbiot, G. (2017, November 30). *The* age of loneliness is killing us. *The Guardian.* https://www.theguardian.com/commentisfree/2014/oct/14/age-of-loneliness-killing-us

2. Baumeister, R. F., & Leary, M. R. (1995). The need to belong: desire for interpersonal attachments as a fundamental human motivation. *Psychological bulletin, 117*(3), 497.

3. Holt-Lunstad, et. al, 2015. Loneliness and social isolation as risk factors for mortality: A meta-analytic review. *Perspectives on Psychological Science* 2015, Vol. 10(2) 227–237

4. *Doing Something is Better Than Doing Nothing for Most People, Study Shows.* (2014, July 3). UVA Today. https://news.virginia.edu/content/doing-something-better-doing-nothing-most-people-study-shows

5. Cacioppo, J. T., Hawkley, L. C., Crawford, L. E., Ernst, J. M., Burleson, M. H., Kowalewski, R. B., ... & Berntson, G. G. (2002). Loneliness and health: Potential mechanisms. *Psychosomatic medicine, 64*(3), 407-417.

6. Coric, D., & Murstein, B. I. (1993). Bulimia nervosa: Prevalence and psychological correlates in a college community. *Eating Disorders, 1*(1), 39-51.

7. Schumaker, J. F., Krejci, R. C., Small, L., & Sargent, R. G. (1985). Experience of loneliness by obese individuals. *Psychological Reports, 57*(3_ suppl), 1147-1154.

8. Gupta, S. (2015, August 4). *Why You Should Treat Loneliness as a Chronic Illness | Everyday Health.* EverydayHealth.Com. https://www. everydayhealth.com/news/loneliness-can-really-hurt-you/

9. Perissinotto CM, Stijacic Cenzer I, Covinsky KE. Loneliness in older persons: A predictor of functional decline and death. *Arch Intern Med.* 2012;172(14):1078–1084. doi:10.1001/archinternmed.2012.1993

10. Schultz Jr, N. R., & Moore, D. (1988). Loneliness: Differences across three age levels. *Journal of Social and Personal Relationships, 5*(3), 275-284.

Schumaker, J. F., Shea, J. D., Monfries, M. M., & Groth-Marnat, G. (1993). Loneliness and life satisfaction in Japan and Australia. *The Journal of psychology, 127*(1), 65-71.

11. Baumeister, R. F., & Tice, D. M. (1990). Point-counterpoints: Anxiety and social exclusion. *Journal of social and clinical Psychology, 9*(2), 165-195.

12. Perlman, D., & Peplau, L. A. (1982). Theoretical approaches to loneliness. *Loneliness: A sourcebook of current theory, research and therapy,* 123-134.

13. Baumeister, R. F., & Leary, M. R. (1995). The need to belong: desire for interpersonal attachments as a fundamental human motivation. *Psychological bulletin, 117*(3), 497.

14. Weiss, R. S. (1974). The provisions of social relationships. *Doing unto others,* 17-26.

15. Hawkley, L. C., Burleson, M. H., Berntson, G. G., & Cacioppo, J. T. (2003). Loneliness in everyday life: cardiovascular activity, psychosocial context, and health behaviors. *Journal of personality and social psychology*, *85*(1), 105.

16. Weiss, R. S. (1973). Loneliness: The experience of emotional and social isolation. JAI Press.

17. DiTommaso, E., & Spinner, B. (1997). Social and emotional loneliness: A re-examination of Weiss' typology of loneliness. *Personality and individual differences*, *22*(3), 417-427.

Weiss, R. S. (1973). Loneliness: The experience of emotional and social isolation.

18. Social = a lack of a social network or friends, resulting in feelings of boredom, aimlessness, and anxiety

19. Emotional = lack of a close, intimate relationship, resulting in feelings of emptiness.

20. Bretherton, I. (1992). The origins of attachment theory: John Bowlby and Mary Ainsworth. *Developmental Psychology*, 28(5), 759.

21. Cacioppo, J. T., Ernst, J. M., Burleson, M. H., McClintock, M. K., Malarkey, W. B., Hawkley, L. C., ... & Spiegel, D. (2000). Lonely traits and concomitant physiological processes: The MacArthur social neuroscience studies. *International Journal of Psychophysiology*, *35*(2-3), 143-154.

22. Weiss, R. S. (1973). Loneliness: The experience of emotional and social isolation.

Henwood, P. G., & Solano, C. H. (1994). Loneliness in young children and their parents. *The Journal of genetic psychology*, *155*(1), 35-45.

Jones, W. H. (1981). Loneliness and social contact. *The Journal of Social Psychology, 113*(2), 295-296.

CHAPTER 10

1. Shapiro, E. G. (1983). Embarrassment and help-seeking. In B. DePaulo, A. Nadler, & J. Fisher (Eds.), *New Directions in Helping: vol. 2. Help Seeking.* (pp. 143-163). New York: Academic Press.

2. Tessler, R. C., & Schwartz, S. H. (1972). Help seeking, self-esteem, and achievement motivation: an attributional analysis. *Journal of Personality and Social Psychology*, 21(3), 318.

3. Bretherton, I. (1992). The origins of attachment theory: John Bowlby and Mary Ainsworth. *Developmental psychology, 28*(5), 759.

https://www.psychologytoday.com/us/blog/love-and-sex-in-the-digital-age/201509/the-opposite-addiction-is-connection

4. Huang, K., Yeomans, M., Brooks, A. W., Minson, J., & Gino, F. (2017). It doesn't hurt to ask: Question-asking increases liking. *Journal of personality and social psychology, 113*(3), 430.

CHAPTER 11

1. https://www.merriam-webster.com/dictionary/ambition

2. I mean this with love and in jest. I feel like I'm going through life with my flag on display.

3. Pury, C. L., & Lopez, S. J. (2010). *The psychology of courage: Modern research on an ancient virtue.* American Psychological Association.

4. https://www.psychologytoday.com/us/basics/groupthink

5. Choi, J. N., & Kim, M. U. (1999). The organizational application of groupthink and its limitations in organizations. *Journal of Applied Psychology, 84*(2), 297.

CHAPTER 12

1. We know a lot more about Bill Cosby now than we knew then. At the time, the show was a hit, and he was America's beloved TV dad.

2. Erickson, E. H. (1958). *Young Man Luther: A Study in Psychoanalysis and History.* New York: Norton.

Erikson, E. H. (1963). Youth: Change and challenge. New York: Basic books.

3. Psychosocial crises: facing critical issues as we pass through life

4. I should note that, while forty is a common age for this revelation, it is not an exclusive timeframe; this awakening to our own mortality can occur much earlier or much later.

5. Jaques E. Death and the mid-life crisis. *Int J Psychoanal.* 1965;46(4):502-514.

Wethington, E. (2000). Expecting stress: Americans and the "midlife crisis". *Motivation and Emotion, 24*(2), 85-103.

6. Becker, E. (1973). *The denial of death.* Free Press.

7. Solomon, S., Greenberg, J., & Pyszczynski, T. (2015). *The worm at the core: On the role of death in life.* Random House.

8. Becker, E. (1962). *The birth and death of meaning.* New York: Free Press.

Becker, E. (1975). *Escape from evil.* New York: Free Press.

Greenberg, J., Solomon, S., & Pyszczynski, T. (1997). Terror management theory of self-esteem and cultural worldviews: Empirical assessments and conceptual refinements. In *Advances in Experimental Social Psychology* (Vol. 29, pp. 61-139). Academic Press.

9.   Fox, M., Tost, L. P., & Wade-Benzoni, K. A. (2010). The legacy motive: A catalyst for sustainable decision making in organizations. *Business Ethics Quarterly, 20*(2), 153-185.

10.   Pyszczynski, Tom & Greenberg, Jeff & Solomon, Sheldon. (1999). A dual-process model of defense against conscious and unconscious death-related thoughts an extension of terror management theory. *Psychological Review.* 106. 835-45. 10.1037//0033-295X.106.4.835.

11.   King James Bible: Hebrews 11:1. https://www.kingjamesbibleonline. org/Hebrews-11-1/

12.   Wade-Benzoni, K. A. (2002). A golden rule over time: Reciprocity in intergenerational allocation decisions. *Academy of Management Journal, 45*(5), 1011-1028.

13.   Wade-Benzoni, K. A., Tost, L. P., Hernandez, M., & Larrick, R. P. (2012). It's only a matter of time: death, legacies, and intergenerational decisions. *Psychological Science,* 23(7), 704–709. https://doi.org/10.1177/0956797612443967

14.   Halasz, N. 1959. *Nobel: A biography of Alfred Nobel.* New York: Orion Press.

15.   Erikson, E. H. (1950). *Childhood and Society.* New York: Norton.

CHAPTER 13

1.   Perls, F. S. (1969). Gestalt therapy verbatim.

Made in the USA
Las Vegas, NV
19 August 2021